Sex &

BELONGING

ON THE
PSYCHOLOGY OF
SEXUAL RELATIONSHIPS

TONY SCHNEIDER

AUSTRALIANACADEMICPRESS

First published 2019 by:
Australian Academic Press Group Pty. Ltd.
Samford Valley QLD Australia
www.australianacademicpress.com.au

A catalogue record for this book is available from the National Library of Australia

ISBN   9781925644234   (paperback)
ISBN   9781925644241   (ebook)

Disclaimer
Every effort has been made in preparing this work to provide information based on accepted standards and practice at the time of publication. The publisher and author, however, make no warranties of any kind of psychological outcome relating to use of this work and disclaim all responsibility or liability for direct or consequential damages resulting from any use of the material contained in this work.

Publisher: Stephen May

Copy Reader: Dianne Wadsworth

Cover design: Luke Harris, Working Type Studio

Typesetting: Australian Academic Press

Printing: Lightning Source

I dedicate this book to my beloved wife of forty years, Moira, whose patience, encouragement, and grace has allowed it to come to fruition.

Contents

Scientists prefer explanatory models that are simple with few variables. Psychologists prefer more comprehensive models that allow them to better describe and understand clients' behaviour. In this book, I describe a model that is no doubt too complex for scientific modelling but hopefully provides psychologists with a useful map to understand sexual behaviours.

The 'sex drive' has long been seen as one of the most powerful drives directing human behaviour, and played a key role in Freud's psychoanalytic theory. I argue that the 'sex drive' is better understood as a composite of drives including both biological and subjective factors. Its composition will vary between people and over time. However, such a conceptualisation does not in any way diminish the power it has in human affairs. Equally influential in directing human behaviour are the twin notions of attachment and belonging, which guide relationship dynamics. The various neuro-chemicals activated in the sexual response represent a powerful reward system in their own right; but when these interact with relationship dynamics, their centrality in human affairs becomes so much greater.

I present in this book a theoretical argument, research findings, and clinical narratives to develop and illustrate a dual-source, multiple drive model that integrates the various factors that can affect sexual relationships. Such a model needs to meet a number of criteria. As is evident in the various narratives, the model needs to allow for intra-psychic conflict as well as external (social) conflict. It needs to allow for fluidity in sexual behaviour patterns, yet recognise the inherent stability of such patterns once established (this being a function of the particular outcomes of sexual expression). It also needs to reflect the non-deterministic nature of sexual behaviour (that is, the decisional process).

The composite of drives in sexual relationships is not only powerful, but also complex, and various conflicts easily develop. Conflict can exist in the drive profile itself, with inhibitive and sexually activating drives operating simultaneously. But conflict can also exist between the ascending drives and the ultimate decisions made. This decisional process makes prediction and scientific investigation in general, difficult. Then there is also the matter of a potential conflict between the sexual behaviour embraced and the prevailing sociocultural sexual scripts. Furthermore, conflict can occur where the outcomes of sexual expression do not meet the goals of the prevailing drives, and conflict can arise where the physical self and the subjective self is not aligned. (Similarly, the sexual and relational selves may not be aligned.) Although such conflicts in themselves do not constitute mental health problems, their lack of satisfactory resolution over time certainly *can* lead to such problems. On the other hand, where the sexual behaviour aligns with secure attachment and belonging, where there is good intra-psychic alignment, and where sexual behaviour conforms to sociocultural norms, good mental health outcomes would normally be anticipated.

Moreover, to the degree that the drive profile can fluctuate, so can the patterns of sexual behaviour that are expressed; and yet once a narrative is established, it can be self-sustaining both in conditioning patterns and in the internal consistency patterns of the neural systems. This model is relevant to both heterosexual and homosexual behaviour patterns, and contributes to the explanation of sexual variation in general.

Regarding the case studies featured throughout this book — naturally, all names have been changed and identifying features have been omitted from the clinical material to protect the identities of those involved. The stories have been chosen not because of their unique characteristics, but precisely because they are representative of the many common experiences that are aired in the psychologist's room.

It is my hope and desire that this book helps in some way to motivate a regulation of sexual behaviours that will enhance the wellbeing of those engaged in sexual relationships. This helps not only the parties in the sexual relationship itself but also the community of which they are a part.

My thanks to all those people from whom I have learned so much, and that have made this book possible. Thanks also to Dr Cynthia Dixon and Dr Shaun Dempsey who read earlier manuscripts, and to Stephen May and his team for graciously taking this project on board.

Tony Schneider
March, 2019

About the Author

Tony Schneider is a clinical psychologist who studied at the University of Western Australia and Murdoch University. After five years as a full-time academic in psychology at Murdoch University, Tony worked as an educational and developmental psychologist in childcare centres and in the private schools sector. He entered private practice in 1989 and has remained in full-time private practice since. Tony has maintained a consultancy for schools, but also branched out into trauma debriefing and consulting at a pain management clinic. For many years he also provided supervision in Murdoch University's Master's programs, both in clinical and educational psychology. Tony's work as a clinician in private practice exposed him to a range of common clinical and relational issues, including trauma, grief and depression, anxiety, addictions, chronic pain, and problems in sexual relating. He has published several academic articles and book chapters. In 2013 his first book *The Brain, the Clinician, and I: Neuroscience findings and the subjective self in clinical practice* was published by Routledge.

Introduction

In an era of great mobility and frequent dislocation, the idea of 'home' is profoundly important. Without home we are nomads, refugees in an alien place. We can become alone and disconnected, unknown and unacknowledged, without purpose or role, unstable and directionless. And when we are exiled from home, or simply leave the home we knew for somewhere 'better', does the longing for the home we first knew ever cease? Home is the safe place where we can rest and find refreshment, support, and encouragement. Home is where we began and where we wish to end, even if the place defining home changes.

Probably one of our most powerful drives is the desire for 'home', the place where we belong and where others agree we belong. MacKay (2013) lists the desire for 'my place' as one of the ten basic desires that drive us:

> 'Home may be a multilayered concept but, for most of us, the deepest layer is located in our desire for a place that is unambiguously ours; a place that seems in harmony with us; that welcomes and comforts us; that says things about us we're pleased to have said… [It] is partly an anchor, partly a refuge, partly a stable reference point in a world that seems kaleidoscopic in the complexity of its shifting patterns… [It] helps not only to locate us, but to frame us, to contribute to our sense of who we are' (pp. 36–7).

It might be said that I belong to my home as much as it belongs to me. And although I belong to it, in a sense, I cannot really 'own' it as I might own a house. Mackay (2013) notes:

> 'Once you look beyond the economics and the aesthetics, you realise that "home" can't actually be owned at all. It's an idea too deeply lodged, too big, too rich, too complex, too subtle for ownership' (p. 65).

Nevertheless, ownership commonly associates with home and can become a basis for conflict where a home is shared. Furthermore, we might assert rights relating to our home — the right to stay where I belong; the right to express myself in the safety of home; the right to contribute to its arrangement and presentation; and the right to prevent violation of that space. Where home is shared, there will be rules, but good rules will feel familiar and natural, an expression of respect for each one sharing our home.

While 'home' is normally seen as a place in the external world, my *body* may also be thought of as home the place my subjective self necessarily lives. And, by extension, the person I share my body with in a sexual relationship also becomes associated with the 'home' that my body represents. If 'home' is about 'belonging', then the person I belong to and that belongs to me — that is, the relationship — might be considered a part of 'our home'.

Typically there is a crisis in the idea of 'home' during or following adolescence, as the adolescent prepares to leave the home of childhood in order to establish a new home. And so it was that I left the home I was born into so that I might make a new home with my wife. My parents and I once shared the same home; but then I left that home. Subsequently, my wife and I became united both in our sexual relationship and in our living arrangements — we came to belong to each other and shared a new home in every sense. The context that oriented me and contributed to my identity shifted from the home of my birth and the people of my upbringing to that of my wife and the children we subsequently had. Here again I became known, accepted, loved and respected. Here was my new 'home', both physically and psychologically, with a purpose and role recognised and needed by my wife and family.

In this book I argue that, like procreation, bonding and belonging constitute primary functions of a sexual relationship, a relationship that might be conceptualised as a person's psychological 'home'. However, we will discover that there are also other functions in the sexual relationship which are not necessarily aligned with these functions. Indeed, there are many different kinds of sexual experience and sexual expression, some of which are not relational at all, either because they are fleeting experiences, or because they don't involve another person. Our many drives and life experiences can bring dimensions into our sexual experiences that exclude the functions of procreation and belonging. A sexual relationship can create the foundation for belonging through the intimacy, love, trust, familiarity and commitment that accompanies such a relationship, and upon which such belonging depends. It can also serve as a vehicle for self-discovery and passing pleasure. At the same time, it can result in disappointment, emptiness and loneliness. Furthermore, belonging can be established but then be destroyed by the unauthorised entry of another person, leaving a sense of betrayal, disconnectedness, loss of self-esteem, and disorientation. A kind of 'home-invasion'. In other words, while a sexual relationship can create the context for wellbeing and belonging, it can also result in alienation and mental anguish.

An understanding of the complexities of sexual behaviour is critical when working with mental health problems that give rise to, or result from, sexual behaviour. Whether dealing with the trauma of sexual abuse, the pain of infidelity, self-rejection that leads to social withdrawal, or crises in sexual orientation; the need to understand sexual behaviour will play an important role in clinical practice. Surprisingly, until recently research and theory relating to sexual behaviour has received disproportionately small attention in the psychological literature compared to the attention it receives in politics and the media. The sexualisation of advertising, sexual themes in the arts, child sex abuse scandals, the same-sex marriage debate, the frequent failure of marriage giving rise to blended families and acrimonious court battles, the prostitution containment debates, the flooding of pornographic sites on the internet, and the problem of sexual predators using the internet, gain considerable political and media attention. Moreover, not only is the psychological literature on sexual relationships struggling to keep up with the social questions and controversies relating to sexual relationships, in the tradition of science it frequently provides impersonal perspectives and mechanistic explanations about an intensely personal event. Such perspective can contribute to the depersonalisation of the sexual experience.

Nevertheless, significant contributions have been made over time to the psychology of sexual behaviour and relationships, especially in more recent years. But the field continues to lack conceptual coherence, as Kleinplatz & Diamond (2014) observe: 'There is a lack of conceptual clarity regarding the entire spectrum of sexuality, from problematic to normal to optimal' (p. 247). Conflicting sociocultural sexual scripts and subscripts defining what sexual behaviour is acceptable has created further confusion and debate, clouding the issues of the role and function of the sexual relationship both personally and socially. Furthermore, the inherent complexity in the forces that drive sexual behaviour has made research design and interpretation difficult.

And so we are left to piece together a montage of ideas, research findings, clinical insights, and ideological sensitivities when formulating key principles or developing an integrative model of sexual relationships. Researchers acknowledge the complexities involved, referencing the varying contributions of biological, psychological, and sociocultural factors in sexual behaviours, and contributions have been made towards such integration (see, for example, Halpern (2006), Pfaus (2009), and Toates (2014)). The purpose of this book is to build on these contributions, working to integrate and apply recognised psychological principles towards a model of sexual relationships, especially with a view to better equipping those counselling in the area of sexual relationships. It is my hope that this book will provide a psychological map to navigate the complexities of sexual relationships, to better interpret individual subjective experiences of sexual events, and to better appreciate how the dynamics of a sexual relationship can influence a person's mental health.

I present a model that recognises multiple drives from two sources, biological and subjective, that operate within a context of sociocultural sexual scripts. These drives relate to various functions that the sexual relationship serves. The critical role of the perceptions and decisions of the subjective self, and the central functions of bonding and belonging in sexual relationships (helping make such relationship a psychological 'home'), receives particular attention. Indeed, I propose that when sexual activity serves to build belonging and attachment, good mental health is promoted. I also seek to restore a personal perspective to the psychology of sexual relationships.

Chapter 1

The Challenge of Explaining Sexual Behaviour

As he left the prostitute's premises, Karl regretted what he'd done and found himself with mixed feelings towards her for her part in the arrangement. It wasn't the money. He felt empty — he just didn't like himself. Karl wanted something more, but couldn't define what that more was. He'd looked forward to having a good time. And he did have a good time for a short time. He'd found adventure and release. Yet he felt cheated — and a bit stupid. Vague feelings of loneliness seemed only to have intensified. He resolved he wouldn't do it again, but knew in his heart that he probably would — and he would want similar sexual activities to happen, things his mates had talked about. He wanted to enjoy sex without the complications of a relation-ship (which he hadn't been much good at anyhow), and he was at a loss to know why this experience had left him like this. After all, she'd done every-thing he'd wanted, and he'd felt great while he was with her. From where did this urge to see her come, and why did he feel this way now? Was he really looking for something else?

Indeed. What causes me to do a thing? What is the origin of the drives and motives that energise my behaviour, and how do these affect my choices? How do I understand the behaviour I engage in, and what meanings do I attribute to such behaviour? For that matter, am I *able* to discern the motives of my own behaviour — can I always identify what moves me to do a thing? Or do I, like Karl, sometimes find myself doing things, and wonder why I do them? These questions are fundamental to psychology in general and no less so to the psychology of sexual behaviour and relationships. Sexual behaviour, moreover, has features that differentiate it from other behaviours. Although non-sexual motives and drives play a role in sexual behaviour and relationships, there are also drives unique to them. And this raises the question: what motives or drives make behaviour and the relationships in which such behaviour occurs 'sexual'?

Deeply embedded in both our physical and subjective selves are sexual differences. Indeed, this is true throughout the animal kingdom. Why might this be so, and what function does such sexual difference serve? We will look at this thing called 'sexual'. 'Maleness' and 'femaleness' is explored; and what is and isn't 'sexual'. Intrinsic to the sexual relationship is the expression of sexual motives — what is their function in relationship? We will ponder the other component to the sexual relationship — the 'relationship' — and what it has to do with sexual behaviour. We will consider the role of internal drives, introducing the idea that drives have two sources — a biological one and a subjective one. I will argue that we are influenced by a changing drive profile comprising multiple drives which in turn help predict the sexual behaviour and relationships in which we might engage. I will later identify factors that help shape a person's drive profile, paying particular attention to the notion of belonging.

On 'maleness' and 'femaleness'

A unique aspect in sexual behaviour that differentiates such behaviour from other behaviours is inherent in the notion 'sexual'. But what does this mean? According to my dictionary, 'sexual' has to do with the sexual act, the intentions and motives leading to the sexual act; and with the respective sexes, male and female, and the behaviours (essentially the gender predispositions) and physical characteristics unique to each defining their maleness and femaleness. We understand, of course, that there is a biological imperative that male and female should desire sexual encounters between each other (a primary and normal function of sexual behaviour): to create offspring.[1] Yet while sexual attraction between male and female might be mutual, there will be differences in the basis for that attraction between male and female, reflecting inherent differences in their maleness and femaleness. Indeed, it is the very *difference* that contributes to mutual attraction and desire. But this is not so for everyone: same-sex attraction and other forms of sexual expression reveal further complexities in the notion of what is and isn't 'sexual'.

We begin with the notions of 'maleness' and 'femaleness'. These are surprisingly difficult to define, even though the idea of consistent differences in male and female experience and behaviour resonates with popular perception and the observations of experienced relationship counsellors. Gray, for example, famous for his 1993 self-help book *Men are from Mars, Woman are from Venus*, suggests a number of such differences: men are 'solution-focused' rather than 'feeling-focused'; under stress men withdraw while women prefer to talk issues through; men and women have different needs for, and patterns in, intimacy; men need to be 'needed' while women need to be 'cherished'; men need a love that 'is more trusting' while women look for a love that is caring, understanding and respectful; and a man's need is to overcome his resistance to giving love while a woman's need is to overcome her resistance to receiving it. Is Gray right? And if so, are these differences inherent in maleness or femaleness, or are they learned gender roles?

While sexual differences are genetically determined and easily seen in the physical differences between a man and woman, the subjective aspect of maleness and femaleness is not so easily seen or understood. The experience of one with Gender Dysphoria highlights this subjective dimension: 'I feel that I (my subjective self) am female, even though I am in a male body.' Whatever the reason for this dysphoria, it seems that it is possible for the physical self to be male, while the inner self — the subjective experience or awareness - does not identify as such. This is not simply about a male *behaving* as a female - a cultural construct; it is about *feeling* or *identifying* as 'female', the self-perception of being female in a male body. Furthermore, even though feeling or identifying as female is not the same as having a female body, there is a need to have a female body to properly express such experienced femaleness: at least, this is what the person suffering Gender Dysphoria would argue and why the relevant treatments are sought.

But what does it mean for the inner self to be 'female' or 'male'? And why is it necessary for the body to reflect this?[2] This difference has historically been seen as the basis for the differences in the emotions, the psychology, and the motivations found between a man and a woman: commonly referred to as gender difference. Is this difference also reflected in the dynamics of sexual desire and attraction? And is the subjective experience of 'maleness' and 'femaleness', the basis of gender difference, innate? And then, how is it possible for these not to be aligned to physical sexual characteristics, as is the burden for those suffering Gender Dysphoria?[3]

Prenatal hormonal influences play a role in the masculinisation or feminisation of the brain, a process separate from the development of physical sexual characteristics. Nevertheless, to the extent that the body is the vehicle of expression for the inner self,[4] and that the neural and hormonal activity of the brain orients that self; we would expect the experienced maleness or femaleness of the self to correspond to the relevant physical sexual characteristics. And so, given that a female body is required to express the female self, and the male body is required to express the male self, reviewing the sexual features and functions of the physical body should be a legitimate source of clues as to what might define subjective 'maleness' or 'femaleness' — the gender identity.[5]

Whether or not it actually occurs in any particular sexual act, the biological fact is that a man's body is designed for sexual entry into a woman's body and to release his sperm within her. The testosterone that motivates and makes possible such entry by generating sexual desire and physical arousal is generally activated by seeing and thinking about sexual stimuli — the sight of an attractive woman may be enough to stimulate testosterone and arousal, an event of which he quickly becomes aware.[6] In this regard, the man has better capacity for keeping separate sexual arousal and the emotions associated with intimate encounter: he can easily be aroused outside a relationship, which may predispose him towards sexual curiosity and adventure.[7] Testosterone release is associated with dominance, competitiveness and territorial behaviours in general[8] — where strength of character or physical prowess is to advantage. Such predisposition can be used to overcome obstacles or protect a mate. However, it is more territorial than relational, and so the idea of 'belonging' might have a territorial flavour for the male.[9] Having released his sperm within the woman — that part of him is now in her — the man may be inclined to treat her as his 'territory', both then and when children are born into the relationship. She can be emotionally close to other people, but she mustn't give her body to anyone else: her body now belongs to him.[10]

These observations suggest that the meanings associated with 'maleness' might feature curiosity, adventure, the capacity to sexually respond to a woman's physical beauty, strength and forcefulness,[11] and the drive to claim, retain and protect territory. As such, these 'maleness' characteristics may feature strongly in the drive profiles of many men. We might also argue that these are the qualities women associate with 'maleness', although the characteristics of strength and the capacity to protect and provide are also primary issues for many women.

The woman's body, on the other hand, is designed to allow her to sexually receive the man and his sperm, while her breasts allow her to nurture new life. Her hormonal cycles mean that sexual desire and the associated sexual receptivity are affected by ovulation, which in turn prepares her for new life. This suggests a biological connection between her sexual receptivity and nurturance, an integration of sexual arousal, emotional intimacy, the possibility of new life, and concerns with the future — the establishment of a home or safe place both for herself and for her children.[12] In this context, for the woman, 'belonging' is more about shared experience, acceptance, identity, and affiliation. To the extent that she is receptive, she needs to be trusting of her man.[13] But she also needs to be socially and emotionally aware. Her man must not become emotionally involved elsewhere: she should be his only or primary influence, and so she learns to read emotions well.[14] She wants him to be protective and appreciate her physically and desire her body (and hers only — she watches for straying eyes). Yet she is careful about entering a relationship: to the extent that some dependence upon him may become necessary, it is important that she gets the 'right man', because she will need his support, strength, presence and understanding in the longer term, especially once she has had children.

These observations lead us to expect the meanings associated with 'femaleness' to feature integration between intimacy, emotional sensitivity and vulnerability, receptivity and an inclination to trust, nurturance and new life. We might argue that these are the qualities men associate with and perhaps desire in femaleness. Femaleness means the readiness to accept and receive what a man gives sexually, to trust for and desire his protection, general emotional sensitivity, and the capacity to create a place of nurturance.[15] Yet I suspect that for all the woman's complexity, a man is more likely to be initially drawn to and aroused by the simpler elements associated with femaleness: the physical and biological attributes of her femaleness and her sexual receptivity.

While the biological differences between a man and woman colours psychological and behavioural differences, the notion of maleness and femaleness — and especially how such maleness and femaleness is expressed — is also informed by cultural contexts and expectations.[16] Although not everyone will embrace these cultural expectations, they nevertheless serve to orient the inner self in the subjective experience and expression of maleness or femaleness in the social sphere. I will later review some major sociocultural sexual scripts which affect the drive profiles of male and female, and contribute to the emerging relationship dynamics.

The male/female distinction lends itself to the idea that each makes different contributions to a relationship on the basis of their inherent differences. Together they form a functioning social unit; the functions of one being intimately balanced by the functions of the other at a biological and psychological level. For one to enter, the other needs to receive. For one to respond, the other needs to initiate. The strength of one needs the trust of the other. The social and emotional awareness of one stabilises the tendency to adventure in the other. And for such a social unit to function over time, we find that a sexual relationship generally becomes integrated with the processes of bonding and belonging, which further contributes to emotional and psychological stability and satisfaction. This circumstance provides a secure setting for children born into the relationship; and the growing social unit continues to be coloured and balanced by the gender differences. Yet the diversity of drives found in a person's drive profile means that many sexual relationships don't fit this pattern, and that sexual behaviour will find broad expression — but often at cost.

On what is and isn't 'sexual'

We have seen how 'sexual' has to do with the respective sexes, male and female, and the behaviours (essentially the gender predispositions) and physical characteristics unique to each which defines their maleness and femaleness. But it also has to do with the sexual act and the intention (with its associated drives) and behaviours leading to the sexual act. This includes physiological arousal in which certain hormones and neurotransmitters are activated, creating tension and priming for sexual (genital) release (or intentionally stimulating this in another person); and the desire for, and experience of, sexual pleasure resulting from either their own or another person's actions. And, of course, it relates to entering another person's personal space with the intent of stimulating sexual interest and perhaps of establishing a subjective connection with that person, and ultimately the act of copulation.

Some of these components have to do with the sexual experience itself, but some associate with the relationship more generally, so that the two become intertwined. For example, one component involves physical touch and sexual entry, which stimulates a bonding process through the release of oxytocin and vasopressin. Along with this, a parallel event occurs: the entering into another person's subjective personal space, so that personal space becomes a shared space. Such intertwined components in sexual behaviour create associations (with corresponding neural connections) which link it to the notions of both belonging and bonding.

But first: what makes behaviour 'sexual'? A range of behaviours might attract the label 'sexual' but involve few of the above-mentioned components, while there are also behaviours that are decidedly nonsexual, yet have components associated with the idea 'sexual'. A key distinguishing factor is *intent* — that is, the meaning or purpose of the behaviour. For example, because love and intimacy associate strongly with sexual behaviour, behaviours relating to either love or intimacy may be interpreted as sexual, yet they may be without sexual intent: one need not imply the other. Two people can love each other deeply without sexual intent, such as a child and parent, or siblings, or two men or two women who are drawn together, perhaps through shared life experiences. Similarly, there are behaviours and experiences that might approximate aspects of sexual behaviour or experience, but, lacking sexual intent, are not considered 'sexual'; such as an adult caressing a child, a child suckling at the breast, a person receiving therapeutic massage, or a doctor conducting an intimate examination.

On the other hand, there are situations, behaviours, or comments that might be described as 'sexualised' because there is an intended association with sexual desire or behaviour, even though there is no actual sexual component to the situation, behaviour, or comment (such as may be found in advertising). Then there are behaviours where the boundaries and motives are blurred, and it is difficult to interpret whether or not the behaviours are 'sexual' (that is, whether there is sexual intent) — when one person meets the gaze of another; an affectionate embrace or physical touch; unintended sexual innuendo in conversation, and so on.

In making links between neurobiological processes and sexual experience and behaviour, it is necessary to differentiate between *sexual arousal, sexual desire* and *interpersonal sexual attraction*, even though these experiences can overlap and the distinctions can become blurred.[17] Nevertheless, these distinctions become important when analysing and deconstructing a person's prevailing drive profile: sexual arousal, desire, and interpersonal attraction are not always aligned, and nor does their combined presence necessarily predict a successful or functional sexual relationship. Furthermore, the blurring of these distinctions can sometimes create confusion in interpreting one's own physiological and psychological responses to a situation — for example, the experience of sexual arousal does not always correspond to sexual desire, nor is it always a valid indicator of sexual attraction. Let us consider these distinctions.

Generally, *sexual arousal* has to do with *eroticism* — the capacity of a stimulus to excite a genital response. Such a stimulus may be the presence of another person, or of sexual images or fantasy; it may even be a pleasant awareness of one's own sexual attributes. However, such genital response does not always reflect sexual desire; and sexual desire, on the other hand, can occur without a genital response. Consider, for example, masturbation without erotic images; a child sexually stimulated by an adult; therapeutic massage; and physical closeness. The one responsible for the sexual arousal does not necessarily represent an object of sexual desire for the one experiencing the arousal.[18] To be aroused simply means that physiological changes have taken place within the neuroendocrine system, typically involving the release of dopamine and melanocortins. Sexual arousal is a physiological event generally reactive to certain stimuli associated with sexual behaviour, but does not constitute a sexual drive as such, even though it is a critical link in the chain of sexual behaviour. Nevertheless, we will see that sexual arousal without interpersonal attraction or pre-existing sexual desire can result in the conditioning of subsequent sexual arousal responses, which in turn can create a sexual drive.

Distinguishing between *sexual desire* and *interpersonal sexual attraction* is more difficult. They involve rather nebulous dynamics comprising interrelated meanings, attributions, values, perceptions and expectations. Interpersonal attraction may involve admiration, love, or pleasure in the company of another person, and can occur without concomitant sexual desire, although the basis of attraction does normally include gender traits. Of course, interpersonal attraction can prime someone for sexual desire (just as sexual desire can prime someone for interpersonal attraction). Importantly, interpersonal attraction — whether sexual or otherwise — involves being drawn to a person because of certain qualities of the person to whom one is drawn: its focus is the other person, including their maleness or femaleness; not sexual activity as such. The experience of falling in love typically reflects this, as I will explain later.

More generally, desire relates to wanting an object or experience, so it generally emerges in the context of a perceived *lack* of something. It translates into an impulse to *own, consume* or *experience* something: its focus is one's own fulfilment. *Sexual desire*, then, has to do with wanting the fulfilment that comes through sexual experience. However, it can also refer to that sexual experience as an avenue to wanting, consuming, or experiencing someone, or certain aspects of that person. Being 'joined' to a person is subjectively accomplished through the sexual act — it can be a way of subjectively 'capturing' that person and what that person represents. In this case, the goal is not the sexual experience per se; but the sexual experience is used to obtain the goal — the getting of something which is seen in a person or associated with that person. The origin of such desire might reflect any combination of underlying drives that finds expression in the sexual act. To understand sexual desire in a person, we need to establish what that person wants to own, consume, or experience.

Of the attributes most men want to experience or own in another person, perhaps the most important is the femaleness of the woman — both of her body and her inner self; and for most women, the maleness of the man. But when sexual desire is 'desire for sex' only, it is essentially indiscriminate in terms of with whom a man or woman might have sex (especially where alcohol is involved), drawing a man or woman into sexual activity where there may be little interpersonal attraction outside the essential femaleness or maleness of the other body (as Karl discovered in his encounter with the prostitute).[19] Sometimes, of course, a man desires the maleness in another person (and a woman the femaleness in the other person); and then, sometimes, the sex of the other person is irrelevant, either because the sexual desire lacks all discrimination in what is desired except for the pleasure of sex itself, or because the desire is to own or experience certain inner qualities of the other person other than their maleness or femaleness. Where sexual desire relates to a particular person, then the desire is for the qualities seen in that person, a desire that finds momentary consummation through the sexual act with that person.

The relational goals of connection and belonging

We have considered what makes behaviour 'sexual'. Sexual behaviour, however, is one thing; a sexual *relationship* is another. And because sexual behaviour generally occurs in the context of relationship, relationship dynamics necessarily play a role, affecting the quality of the sexual encounter. Indeed, sexual and relationship satisfaction are closely linked.[20] A relationship has to do with relating to and connecting with someone else. But where a relationship is *sexual*, that relating and connecting necessarily has a sexual dimension. Belonging comprises an important element of sexual relationships. Love and intimacy add further elements addressing relational needs, forming the basis for *romantic relationships*. Of course, not all relationships are sexual; nor does all sexual activity occur within relationship — romantic or otherwise.[21] We will find that these variations are the outcomes of different drive profiles.

But first we need to make a distinction. While the ideas of belonging and attachment overlap, they are not the same. I can belong and not be attached; and I can become attached but not belong. A child can belong to its parents and not be attached to them, while a person who has fallen in love may feel an attachment to someone that doesn't yet belong to them. One aspect of belonging has to do with social *identification* with somebody. Such identification might cause me to be embarrassed by a person's behaviour when I feel I belong to them, which I wouldn't if they didn't belong to me. By the same token, I would feel proud of their achievements because they are a part of me, and represent me as much as they do themselves. Ours becomes a *shared* experience, with shared ownership of decisions, accomplishments, failures, and so on. It is primarily a matter of *social position*: others also perceive and respect that the couple belong to each other. When something happens to the person that belongs to me, it also vicariously happens to me. I will argue that the need to belong is a central psychological drive, and that one function of the sexual relationship is to meet that drive.

While attachment is also about shared experience, its focus is different. It has to do with the *nature* of the bond that has been created — with intimacy and being close to someone. What matters is a person's acceptance, interest, and understanding of me, regardless of how they might come across socially. I am less likely to be embarrassed by or proud of the person I am attached to: so long as they are there for me. What is important is the connection, the interpersonal need for recognition and validation, the mutual encounter. With attachment, what *others* think of the person is not as important as what the person thinks of *me*. Secure attachment is built on a person's ongoing emotional presence and availability when I need them; it also involves my desire to be emotionally transparent with them in order that they might know me and validate me.

Belonging is a fundamental drive that associates with relatedness and attachment. Although they don't distinguish between attachment and belonging, Baumeister and Leary (1995) conclude 'that human beings are fundamentally and pervasively motivated by a need to belong, that is, by a strong desire to form and maintain enduring interpersonal attachments. People seek frequent, affectively positive interactions within the context of a long-term, caring relationship… The desire for interpersonal attachment may well be one of the most far-reaching and integrative constructs currently available to understand human nature' (p. 522).[22] Rokach (2014) echoes this observation: 'There is a basic human need to belong, to be part of an intimate and caring relationship with a partner who is close, and deeply concerned about us [so that] we are driven to establish close contact with others, and participate in intimate relationships' (p. 155). Furthermore, research has found that relatedness, or the sense of belonging, is important for our mental health. It is associated with better functioning and greater resilience to stress.[23] In its absence, sadness, depression, jealousy, health problems, and loneliness may emerge.[24] Belongingness helps to orient us socially, and its connections contribute to our sense of meaningfulness.[25]

Given the centrality of the human need to belong and establish attachment, it comes as no surprise that it might constitute a primary function of a sexual relationship.[26] There is a drive to belong, and attachment reflects the quality of the associated intimacy. Ideally, significant relationships are characterised by both belonging and attachment, and this is especially true for sexual relationships. There is a sense of mutual identification, closeness, acceptance and embrace that has a different quality in such relationships than in other relationships, because of the unique physical sharing of self that does not occur in other relationships. Besides this, there is a cooperative component involving mutual consent and the fulfilling of various needs and desires not fulfilled in non-sexual relationships. In fact, for many people such relationship represents both the goal and proper integration for their sexual expression.

It is the difference between sexual expression within relationship and that occurring casually that had left Karl vaguely dissatisfied after his visit to the prostitute. Whatever Karl thought he wanted, he didn't get. Even though he could buy sex, *she* was not for sale. He didn't get her or what she might have represented to him. He glimpsed her femaleness, but didn't encounter her as a person. He gave nothing of himself except money and his body: she gave nothing of herself except her time and her body for sexual performance. Perhaps he needed to express and explore his masculinity, and he needed the femaleness of a woman to do so. Karl was not attracted to a male prostitute; this was not the focus of his need or desire. Even though he didn't know the woman, it was the woman he thought he wanted. But all he got was a sexual encounter: the enactment of his sexual fantasy, a reassurance of his maleness, and the temporary amelioration of his sexual tension. Oddly, although he knew from the beginning what the deal was, the experience stimulated something else: it stimulated a vague desire for more of her and of her femaleness, to have her indefinitely and exclusively, and perhaps connect with her more deeply. Multiple drives were at work.

Karl knew he would come again even though this experience had left him feeling vaguely depersonalised and disconnected. His identity as a person had been irrelevant, and she would never belong to him, or he to her. He felt 'short-changed'. The event was not without consequence. From the prostitute Karl learned that 'loving care' did not mean loving care at all; and that sex had nothing to do with the 'giving' by the woman of herself to him. He learned about deception and pretence; he learned meanings of the sexual event that left him empty and cynical; he learned about a world of unfulfilled promises. The sexual experience came to have negative associations for him. He was disillusioned and lonely. Nevertheless, he kept her number and knew he would probably be back. Although he was conflicted, the sex he had purchased for his masculinity had been pleasurable in itself; it had given him release, and she had done nothing wrong by him. She was a good business woman and had kept to the agreement. For Karl, his confusion related to a mixed drive profile that also included unmet needs to connect and belong.

On belonging: Further considerations

What does it mean to 'belong' in a sexual relationship? We might think of belonging as having a shared history or shared values with someone else, things in common, promoting a sense of connection: 'I belong to this person because we both came from the same town and we both love fishing.' Alternatively, to belong might involve a sense of ownership: 'She belongs to me because I have invested so much in her.'[27] Then again, to 'belong' might mean that I have a role or place that fits a specific need or purpose: for example, 'you belong in our organisation (that is, you have this role) because of the particular skills you have.' In each case, we see that 'belonging' is a *relational* notion, reflecting some investment, connection, obligation, meaning or role in a relationship. Each nuance of meaning may also find its way into a sexual relationship.

To better grasp this idea, consider my relationship with my mind and body. I normally experience my mind (here I mean my perceptions, thinking and emotions) as belonging to me — that is, belonging to my subjective inner self,[28] just as my body belongs to me. I normally protect myself (my mind and body) and maintain the integrity of my uniqueness and separateness from others (other minds and bodies). For example, I protect my body by clothing it, shielding it from pressure and harm, and guarding it from unwanted and invasive eyes and touch.[29] I do this because my body is private territory, my 'home': it is not just a physical body indifferent to the effects of the physical world and the presence of others as a dead body might be. It is 'owned' by me; it *belongs* to me — that is, to my inner self. I have an intimate relationship with my body, expressing myself through it, embracing it, looking after it, protecting it, and investing in it. There is a union between me and my mind and body, but also autonomy and separateness of my mind and body from others: my mind and body belong only to me. One might argue such exclusivity (that is, that it belongs only to me) to be an inherent right.[30] Nevertheless, given my mind and body belong to me, I have a right to choose to share these with another person. And to the extent that my inner self is expressed through my mind and body, then, when I share my mind and body with somebody else, I also share my inner self.

How can sex associate with 'belonging'? When I choose to share my body sexually with a person, it is not just one body encountering another body — each reacting physiologically to the other, giving energy and life to the other — but it is also our inner selves doing so, finding expression in each body's activity, giving and receiving, and (ideally) at the same time discovering and enjoying subjectively the inner self of the other person.[31] In this way, both selves are changed by the encounter, a change imprinted on the brains and inner worlds represented by our respective bodies. In effect, I am giving both of my inner self and my body, and in return, I am receiving from the other person both their body and inner self.[32] We become vulnerable to each other, each trusting that what has been given to the other will be treasured and protected, just as each treasures and protects what was given. This shared investment and the intense experiences associated with the sexual relationship bond us together and typically generate a sense of mutual belonging. And so it is not surprising to find that high relationship satisfaction is strongly associated with high sexual satisfaction — it is a bi-directional relationship.[33]

In a sexual encounter the physical interpersonal boundaries maintaining separateness are removed, and the respective bodies become shared territory. The body of the other person for that moment comes to belong to me as much as my own body belongs to me — in a sense we share ownership. Two 'homes' become one shared 'home': we are joined together. I enjoy the other body as much as I do mine, just as I protect the other body as I do mine. And again, the other person equally enjoys and protects my body as they do their own. The mutual vulnerability this creates needs protective factors. It requires interpersonal sensitivity, trust, and a mutual commitment to each other's wellbeing (that is, love for one another), so that the shared 'home' remains a safe and beneficial place to be.

The sense of belonging is not just momentary: a union is created.[34] From now on, if someone else should approach the other (shared) mind and body threatening to take it from me, I may be provoked to jealousy or anger — I view it as someone invading our shared territory and home.[35] Indeed, if the relationship is under threat, sexual intimacy may be activated to ensure closeness and reassurance, and to ensure the integrity of the relationship.[36] Once I kept *my* mind and body separate from others; now I want to keep *our* minds and bodies separate from others. The sense of belonging insists on exclusivity in the sexual relationship,[37] and where this is violated through infidelity, relationship dissolution generally follows,[38] even though feelings of belonging, attachment, and sexual desire can still linger for a considerable period.[39] If we allow invasion into 'our territory', our sense of 'ownership' over our shared selves is diminished, our sense of self is affected, and we become disempowered and weakened in a moral sense. The third party threatens to take what we perceive has come to belong to us. This sense of belonging is invisible and unmeasurable, but powerful in its implications, both personally and socially.[40]

In both sexual and non-sexual intimate relationships, the boundaries protecting the inner self are relaxed, so that our respective inner selves become shared territory to the extent that our thinking and emotions are shaped by each other's presence.[41] With interpersonal attraction (as against sexual attraction), there is a desire to encounter the inner self of the other person so that our inner selves might become 'shared territory', as well as enjoying the more 'superficial' qualities of the person. In these circumstances there is no sharing of our respective bodies. But in a functional *sexual* relationship, there is a desire to encounter both the inner self and the body of the other person: the sharing of interpersonal territory occurs at both physical and relational levels.[42] And probably the most profound and enduring extension and expression of this 'shared investment' or 'mutual belonging' is in the birth of a child into the relationship — the child belongs to both parties and both parties belong to the child. Belonging forms a primary function in a sexual relationship, and the drive to belong quite appropriately finds expression in sexual behaviour.

Chapter 2

Drives and Sexual Behaviour

Karl's reaction after his visit to the prostitute revealed that drives were present of which he was not aware — his visit had satisfied some drives, but not others. What was the nature of his various drives? What made him visit the prostitute, a visit that left him vaguely unhappy? What makes him do anything? This is another way of asking: what are the underlying forces or motives that energise and direct Karl's behaviour? What was he wishing to achieve in his visit to the prostitute — what was his conscious or unconscious goal? Is there such a thing as a biological 'sex drive' that 'caused' him to desire and engage in sexual behaviour with the prostitute? But how might such a drive discriminate with whom and under what circumstances he should have a sexual encounter? Karl's experience suggests that it was not a single drive, biological or otherwise, conscious or otherwise, that energised his actions: several drives appeared to be operating simultaneously, and not all those drives were fulfilled in his case. Moreover, in this mix of drives, some serve to make him want something, others to actively avoid something. But what were these drives?

The idea that a mix of drives prompted Karl to do what he did can also be used to explain why others enter into sexual encounters and relationships of one sort or another. Moreover, to explain the many ways in which sexual behaviour is expressed, I propose that the composition of drives varies between people, and over time in any one person. Theoretically, identifying different drive combinations might help us predict with whom and under what circumstances a person has a sexual encounter or relationship. Fleeting sexual encounters will generally involve different drive combinations than long-term sexual relationships, while relationships of convenience will generally involve different drive combinations than romantic ones. In like manner, sexual variation emerges from variation in drive combinations. But what drives comprise these drive combinations? How can such drives be identified and measured, and how might different drive combinations form? I will argue that there are both biological and subjective aspects to these drives, forcing us into a dualism of some kind. I will argue for an interactive dualism, rather than for parallel and independent processes in the biological and subjective spheres.

Drive theory: What prompts me to do something?

A drive is a subjective motivating urge that stimulates behaviour. It is a force that energises and directs an action or activity. It reflects an incentive towards a particular goal and is the basis upon which we might say 'the reason or purpose for doing something is such and such.' However, the term 'drive' has had particular meanings in the history of psychology. Early drive theorists conceptualised drives (or 'instincts') as essentially mechanical and deterministic in nature, where an irresistible physiological need aroused and energised a person to activity, reducing discomfort or maximising pleasure in relation to the physiological need.[43] While avoiding notions of goal or purpose in describing behaviour, behaviour theorists argued that the behaviours such drives energised were shaped by a person's learning history, whereby the learned habit patterns determined how a person might satisfy relevant physiological needs.[44] Reinforcement schedules and conditioning theories explained the links between drives and observed behaviours. The satisfying of the physiological drive established the reinforcement value of the relevant behaviours, thus forming the basis of the habit pattern. This conditioning theory underpinned psychological interventions of the 1960s and 1970s, including interventions relating to sexual behaviour and orientation, with varying success.[45]

However, the idea of a drive as simply a physiological energy system directing behaviour failed to explain many behaviours. There needed to be a subjective dimension to drives — a dimension involving a person's perceived needs and desires. Indeed, we know that subjective perceptions and their associated desires can overpower physiological needs. And so some earlier theorists cast a wider net to the question of what motivates us to do things, such as Murray in his 'universal needs', Miller in his 'conditioned motives';

and others who proposed various 'mini-theories' of motivation.[46] Each of these contributions offered particular insights into the complex interaction of drives that energise behaviour.

Nevertheless, because of the problems inherent in measuring and predicting drives, motives, incentives and intentions, and because of the complexities such notions added to experimental design, they lost their appeal as explanatory mechanisms in evidence-based psychological theory and research in subsequent decades. But this did not mean the notions themselves were invalid or outdated; from a clinical perspective, they remained central constructs.[47] We return to these ideas, but make distinction between our use of the term 'drive' and that used in traditional drive theory. Our focus is on the subjective aspect of drives — whether the drive source be subjective or physiological. To gain insight into the interplay of the subjective and physiological components of prevailing drives, let us leave the subject of sex for a moment and consider an equally fundamental activity: eating.

We all understand the need to eat. This need has an obvious primary physiological function: that is, to provide nutrition for the body. Normally, when the physiological need arises, the body generates hormones creating a desire to ingest food — that is, it creates hunger signals.[48] While the source of these signals may be biological, they are apprehended by the subjective self, creating a felt urge — a 'drive' to eat. Yet the need to eat does not discriminate what food is good for the health of the body, even though a primary function is to keep it healthy. Furthermore, competing motives affecting eating behaviour may have little to do with this physiological need and primary function. Take, for example, the person suffering an eating disorder,[49] or choosing to fast until they get political demands met: here the physiological 'need to eat' is suppressed. If we were to define a drive by its goal, we would find many different goals for eating (or not eating): I might eat because it is dinnertime, because I am bored, because I feel sad, because the food looks/smells good (for pleasure), to celebrate, to be nurtured emotionally, to be social, to make a political statement and so on. The goal becomes the defining element of the subjective drive, a drive that can have more to do with the state of the inner self or with social demands than with bodily needs.

And so we see that different subjective drives can relate to the same behaviour: in this case, whether or not to eat. A drive can be linked to a physiological need (eating to satisfy felt hunger that signals physical needs), or to other subjective desires and goals (such as eating in order to respect the hospitality of the host). 'The reason for' may relate to a conscious awareness or decision (a decision to lose weight), but it might also be an unconscious process (to meet emotional needs).[50] Furthermore, the goal of the drive, though expressed in certain behaviours, exists independent of those behaviours. That is, I can desire something long before that desire finds consummation in my behaviour, and the behaviour in which it finds consummation (if indeed, I choose to consummate that drive) can vary: I can feel hungry for some time before I decide to eat; and where, how, and what I eat can vary depending on other coexisting and competing drives, as well as on prevailing environmental and social circumstances.

Various drives can act simultaneously in relation to eating behaviour. I can eat both because I am hungry and I wish to please my dinner host. Different functions are being met at the same time. But co-occurring drives may also be in conflict: I may want to eat because I am hungry, yet not want to eat because I have been putting on too much weight. Some drives may be ego-dystonic: that is, I experience an urge I would rather not have (I continue to feel hungry although I've already eaten too much). And so I may need to manage drives that create conflict, as conflict creates psychological distress. The management of drives involves optimising the fit between drives, their possible expression, and my values and beliefs, so that internal and external conflict is minimised. In such a process, a particular drive may be rationalised by changing or amending a value or belief, or a particular drive may be inhibited or embraced behaviourally to match an underlying value or belief. Situations may be avoided altogether to limit the activation of unwanted drives. Furthermore, the meanings attributed to a drive can be coloured to match the underlying values and beliefs.

There are other complications. For example, eating might satiate a physiological drive. However, when eating is motivated by loneliness, no satiation occurs. In this case, eating may help someone feel better momentarily, but it is unrelated to bodily needs, and it won't fulfil the need for company. In other words, the outcome of the activity doesn't meet the goal of the drive that set it in motion. The circumstances of eating can also change the extent to which related subjective drives are met. I can eat a burger alone, but the experience will be different when I eat a burger prepared for me by a friend. When this happens, I don't only eat a burger; I am also the recipient of my friend's love and intent to bless me. I feel special and significant by the intent and energy and sacrifice of my friend. The event becomes not only an act of eating; it now carries layered meanings in regard to relationship. Eating alone accentuates loneliness: eating with another might mean acceptance and recognition by another person. Without these other meaning layers, I might eat simply to combat my loneliness, which can result in overeating — even though my body has had enough, my loneliness remains, and so I keep eating.

Alternatively, I might lose interest in eating altogether where other critical needs are not being met.

And so we see that eating has a primary physiological function, but also has psychological and social functions. Moreover, the motives relating to eating may be mixed and vary greatly and independently of its physiological function; and the circumstances of eating further affects what drives are met. This is also true for functions and drives relating to sexual behaviours. While I might argue that sexual relating has the physiological function of procreation, and the psychological and social function of belonging, the drives relating to sexual activity and the goals they represent can vary considerably and independently of these functions. Furthermore, like eating, the need for sexual expression does not discriminate what sexual behaviour is good for the health of a sexual relationship. In this respect, the term 'sexual drive' is similar to the term 'eating drive', in that it gives no information about the great variation of possible drive goals except the implied biological imperative, nor does it identify what constitutes a 'healthy' or 'functional' expression of such drives. There are drives that shape behaviour that have little to do with the primary functions of that behaviour. For example, eating or sexual behaviour in order to 'prove a point' may have some fleeting social or psychological value, but it does not serve any enduring purpose. Similarly, eating junk food alone or masturbating to pornography may provide some fleeting pleasure, but again, such behaviour does not serve a functional personal or wider social goal.

And so 'sexual drive' is best thought of as a complex profile of any number of drives. It is coloured by hormones, mood, situation, personal history, and personal and societal expectations and values which relate to both primary or secondary functions of sexual behaviour. The relative strength of each drive can vary, affecting a person's overall drive profile from one circumstance to the next, and so affecting the person's ultimate decisions and behaviour. There will naturally be debate as to what might be considered 'primary' and 'secondary' functions of behaviour: is this relative to a person's drive profile (reflecting the most powerful prevailing drives), to sociocultural values and expectations, or to biological imperatives? Each no doubt plays a role, and it is up to the reader to decide whether the argument for what serves as primary functions in sexual behaviour is convincing, and whether the various expressions of such drives might be seen as 'healthy' or 'functional'.

The notion that sexual behaviour involves both multiple drives[51] and multiple functions has important implications. It is the particular mix of drives that predict whether the resulting sexual behaviours are likely to promote the long-term wellbeing of the parties involved, and to perform the multiple functions required. As such, it might be argued that a healthy mix of drives serves a protective function. For example, if pleasure and enjoyment is the only motivating drive, it might find expression in such behaviours as binge-eating, smoking, and recreational drug use, negatively affecting a person's long-term wellbeing. Similarly in sexual behaviour, where the attainment of pleasure and enjoyment is the only or pre-eminent drive and function, the long-term wellbeing of the persons involved may be compromised. Various forms of sexual exploitation come to mind. If pleasure and enjoyment is the only function and goal of sexual behaviour, the relevance of with whom, how, when or where I have my sexual experience relates only to the degree of pleasure I might anticipate. Once this drive is paired with the need for intimacy and to belong, however, a different picture emerges.

There is further a principle that moderates sexual behaviour (and behaviour generally) which might for our purposes also be thought of as a drive. It is the drive to homeostasis at the biological level, and its counterpart at the psychological level; the drive to internal consistency — that is, to think and behave in a manner consistent with one's self-image and past history.[52] This drive to homeostasis results in the maintenance of the existing equilibrium in biological systems, while the drive to internal consistency results in interpretation of subjective events so that such interpretation remains consistent with the existing decisions and perceptions that define a person's sense of self — that which orients that person. For example, if a woman decides she is unattractive because she is carrying too much weight, even though her doctor sees her as dangerously underweight, she will nevertheless experience a strong drive to starve herself in keeping with her perception and orientation. Meanwhile, her body has adjusted to very low food intake and seeks to maintain its current internal equilibrium. Because of the stability of her self-image, this behaviour becomes very difficult to shift. And so, although the drive profile is dynamic, the brain seeks stability, consistency and familiarity. These two opposing forces — the brain's capacity to adapt to hormonal and social changes with accompanying drive profile changes, and the brain's competing need to create a stable and familiar sense of self (internal consistency) — creates a dynamic of its own, potentially with its own conflicts.

A person makes decisions and develops perceptions in their early years that shape their sense of self, and that emerge as basic schemas or belief systems.[53] These are not inherent or inevitable, but they are nevertheless powerful and difficult to change, because of this drive to homeostasis. The motivation is to match subsequent behaviour to the self-image, reinforcing the image. Such decisions and self-perceptions might include: 'I'm unattractive'; 'I don't belong'; 'I'm not good enough'; 'I'm worth more'; and so on. Perceptions of this kind result in a person not attempting activities that are inconsistent with their self-image, or feeling anxiety or dysphoria should they find themself in situations that require them to attempt activities inconsistent with their self-image.

This principle also operates in relation to a person's sexual self-image — and perhaps, to an extent, their sexual orientation. Labelling a person in relation to their identity or orientation tends to reinforce this process. The younger the person is when the perception is established and the longer it is held, the more difficult it is to change. Whatever other drives might subsequently contribute to sexual attraction and desire, the subjective drive to internal consistency regarding a person's sexual self-image plays an important role in the behaviours enacted. And so, should Karl see himself as not 'good enough' for a relationship with a girl, he remains consistent with that self-image by trying to purchase from the prostitute what he believes he is not good enough to receive in relationship.

A dual drive-source, multiple-drive model

We have considered some of the complexities involved in explaining sexual behaviour and relationships. These complexities have made it difficult to integrate theory and the wide-ranging focus of research relating to sexual behaviour and relationships. This section introduces a model designed to bring together the disparate issues and complexities confronting the psychologist when working with sexual behaviour and relationships. *Figure 2.1* outlines this model, which provides a map to enable us to navigate our way.

There are several features to note in this model, which I explain more fully later. First, the subjective (top half in *Figure 2.1*) parallels the biological (bottom half in *Figure 2.1*) at all points of the sexual relationship process, from the initial drives to the relationship outcomes. Second, the decisional aspect (a part of the subjective self), prevents the model being a deterministic one. Third, there is an interactive dynamic between the subjective and biological aspects whereby each continually influences the other. Fourth, although interpersonal attraction, sexual desire, and sexual arousal generally interact, they can also act independently of each other. Fifth, while the drives and sociocultural scripts orient the *circumstances* of sexual behaviour (with whom, when, and where sexual behaviour might occur), sexual desire and arousal prime for actual *expression* of these drives: both aspects have a direct bearing on the sexual behaviour itself. Sixth, while the model has linear aspects, it also loops back so that the outcomes help shape the subsequent drive profile, maintaining consistency over time, as shown in *Figure 2.2*.

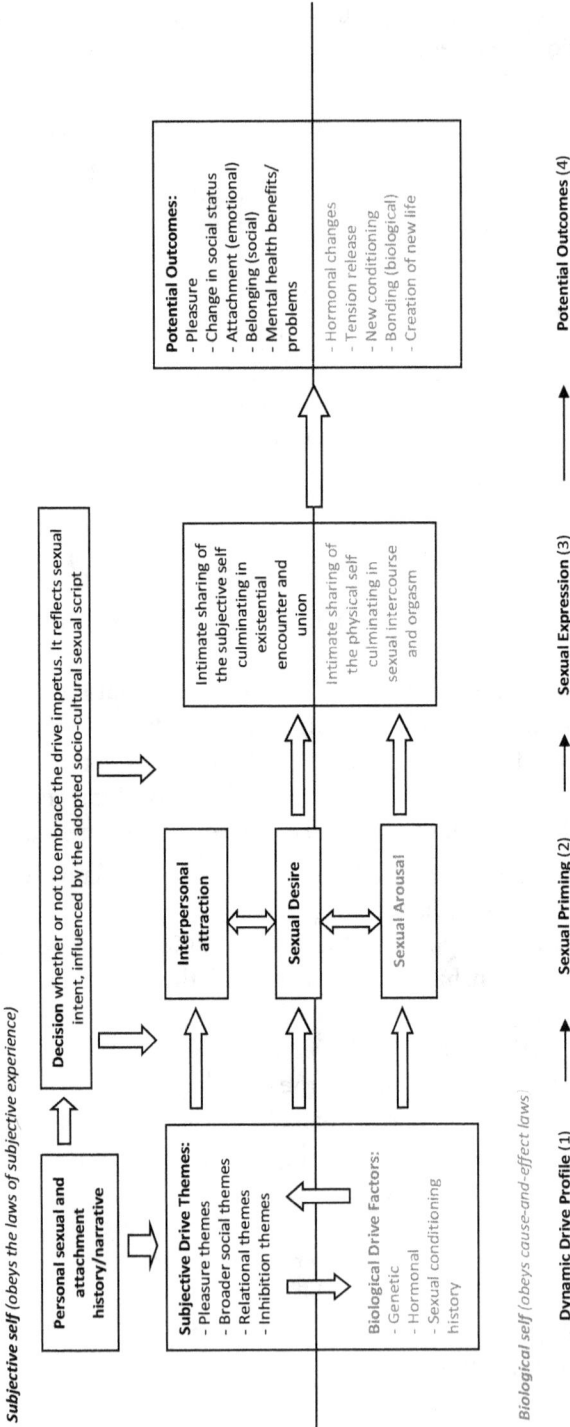

Multiple Drive Model of Sexual Relationships

FIGURE 2.1

(1) Subjective drives help orient and prime biological systems, while biological drives help orient and prime the subjective self. The fluctuating multiple drive profile orients the person for sexual priming; depending on the mix of ascendant drives, it either activates or inhibits sexual priming. Elements of the drive profile also play a role in sexual identity and sexual orientation. (2) While they are separate events, interpersonal attraction may prime for sexual desire, and vice versa. Similarly, while they are separate events, sexual desire may prime for sexual arousal, and vice versa. (Sexual arousal can also result from non-sexual events.) (3) For intimate sharing to happen, sexual expression needs to take place within a relationship, which of course is not always the case. Furthermore, sexual experience does not always occur in the context of sexual priming (for example, in some abuse situations) (4) These short and long-term potential outcomes, some of which are only possible within a relationship, may or may not satisfy the goals of the original drives; several of these outcomes (for example, pleasure, belonging, hormonal changes, and conditioning) in turn will affect the subsequent drive profile.

Sexual Relationship Cycle

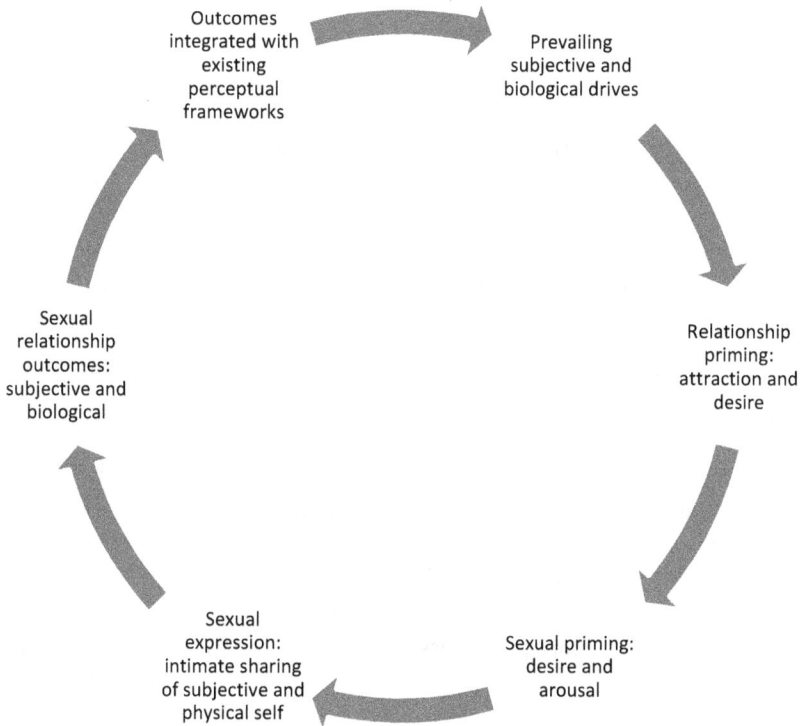

Outcomes integrated with existing perceptual frameworks

Prevailing subjective and biological drives

Relationship priming: attraction and desire

Sexual relationship outcomes: subjective and biological

Sexual expression: intimate sharing of subjective and physical self

Sexual priming: desire and arousal

FIGURE 2.2

This diagram depicts a circular process, rather than the linear process that is typically shown to explain sexual behaviour. Here we see that each sexual encounter has outcomes that are integrated into our perceptual frameworks, helping shape the prevailing drive profile, which in turn plays a role in future sexual behaviour. The outcomes of sexual expression may be positive or negative, which has an activating or inhibiting effect for future sexual encounters. Relationship priming is here presented as preceding sexual priming, but of course such relationship priming may be minimal or even non-existent in some circumstances. Decisional aspects or the effects of the prevailing socio-cultural context are not shown here.

This model of the psychology of sexual behaviour is based on the idea that there are two drive sources that orient and energise the subjective self. There is a biological source that mostly involves neuroendocrine processes, and a subjective source that involves social and psychological motives. Each drive source represents a complex mix of dynamic forces, an ever-changing profile of drives, rather than a simple and stable force. The stability of the drive profile will vary between people: the strength of certain drives might fluctuate hourly while others are much more stable; the overall drive composition can also fluctuate over the lifespan. Nevertheless, this fluctuation is constrained by the drive to homeostasis and internal consistency.

Early theorists have described drives involving both biological and non-biological aspects.[54] One of the ongoing debates in the literature concerning sexual behaviour is between the essentialists, who focus on biological explanations for sexual behaviours, and the social constructionists, who focus on sociological explanations for sexual behaviours:[55] both aspects clearly play a role. Of course, neither tells the full story, and other theorists have argued for a more integrated dual-source model of sexual behaviour.[56]

My model distinguishes between natural laws and laws relating to the subjective self. The natural laws that comprise the world of science describe cause-and-effect relationships. However numerous and interactive the various natural factors acting upon something (think chemistry and physics), the combination of these factors will theoretically predict the outcome. If we can identify the strength of all relevant factors, we can accurately calculate the outcome. These factors are irresistible and inevitable, they can be measured and their action predicted: they just are. These cause-and-effect relationships remain true and unchanged, across time and across people. It is a closed and deterministic system. Scientific explanation is an explanation that describes events in terms of these cause-and-effect laws.

Psychological science, however, needs to deal with another dimension that interacts with natural laws and their inherent predictability: the dimension of the subjective self. This is the dimension of ideas, meanings, and reasoning, of decision-making and independent initiative. The laws it obeys are not the same as those of natural laws. It is no longer a closed and deterministic system. Rather than cause-and-effect, it is about subjective perceptions that form the basis for reasoning and action. It is about the purpose and function of behaviour — the intent and motives. The rules that govern these are not irresistible or inevitable as natural laws are, and they are not easily measured or accurately predicted. They have the capacity to change across time and across people. Nevertheless, they are not random or without reason. But the reason for such behaviour relates to subjective perceptions, prevailing emotions, and personal goals — behaviour is not just the inevitable outcome of prevailing forces; it can be said to have a purpose.

We might say there are natural laws and supernatural laws, in the sense that the latter deal with laws that may be superimposed upon the former natural laws. The natural laws are never suspended, but may be interfered with by 'supernatural' laws that govern the actions of the subjective self. And so the study of natural laws remains relevant in psychology. As human beings, we simultaneously inhabit bodies subject to natural cause-and-effect laws, and have minds that can make subjective decisions that 'interfere' with these natural laws, bringing about different outcomes. These, then, are reflected in the two drive sources, one obeying natural laws; the other obeying 'supernatural' laws. It is the 'supernatural' laws of the subjective self that submit to legal and moral considerations in a way that natural laws never could.[57]

In the present conceptualisation of a dual-drive model, the first drive source is neurobiological and governed by natural laws. That is, the drives involve the neuroendocrine system with its associated hormones, peptides, and neurotransmitters which either prime for and activate or inhibit sexual desire and sexual arousal. These drives originate from the chemistry of our biological selves and are sensitive to ever-changing neurobiological processes. They are affected by external environmental conditions (through classical conditioning) or by the internal physiological environment (including various mood and emotion states) and can fluctuate hourly, monthly, and more subtly over the lifespan. The classical conditioning processes relate to automatic associations the brain establishes with pleasure and pain, and which involve automatic physiological and behavioural responses, rather than ideas-related responses, and so are included under this umbrella. And although subjective ideas and perceptions can emerge from various mood or emotion states, the source of the idea or perception in such instance is the physiological event itself. Furthermore, genetic predispositions (including temperament) and diseases (such as diabetes, polycystic ovarian disease, and various psychiatric illnesses) as well as events such as traumatic brain injury[58] may also play a role at this neurobiological level. I refer to the prevailing collection of drives sourced from the biological system as the Biological Drive Profile, or BDP.

But we are as motivated by ideas as we are by hormones and conditioning, perhaps more so.[59] Although the source is different from physiological imperatives, the result of both is the energising and directing of sexual behaviour. And so we come to the second drive source, governed by 'supernatural' laws, whose collection of drives I refer to as the Subjective Drive Profile, or SDP. This second drive source comprises drives that derive from ideas, beliefs, meanings, memories, values, perceptions and decisions apprehended by the subjective self — critical components of the evolving mind map that orients the subjective self.[60] These meanings and ideas include those relevant to the expression of the inner self, and those relevant to a person's role in wider society. Some of these drives are relatively stable, although changes in circumstance may cause the profile to fluctuate. Although these meaning-based drives can generate emotions (and therefore activate physiological processes), in such cases the source of the drive is not the emotion itself, but the idea or perception giving rise to the emotion.

Ideas relate to an intangible and unmeasurable dimension, yet play a critical role in the physical world of tangible and measurable events. Consider how an architect's thoughts ultimately shape a building, or how the coach's ideas influence the movement of players in the field. The physiological event of hormonal release and the subjective event of ideas and meanings can occur simultaneously, one activating the other, just as multiple ideas can reflect complex associations; and all of these interact. The latter are difficult to explicate, depending largely on introspection and self-awareness. Through introspection, people are generally able to identify at least some reasons that contribute to the way they might behave: for example, why they might be attracted to (or repelled by) another person. Identifying underlying belief systems and emotional responses also give clues to the drives that comprise a person's SDP, as we will see.

The differentiation and labelling of drives in the SDP is inherently problematic, however. The brain is associative in nature,[61] and so drives based on subjective perceptions will reflect meaning clusters that vary from one person to the next. And so I do not conceive the different drives as representing discrete categories or entities that mean the same thing from one person to the next: rather, I describe approximate and interdependent motivational themes, referencing motives and drives described by other theorists. These drive themes comprising meanings clumped together by association, representing various emotional[62] and social needs, perceptions, attitudes, hopes and desires. Some drive themes relate more to the relational needs of the desirer and are less discriminative of the qualities of the desired one, while other drive themes are more discriminative, focusing more on the attributes of the object of desire. Some drive themes are more strongly related to sexual desire and/or arousal, while other drive themes relate more to broader emotional, social, or even practical considerations relating to interpersonal attraction and pairing. Interpersonal sexual attraction is shaped by the particular mix and prevailing ascendancy of drives in a person's drive profile. Any one person's drive profile is unique to that person, although various themes and trends will emerge that are common to groups of people. This drive profile changes over time, depending on personal and environmental circumstances, and on normal developmental processes.

The two sources, one essentially biological in nature, the other related to the perceptions and attributions of the subjective self, are governed by different laws and principles. Yet they interrelate, each finding context in the other, each informing the other. It may be fair to say that sexual arousal and sexual desire have more to do with the BDP, while interpersonal attraction and pairing, relating to subjective and social events, have more to do with the SDP. Nevertheless, the BDP and the SDP interact, so that the subjective self seeks to make meaningful attributions to the emotions, moods, and general experiences emerging from neuroendocrine activity, while patterns of neurochemical activation and neuroendocrine fluctuations respond to subjective perceptions. We will discover that the sexual relationship encompasses a complex mix of these drives which need to be integrated so that interpersonal attraction, sexual desire, and sexual arousal become aligned. The subjective self interacts with both drive sources, playing a critical role in the interpretation of meanings, choice of focus, and the behavioural decisions that result in the unique patterns of sexual behaviour and relationships entered into. In the process, it seeks internal consistency through minimising internal conflict, while also minimising external conflicts.

Features of the biological (BDP) and subjective (SDP) drive profiles

We have seen how 'sexual' has to do with the respective sexes, the sexual act, and the intentions and behaviours leading to the sexual act. But we have also seen how complex sexual behaviour is — in the factors that make it sexual, and in the circumstances that might lead to such behaviour, including relationship factors. We have further observed that the associative nature of neural functioning contributes to this complexity. This associative process connects ideas and overlaps meanings, so that, through these associations, diverse behavioural events can attract the label 'sexual'. For this reason, the idea of a single 'sex drive' is manifestly inadequate. We find a variety of drives can find expression in what we call 'sexual behaviour' — drives for pleasure, social acceptance, power, love, belonging, and so on; because these drives have become associated with sexual expression, most frequently in the context of relationship. Yet many of these drives can also find expression in non-sexual behaviour. Furthermore, the wide range of drives results in a diversity of sexual behaviour, both heterosexual and homosexual. And so sexual expression might be associated with romantic relationships and mate selection where drives relating to love and intimacy are ascendant; it might be associated with pursuance of prostitution and pornography where drives relating to curiosity and adventure are ascendant; or it might be associated with other psychological and social events, each with their respective relevant drives.

Where do these drives come from, and what shapes a person's drive profile? How do some drives become more important than others? And what sexual behaviour will different drive profiles prompt? The sources of the various drive themes vary. They find a basis in a person's sexual and relationship history as well as in their social context: dysfunctional and normal emotional needs, adaptive and maladaptive schemas, sociocultural scripts, conditioning history, attachment and relational history, relational skills, hormonal history, and mental and physical health all contribute to shaping of a person's unique drive profile. Some of these factors we will explore in more detail later. For now, we observe that a person's unique history contributes to how he or she interprets things: that is, it is from their past experiences and beliefs that particular meanings are attributed to people and events. For each person, different meanings might associate with the activation of sexual interest — for example, what another person represents to them affects whether or not they might be sexually attracted to them.

How does this work? A person is not only a physical and sexual being; he or she can represent other things — power, status, energy, nurturance, safety, and so on. The meanings I associate with a person may be idiosyncratic to me, and may not be an accurate representation of that person; but it is these perceived attributions which interact with my SDP. And just as a *person* represents various meanings to me, so does *sexual behaviour*. Behaviour, like words, carries meanings interpreted by the perceiver. Behaviour driven by neurochemical forces is still imbued with meaning: it is interpreted. Sexual behaviour has meanings both parties need to interpret. The perceived drives that inform sexual behaviour contribute to its meaning and accepted function — whether such behaviour means ownership, recreation, acceptance, escape from responsibility, and so on.

How I choose to interpret behaviour (both my own and that of others) may be different from the way others, or society in general, interprets that behaviour. My frame of reference may not coincide with that of the society in which I live, and this can lead to confusion and frustration. The attribution of meaning is also affected by prevailing physiological events and sexual interest and desire. For example, if you happen to feel good when you meet someone, you are more likely to like them: the prevailing mood state colours how you see the other person and may be attributed to good qualities in that person.[63] Similarly, physiological arousal makes easy association with 'being in love',[64] which of course may be the case; but might also be a misattribution.

It is one thing to argue that the drives that inform sexual behaviour contribute to the meaning and accepted function of that behaviour. But given their invisible nature, how can I identify what such drives might be, both in myself, or in someone else? Besides drawing inferences from a person's patterns of sexual behaviour, or asking them about their beliefs and perceptions, a clue to the drives comprising a person's drive profile is the emotions that might result from frustrated drives.[65] For example, I might have a sexual relationship with someone who decides to have sex with someone else. If my preeminent drive is to promote my partner's wellbeing, I might be support her in her adventures and want the best for her. If my preeminent drive is to enjoy the pleasure of sex, I might thank her for giving me a good time, and perhaps find someone else with whom to enjoy the pleasure of sex. If my preeminent drive is to prove that I am acceptable as a person, I might feel a failure, that I am somehow not good enough as a person, and get depressed. If my preeminent drive is to belong to my partner in the sense of shared experience, I might feel sadness or disorientation because I have lost someone who has become part of my shared identity. If my preeminent drive is to ensure my partner belongs to me in the sense of ownership, I might become jealous or angry because someone else has taken what I believe is mine. These different emotions reflect the various meanings and drives involved: of course, my emotional response would probably be varied, belying the multiple drives involved.[66]

These dynamics and associated conflicts may find expression in different ways. Our friend Karl, for example, may have visited the prostitute while he was lonely and while drives of adventure and pleasure-seeking were ascendant, eclipsing other inhibitive drives such as social prohibition, and eclipsing the drive to emotional intimacy and belonging that associated with his loneliness. In fact, he may have associated sexual intimacy with emotional intimacy, assuming that the pleasure of sex, even with a prostitute, might address his loneliness. However, after his pleasure drives were temporarily sated, his drive profile might change so that the latter drives become ascendant, shifting the emphasis in his SDP, so that he now feels cheated, and a measure of regret and self-hatred for the sexual liaison emerges. He might project this hatred onto the prostitute, so that another drive is activated: disgust for what the prostitute represents. At that point, he might resolve never to visit a prostitute again. Nevertheless, conditioning has taken place, so that sexual pleasure remains associated with her. When next Karl is feeling lonely and his drive profile again resembles what it was before, the conditioned sexual behaviour that promises to bring pleasure will no doubt draw him back to her, and the cycle recurs.

We are left with a final question: could Karl have done otherwise? Did he have the capacity to choose not to visit the prostitute, and to find other expression for his poorly understood drives? Despite his disappointment, he knew he would return to her. Could he not control his actions? Was he a helpless victim of his fluctuating drives? Was there no place to make choices according to personal values or prevailing sociocultural mores? If we were to argue that only natural cause-and-effect laws apply, we would conclude Karl had no choice: he was pulled by drives in some deterministic way. But accepting the idea that laws of reasoning can be superimposed upon natural laws allows us to argue that Karl did have the capacity to manage and regulate his drives, whatever their origin, and so determine his sexual behaviour.

Drives are not the same as their expression, and while biological and subjective drives energise and direct behaviour, a person has the capacity to embrace or inhibit their expression, making a decision which is sensitive both to sociocultural mores and personal values. This is the basis upon which adults are held legally responsible, and it is also the basis for their dignity.[67] There is a complex and unseen dynamic of drives and memories, of biology and the subjective self, which underlie the drive profiles. A person needs to manage this confluence of underlying motivational forces, each interacting with the other. These forces are invisible, like the wind above the ocean or the currents below that push a sailing vessel in one or other direction: yet a sailor is able to understand these forces and to keep the vessel on track. The mere existence of the prevailing drives cannot be used to justify the manner of its expression: such expression is always subject to the choices made.

Chapter 3

Biological Drive Profile (BDP) Factors

M any biochemical processes are involved in human sexual behaviour: some activating the sexual response; others inhibiting it. Some of these processes are similar in both male and female; others are different. Genetic and developmental factors play a role, not least in the regulatory functions of the brain and hormonal system. These biological processes are also found in nonhuman mammalian species, so that generalisations from animal research have some justification, although non-human species are unaffected by the overlay of political, sociocultural, moral, and gender issues.[68] The combined activity of the biochemical processes activating and inhibiting sexual motivation at any particular time forms the basis of the prevailing BDP, and this I now outline.

A study of brain regions associated with sexual desire and arousal or inhibition gives insights into the biology of the sexual response. However, it is difficult to separate the brain's activity as a biological *source* motivating sexual behaviour, from its role as a processing *mediator* creating a physiological response to the ideas and perceptions generated by the subjective self. The neuroendocrine system is a key player in sexual motivation and sexual behaviour (and in reward systems more generally), producing various neurochemicals including hormones, peptides and neurotransmitters.[69] We find that although neuro-biological systems are involved in both *priming* sexual interest and in the *expression* of sexual behaviour, it plays a lesser role in the *reason*, *focus* and *object* of this interest and behaviour (why and with whom I might want to have sex), the latter being mediated by subjective attributions relating to the sexual object. This drive source is also independent of the perceived *meanings* of behaviour: at this level, it is the sensory experiences that become the stimulus for sexual interest or arousal.

Genetics and sexual predispositions

Biological systems find their origin in genetics. However, the interplay of environment and physiological development can make it difficult to disentangle those aspects of our biological makeup that are fully determined by genetics, and those which are only partially so determined. It is now recognised that many characteristics with a genetic base nevertheless require environmental events to activate their expression. Wieten (2001) observes: 'the impact of genetic makeup depends on the environment, and the impact of the environment depends on genetic makeup' (p. 86). While there is no doubt some genetic contribution to a person's hormonal profile,[70] what we *do* know is that the environmental contribution to that profile is significant. Twin studies are routinely used on the basis that identical twins share identical genetics, while non-identical twins share the same uterine and family environment, but not identical genetics. Strictly speaking, if something is governed by genetics alone, we would expect a 100% correspondence for identical twins, and some smaller percentage for non-identical twins. Typically, when a less than 100% correspondence is found, we talk of genetic *predisposition*. But this leaves open the question of the nature and extent of such genetic contribution.

When it comes to sexual behaviour, twin research has largely centred on the question of sexual orientation. Questions relating to interpersonal variation in hormonal profiles and temperament and personality factors in sexual attraction and desire have received little attention. Although the nature/nurture debate has long featured in personality research, the extent of the role of genetics in these individual differences remains unclear. Nevertheless, whatever the extent of genetic involvement, research has linked certain personality and temperament characteristics to certain sexual behaviours. For example, extraversion has been linked to having more sexual partners[71] and to sexual risk-taking,[72] while interpersonal assertiveness and dominance have also been linked to having more sexual partners.[73] Also people who are sensation-seeking, that is, who tend to pursue thrilling and risky activities (perhaps to compensate for lower levels of dopamine[74]) are more likely to be unfaithful[75] and to engage in risky sexual behaviours with larger numbers of sexual partners.[76]

Returning to the question of the genetic contribution to sexual orientation, we find relatively low percentages of such contribution have been found in twin studies. Rosario and Schrimshaw suggest that there is a lack of significant findings in more representative samples of the population when it comes to large familial (sibling versus identical versus non-identical twin) studies. They conclude that up to 50% of homosexual orientation may be attributed to genetic factors 'of some kind'.[77] In fact, feminine behaviour in boys, which the intra-uterine hormonal environment contributes to, appears to be a much stronger predictor of male homosexuality.[78] Either way, there remains a significant proportion of men experiencing same-sex attraction for reasons other than genetic predisposition and feminine inclinations. This is certainly also true of women, where a greater incidence of sexual fluidity is reported.[79]

Neurochemicals and the sexual response

The biological mechanisms underlying sexual desire, arousal, and expression involve many different elements. Not least of these is the timely release of various neurochemicals, some of which *activate* sexual priming and some of which *inhibit* it. The continually changing composition of these neurochemicals forms an important component of the BDP.

Let us first consider the neurochemicals associated with sexual *arousal*. Dopamine and melanocortins are released in the hypothalamus and limbic regions when a person is exposed to various sexual cues, heightening attention and desire: these associate with generating sexual interest. Dopamine is typically associated with expectation of reward, and in its link to encoding expectation of reward, it plays a role in the conditioning process — but also in addiction. This alerts us to the addictive potential of sexual behaviour.[80] Dopamine release has a role in 'sexual wanting'. It links with anticipation, excitement, desire, concentration, memory, and learning, as well as enhancing the feeling of meaningfulness in things. It has been linked with sociability, but also to social anxiety.[81] It is not surprising then, that those with a predisposition to high levels of dopamine are more likely to be involved in sexual activity early, and to have many sexual partners.[82] Dopamine interacts with the hormonal profile. Oestradiol and testosterone can facilitate dopamine activation,[83] while dopamine can also stimulate hormone release mediating the body's fight-and-flight response — which may not be so good for the relationship itself. Critical as dopamine activation is to the sexual reward system, it needs to act in concert with other neurochemical and subjective factors to find expression in any particular sexual impulse.

The neurochemicals *noradrenaline, oxytocin* and *vasopressin* are also associated with sexual arousal. Noradrenaline (or *epinephrine*) helps regulate sexual arousal and motivation.[84] Meanwhile, oxytocin and vasopressin are released just before orgasm in both men and women, playing a role in pleasure (motivating future sexual activity), but also in emotional attachment to the person with whom the orgasm is experienced.[85] This mechanism (along with the role of dopamine) can be understood within the classical conditioning paradigm. Lehmiller (2014) notes that the release of oxytocin plays 'a vital role in developing bonds between romantic and sexual partners because it is released during physical intimacy' (p. 99),[86] while Toates (2014) suggests that the raised oxytocin levels in women following orgasm could 'consolidate the incentive value of the partner and sense of belonging with this person' (p. 108). We see here that belonging is not only created by the sense of shared personal space and experience, but is also supported by a biological link between the sexual event and bonding.

Of course, oxytocin is not only featured in the sexual encounter. It is also released in parent-child bonding which should be anything *but* sexual. But there is other hormone activity present in the adult sexual profile to distinguish these events — the release of vasopressin and testosterone, for example.[87] We see here the finely tuned balance of a neuroendocrine system that lays the biological basis for relational experiences; but also the interplay between the bonding qualities of oxytocin and vasopressin, and the territorial and protective aggressiveness with which testosterone release might be associated. Here the source of the bonding experience which associates with belonging is a chemical one. It is easy to see the potential for confusion in regard to the interpretation of one's experiences of intimacy and belonging; that is, to sexualise a nurturing event, or to feel connected in a sexual event where there is otherwise little emotional connection.

With regard to the activation of various brain regions, the orbitofrontal cortex, the prefrontal cortex and the anterior cingulate cortex may be involved in the evaluation of sexual attractiveness. Other regions of the prefrontal cortex and the anterior cingulate cortex may play a role in sexual desire through the evaluation of the reward value of external reward stimuli.[88] Diamond & Dickenson (2012) report that activation of the caudate, insula and putamen brain regions appear to relate both to the experience of sexual desire and romantic love. Pfaus, et al. (2014) note that because of the extensive anatomical and functional connections these neural areas have with many other parts of the brain, ready access is allowed to contextual information to inform both the judgement of sexual attraction and the stimulation of sexual desire. This represents the neural parallel of the many associations made at a subjective and meaning level, and underscores the complexity of the sexual experience.

However, as the arousal level associated with sexual pleasure is prolonged, neural changes occur in regions of the amygdala and the frontal and prefrontal cortex. This adversely affects capacity for moral affiliations, self-other relations, self-awareness, and interpersonal judgements.[89] (Perhaps the reverse is also true: that is, that a strong focus on moral affiliations, self-other relations, self-awareness, and interpersonal judgements act to inhibit sexual arousal and sexual pleasure by way of increased activity in these same regions.) Pfaus, et al. (2014) suggest that the function of such neural changes is to help 'dissolve normal body boundaries, thereby facilitating sexual interactions, which in turn might contribute significantly to the experience of sexual arousal' (p. 174). We observe here a neural equivalent to the notion of shared subjective space in the experience of sexual activity. During orgasm, reward-related regions of the limbic system and the cerebellum are activated, while the regions associated with vigilance are inhibited.[90] Simply put, prolonged sexual arousal negatively affects a person's capacity for objective judgement.

When it comes to sexual inhibition, other neurochemicals are involved. Some prevent a sexual event occurring in the first place; others bring a sexual event to an end. Opiods, for example, are released in the cortex, limbic system, hypothalamus, and midbrain during orgasm, and mediate sexual reward. In providing the experiential reward found in sexual pleasure and thus serving to sate the drive, its release quickly reduces sexual desire and arousal.[91] Both serotonin (which counters the effect of dopamine) and endogenous cannabinoids are released immediately after a sexual event, shutting down sexual arousal, with serotonin creating a sense of peace and sexual satiety, and endogenous cannabinoids mediating sedation.[92]

Not only does sexual inhibition immediately follow orgasm, it can also result from stress or threat.[93] However, the latter is subject to individual differences in perception of the degree of threat: a limited amount of stress or threat can have the reverse effect, stimulating arousal for some (especially in those with a high threshold for the capacity to be aroused) but creating inhibition in others. Generally, stress is associated with negative emotions: of guilt, fear, anger, grief, and shame. These emotions result in cortisol release, contributing to inhibition of sexual arousal. In conditions of sexual inhibition, those areas in the forebrain relating to good judgement, alertness, and saliency detection are activated, preventing focus on sexual desire and arousal.[94] Dual-control theories of sexual arousal such as Perelman's *sexual tipping point* dual control model[95] have been structured around the competing neurochemical activities that determine whether sexual excitation or inhibition ultimately occurs.

The hormonal profile: Priming for sexual desire

We now look at the changing hormonal profile which plays a role both in the priming of sexual interest and in the activation of sexual arousal. Determining the hormonal contribution during various periods of development and determining the effect of various contexts on the hormonal profile is difficult, both in the measurement of hormonal fluctuation and in the isolation of variables — not only in relation to what might *result* from hormonal change, but also in relation to what might *contribute* to it. Nevertheless, it is clear that hormones influence sexual desire in the most general sense, and that various neurochemicals are activated both in the process of sexual arousal and in the subsequent sexual encounter. In a woman, for example, the rhythm of sexual desire is intimately connected with the biology of her reproductive systems as expressed in her hormonal profile, both in her monthly cycles, and in the seasons of her lifetime.

As is true of other aspects of the mind-body relationship, biochemical and psychological processes interact. And so, for example, subjective mood states can affect the hormonal profile affecting sexual desire, while subjective experiences (for example, sexual thoughts or fantasies) can translate into neurochemical activation that creates subsequent conditioned arousal responses to those particular thoughts and fantasies. Furthermore, a person's hormonal profile is in a constant state of flux,[96] responding to physiological events (the internal biological context, such as the menstrual cycle and pregnancy in women[97]), to external circumstances (the prevailing environmental context, such as relationship circumstances), and to developmental and life-cycle changes. The prevailing hormonal profile at critical developmental periods can also have enduring effects, especially when it contributes to subjective associations and conditioning processes. That is, hormones can activate or inhibit certain sexual behaviours at one time, which creates implicit memories affecting later sexual behaviour.

On the basis of such research as has been done in this area, we have glimpses into the complexities of the interaction of the hormonal profile and these various factors. But we begin with the reminder that although both men and women carry the hormones testosterone and oestrogen, their profiles are different. Testosterone, a hormone of the androgen group, has been associated not only with the development of male physical sexual characteristics, but also with the regulation of cognitive and physical energy. Testosterone associates with sexual motivation in men, although it does not affect the ability to engage in sexual activity.[98] In women, the release of oestrogen relates to sexual motivation, while release of progesterone has the reverse relationship.[99]

But the effect of the hormonal profile on sexual behaviour begins long before men and women develop sexual interest. It begins before birth, as a mother's hormonal activity affects the baby within her. The sperm fertilising the egg determines whether the baby will be male or female. However, the baby's physical masculine or feminine characteristics is shaped by the mother's prevailing hormonal profile during the first trimester of her pregnancy. The correct concentration of testosterone at the right time is prerequisite to the physical development of male features; otherwise, female features develop. This in turn sets the biological framework for later patterns of sexual attraction and desire as the baby grows and eventually enters adulthood.

During the second trimester, evidence suggests that the mother's androgen levels shape aspects of the baby's brain, influencing gender formation. Testosterone (converted to oestradiol) contributes to masculinisation in interest and behaviour. Too much testosterone can have a masculinising effect on a developing girl, so that she later comes to prefer 'male' toys, activities, and playmates, has decreased interest in feminine behaviours such as playing with dolls, is more socially detached, engages in less verbal aggression (but more physical aggression) and is later less likely to have exclusively heterosexual orientation.[100] In corresponding manner, a deficit of androgen hormones prenatally may lead to a 'predominantly female differentiated brain' which in a boy has been associated with later homosexual tendencies.[101]

The idea that sexual orientation may be influenced by brain development under the influence of hormonal secretions during critical periods of prenatal development has also found other support.[102] For example, a higher incidence of lesbian orientation has been found among women exposed prenatally to a synthetic hormone used to reduce miscarriage (in their mothers) as well as among women with an adrenal disorder resulting in abnormally high androgen levels during prenatal development.[103] However, while there is evidence that sexual orientation is affected by prenatal masculinisation or feminisation processes, there is no evidence of the biological *inevitability* of sexual object choice.[104] Moreover, the subsequent prevailing hormonal profile in an adult does not appear to determine the choice of erotic desire: when the hormone levels of homosexuals and heterosexuals were compared, no consistent links with sexual orientation were found.[105]

The hormonal profile changes over the life cycle, and does so differently for men than for women. Sexual interest, desire, and arousal often begin before puberty, around age ten, for both boys and girls with the maturation of adrenal glands (adrenarche).[106] Hormone levels begin to change (with sexual interest and hormonal changes influencing each other), the subsequent onset of puberty being managed by hypothalamic sexual control centres.[107] Testosterone levels surge for pubescent boys while pubescent girls experience increasing levels in both testosterone and oestrogen.[108] This results in maturation in primary and secondary sexual characteristics, in increased risk-taking and increased sexual interest and activity in boys, and in depression and identity concerns in girls. Unlike its associations with sexual ideation and motivation in boys, testosterone elevation does not relate strongly to sexual activity in girls.[109] Generally, as testosterone levels begin their steep incline, any potential issues with sexual identity or orientation emerge.[110] Nevertheless, the object of sexual interest appears fluid, especially to begin with. It is not defined by the prevailing hormonal profile: for some boys and for reasons other than hormonal activity, the object of their emerging sexual interest may be other males. These hormonal changes also coincide with changes in relationships with parents, preparing the way for a new attachment with a lover. Perhaps testosterone increase plays a role in motivating the leaving one for the other, along with the establishment of new interpersonal territory. Testosterone levels peak during the 20s, followed by a gradual decline.

Although hormonal levels begin their gradual decline in the 20s, fluctuations continue to occur, affected by both physiological and environmental factors. Testosterone and oestrogen levels fluctuate daily, peaking early in the morning before waking; while seasonal variations also occur, with testosterone levels increasing in autumn in both men and women. Another source of fluctuation is the menstrual cycle in women. Sexual motivation varies systematically during this time. During the peri-ovulatory period of the menstrual cycle, the hormonal profile is characterised by high oestrogen levels and low progesterone levels, with accompanying increase in sexual motivation and likelihood of sexual fantasies,[111] and in greater sexual interest in men — including men other than their current partner.[112] Lesbian women (and to a lesser extent, bisexual women) report a similar increase in sexual interest (in women) during the oestrogen peak of their cycle, although interest in the opposite sex reportedly decreases.[113] The perinatal period in a woman sees dramatic changes in her hormonal profile, lowering sexual interest and enjoyment. With advancing age, testosterone levels continue to drop in men while oestrogen and androgen drops during menopause in women. These changes see a decline in sexual desire and motivation.[114]

Relationship circumstances also affect hormonal profiles, although results vary. Again, testosterone has received most research attention. It seems testosterone levels are higher in more sexually active men,[115] for single men with past relationship experience,[116] and in men who have sex with more than one person or with an unfamiliar person.[117] Continued high testosterone levels seem to associate with instability in a sexual relationship: there is an association between men with high testosterone levels and the likelihood of extramarital sex, or divorce.[118] Some research shows that falling in love decreases men's testosterone levels (simultaneously increasing cortisol, suggesting that falling in love is a stressful event; but the lower testosterone level also suggests that sexual desire may not be the primary drive in the 'falling in love' event) but then, as the relationship becomes more certain, testosterone levels are gradually restored.[119] Other research suggests testosterone levels are again reduced once a man settles into a long-term relationship,[120] or his focus shifts from sexual matters to his children.[121] Parenthood has been linked with lowered testosterone in both men and women. It may be that the need for sexual priming is reduced, and biological processes are responsive to this. But another interpretation may be that testosterone levels in males drop once the business of establishing territory and belonging is completed.

Context also affects the hormonal profile. Various studies give insights in how the hormonal profile might react to perceptions and external events: again, these studies generally measure testosterone levels. For example, it seems testosterone is released (along with accompanying optimism and energy levels) as a man watches a sexually explicit movie, peaking some sixty to ninety minutes after the movie has been seen, whereas such a release does not occur when a sexually neutral movie is watched.[122] No doubt similar testosterone release occurs in relation to viewing pornographic material and whilst engaging in sexual fantasy. Testosterone levels can increase as a man has a brief conversation with a woman, perhaps with the intent to impress her,[123] and more generally (depending on initial level of arousal), when a male relates to a novel female.[124] These findings have implications for the possible effect of exposure to sexual situations (including sexual abuse, sexualisation of relationships, sexualisation in the media, and pornography) on the prevailing testosterone levels in males.

Sexual conditioning: The impulse that repeats the past

While hormones play a role in priming and energising sexual behaviour, other neural systems also contribute to shaping sexual behaviour through behavioural conditioning. Classical (or Pavlovian) conditioning has to do with pairing a neutral stimulus with another stimulus that evokes an automatic response. In this context, a pairing might occur of sexual arousal with a particular image or object. Operant (or instrumental) conditioning has to do with what sexual behaviours are reinforced or punished: this determines whether such behaviours are likely to occur again. Our interest is especially in classical conditioning, which involves automatic physiological responses governed by implicit memories. Being an automatic function of the brain rather than being governed by personal choice, it finds its place as part of the BDP, rather than the SDP. Such conditioned pairing of object or context with a sexual response may be advantageous; but it may also result in a contamination of association, where neural networks make unwanted connections between various stimuli, including ideas and experiences. In the realm of sexual behaviour, this generally means unwanted sexual arousal triggered by various objects, thoughts or contexts; or alternatively, unwanted sexual inhibition triggered by certain thoughts or contexts.

In their research with animals, Pfaus, et al. (2014) found that neutral cues were easily conditioned to sexual desire, arousal, and copulatory behaviour. They explain 'although sexual behaviour is controlled by hormonal and neurochemical actions in the brain, sexual experience induces a degree of plasticity that allows animals to form instrumental and Pavlovian associations that predict sexual outcomes, thereby directing the strength of sexual responding' (p. 147). They further propose that 'endogenous opioid activation forms the basis of sexual reward, which also sensitises hypothalamic and mesolimbic dopamine systems in the presence of cues that predict sexual reward. Those systems act to focus attention on, and activate goal-directed behaviour toward, reward-related stimuli' (p. 147). That is, even though hormonal processes might activate the animal's 'sex drive', learning processes, mediated by dopamine release, were then involved in creating associations with the object or focus of sexual interest, thus affecting later behaviour. The conditioning process stimulated pair-bonding so that an animal would seek out a sexual partner bearing the cue to which it had been conditioned — yet another mechanism connecting sexual activity with the sense of belonging.

Animal studies also show that the environmental cues that come to be associated with opioid release occurring during sexual climax can activate hormonal activity, priming both males and females for sexual activity.[125] The hormones priming for sexual activity can in turn be stimulated by environmental factors previously associated with sexual activity. Pfaus, et al. (2014) observe that 'sexual behaviour epitomises the whole-body relationship between autonomic activation and central nervous function. Yet part of that biological substrate is an enormous adaptive flexibility in the brain that allows individual and idiosyncratic Pavlovian and operant associations to be made between external stimuli, behavioural responses, and sexual reward' (p. 184). In other words, an animal learns to be sexually aroused by things that happen to be associated with sexual arousal in the past.

This conditioning principle predicts that the cues associated with sexual arousal in the past can later contribute to the stimulation of sexual desire. That is, a history of sexual arousal in a certain context can create sexual desire in relation to that context. Sexual arousal can lead to sexual desire, just as sexual desire can lead to sexual arousal. This principle can play a critical role in the development of various sexual fetishes, but also in the longer-term effects of certain fantasies and exposure to various erotic stimuli. And so, for example, because *difference* is an important arousal factor, an adolescent may access increasingly risqué pornographic images (involving, for example, same-sex situations, multiple sexual partners, sexual violence, children, etc.), and sexual arousal responses then become conditioned to those stimuli. A person learns to sexually desire those things that sexually aroused him in the past.

The principles of conditioning theory have also underpinned various therapeutic interventions in sexual behaviour (particularly in the 1960s and 1970s, when a different political climate prevailed regarding acceptable targets for sexual behavioural change). These interventions included 'orgasmic reconditioning',[126] aversive control procedures, and desensitisation (habituation) procedures,[127] practiced especially in relation to homosexual behaviours. That is, therapy was based on the idea that changes in sexual behaviour and orientation could be learned because of the inherent ability of the brain to adapt to experience. Not surprisingly, such therapy had mixed results given the overall complexity of the sexual response. Success was much more likely when therapeutic goals were aligned with personal desire for change, based on other subjective drive factors.

All this means that the early circumstances of a person's sexual experiences may be significant from a conditioning perspective. Animal research suggests that initial sexual experiences play a critical role in shaping sexual responses to particular stimuli. Pfaus, et al. (2014) explain: 'a critical period exists during an individual's early sexual experience that creates a "love map" or Gestalt of features, movements, feelings, and interpersonal interactions associated with sexual reward' (p.147). They argue that there are critical periods in the development of sexual profiles: 'certain critical ages and during certain critical events (i.e., first experiences of sexual desire, masturbation, sexual release, first partnered activity), the sensory, cognitive, affective, and motoric aspects of sexuality become fundamentally integrated, organised by direct experience of reward and pleasure... these integrated experiences crystallise into stable preferences for certain sexual acts and certain partner characteristics.'[128]

Consistent with the principles of classical learning theory, the circumstances and cues that relate to early sexual experiences lay a foundation for subsequent patterns of sexual arousal and sexual desire. This means, for example, that the 'experimental' sexual experiences of adolescence can play a significant role in shaping later sexual expectations and orientation. In this regard, Bem wrote: 'I am willing to entertain the possibility that a process akin to imprinting may also contribute to the eroticization of arousal and the temporal stability of sexual orientation across the life course, again with particular force for the gender-nonconforming child who is taunted by same-sex peers.'[129] Initial learning in sexual experience and behaviour creates neural imprints that play a critical role in later sexual behaviour.

And so we see that the reward systems in sexual attraction are complex. While sexual desire is largely anticipatory in nature, the pleasure anticipated in genital stimulation and orgasm constitute a powerful but small part of the possible reward structure a relationship might provide. Indeed, by its very nature, the arousal linked to genital stimulation and the pleasure related to orgasm are brief events that are quickly sated, compared to other aspects of the reward structure. It is this former aspect of sexual reward that lends itself to classical and operant conditioning principles, while other principles are relevant to the other aspects of reward. In other words, the rewards in sexual behaviour are layered, with physical pleasure and release (with the neural system as source) being immediate but short-lived, while the relational rewards (with the subjective self as source) being more subtle and longer-lasting. We now turn to the subjective drive themes.

Chapter 4

Subjective Drive Profile (SDP) Themes of Pleasure

The subjective drive profile comprises ideas and subjective needs and desires relating to sexual behaviour. These theme descriptions represent an integration of published accounts of sexual motives and drives with those encountered in my clinical work. Some drive themes are pleasure-oriented; others are relationship-oriented, or related to wider social needs. Some drive themes relate to immediate gratification, being more closely aligned to biological events; others take a longer-term point of view. Some are defined by the qualities of the object of desire; others less so. Some motivate sexual behaviour; others inhibit it. Twenty-two drive themes are described in the next four chapters.

These drive themes are not necessarily independent. Just as neural associative processes underlie conditioning, so the associative nature of ideas and the neural networks that carry these ideas means there will be many linkages.[130] This creates a situation where a single theme might accommodate ideas that are similar but not identical, but also where different themes may connect conceptually with each other. What these themes have in common is that they contribute to the shaping of sexual behaviour — especially with whom and under what conditions such behaviour might occur.

The first five themes of the subjective drive profile are about pleasure and desire. These do not relate to relationship factors or to social needs as such: being primarily about self-expression and personal happiness, they tend to be self-focused rather than other-centred. And although two people generally provide each other pleasure in a sexual encounter, here the primary motive is their own pleasure, not the other person's. (To the extent that where the primary motive is to give pleasure to someone else, such a motive is altruistic, and more closely aligned to giving love.) While these drives are not incompatible with the drive to belong, they can find expression outside a relationship. Indeed, some of these drives may find expression without another person being present at all, in such activities as masturbation, and reading or viewing erotic material. Nevertheless, there are other aspects that necessarily reside in another person — whether or not they are present — in which a person might find pleasure, or which that person might desire, such as enjoying beauty or gender traits in someone.

The pleasure themes include: *the compulsion of eroticism; the desire for recreation; the drive to curiosity and discovery; the attraction to beauty;* and *the attraction to gender traits.* I have included *attraction to gender traits* in this chapter on the basis of its erotic and pleasure elements, but to the degree that this drive theme plays a role in relationship dynamics, it might equally be listed under the relationship-need themes of the SDP. I also note that while the *experience* of pleasure is a result of biological events (involving opioid release, etc.), the *desire to pursue pleasure* is itself not a biological event (the role of dopamine notwithstanding), and so is included under the SDP. Furthermore, pleasure is not an enduring outcome, although the associations made between behaviour, the circumstances of that behaviour, and pleasure — the conditioned effect — *is* enduring. And because pleasure tends to be a fleeting experience, any behaviour whose primary purpose is to provide pleasure is likely to be repeated often.

As I have noted, the associative nature of ideas and neural functioning means that there will be overlap between themes. And so we find that having an attractive partner might satisfy a personal desire (*attraction to beauty*), but it might also contribute to social kudos, associating with themes such as the *need for social acceptance* and the *consumer drive.* And as we saw in our discussion of maleness and femaleness, these pleasure themes generally tend to have a higher value in a male's SDP than a female's, although they feature in both.[131] Let us look more closely at these drive themes.

The compulsion of eroticism

We begin with the *eroticism* drive theme. This theme is about the desire for and enjoyment of erotic experience for its own sake — that is, enjoying the feelings of sexual stimulation and arousal.[132] Eroticism can involve the use of sexually stimulating ideas or images in art, literature and drama, or objects designed to stimulate sexual arousal, as much as it might involve another person to create a state of sexual interest or excitement. It is about seeking the orgiastic state of sexual experience rather than any wider benefits of a sexual relationship, and so tends to focus on a person's sexual attributes and behaviours, rather than their attributes as a person.[133] Difference rather than similarity is likely to stimulate the erotic experience,[134] especially for men, and so we would expect this drive theme to associate with the *drive to curiosity and discovery*; although for women there tends to be a greater integration of sexual and relational drives, so that a link with the *need for intimacy and to belong* may remain. Freud argued that this theme (referred to generically as the 'sex drive') underpins much human behaviour, including during early developmental stages, albeit in a subconscious way.

This drive theme can find reward in reading or viewing erotic material in the absence of any relationship at all.[135] Nevertheless, such activity can prime a person for sexual encounters with another person. The *idea* of sexual arousal and pleasure is itself arousing and pleasurable, and so any stimulus evoking such thoughts or imaginations, whether it be words, pictures, behaviours, or clothing, can stir this drive; but *physical stimulation* is also a common source of sexual arousal through masturbatory activity, erotic massage, or the use of sexual objects designed to stimulate sexual arousal. Because of the powerful and inherently rewarding nature of erotic pleasure, this drive theme is closely related to the sexual conditioning drive of the BDP, with ideas, behaviours, or objects capable of becoming conditioned to sexual arousal. There is thus a potential to create a compulsion to access erotic material such as pornography, or erotic experience, at the expense of a relationship. There are of course individual differences in what ideas or images might be considered 'erotic': its key element is the capacity to excite sexual arousal. For some people, even certain levels of pain, of powerlessness (or powerfulness — see *the power motive*), or of social prohibition, can contribute to the experience of eroticism because of their contribution to autonomic nervous system arousal.

The desire for recreation

A drive theme associated with the eroticism theme is the *desire for recreation*, which includes freedom of expression and freedom from responsibility. That is, it is the desire to 'let go' and abandon oneself to the moment. 'Letting go' is a normal part of the sexual experience, as a degree of emotional and physical disinhibition is necessary for interpersonal closeness. This is also paralleled at the neural level, as we have seen. This drive theme may be experienced as an escape from stress and life pressures in general (but also from dealing with life issues), a form of relaxation, of recreation and of tension release.[136] Like the *compulsion of eroticism*, it is a more prominent drive theme in men than women. It associates with having a good time and with general enjoyment, and as such represents an intrinsically rewarding aspect of the event. Such intrinsic reward can act to ward off sadness, boredom, loneliness (and even depression, provided there is sufficient libido), and other negative feelings, by providing pleasure, comfort, companionship, and so on, in the sexual encounter. But it can also do so in a negative sense, as a way of coping through escape from discomfort, stress, and unhappiness, as much as it might in the positive sense of accessing nurturance, enjoyment and emotional support through the embrace of relationship building.

This drive theme represents an important reward component of the drive profile. However, if it is not adequately balanced by other drive themes, it has the potential of promoting one's own happiness and pleasure at the expense of the needs of the other person, or of the relationship itself. Given that to love someone implies focus on the other person's needs and a degree of responsibility, tension may result when this drive theme and the need to love coexist. Nevertheless, mutual abandonment provides necessary reward and enhances connectivity in a sexual relationship.

To the extent that a relationship associates with responsibility and loss of freedom, it might incline some people towards sexual expression outside such responsibilities. It may even find expression in a form of mutual exploitation where two people stay in a relationship for as long as it serves the purpose of their recreation: should this no longer be the case, they leave. (By exploitation, I mean each person is used as a means to an end, and may indeed feel 'used' in this way. In this regard, it also associates with the *consumer drive*.) This drive theme may be ascendant for those that struggle with self-discipline,[137] it may play a role in friends-with-benefits arrangements or in promiscuity, and it associates with media images linking sexuality with freedom and pleasure. Not uncommonly, the sexual encounter can simply become an ingredient, along with alcohol and perhaps drugs, of 'having a good time'. Despite the risk of potentially negative outcomes in the long term where this drive is poorly managed, the recreational aspect of this drive theme is clearly positive and plays an important role in a person's SDP.

The drive to curiosity and discovery

The *drive to curiosity and discovery* is a drive theme not only about the other person, but also about the self (both in relation to self-discovery and the sating of curiosity), and the various and diverse activities and experiences a sexual encounter might allow.[138] This drive is essentially about revealing or discovering something new — in this case, in a sexual context. It involves the thrill of uncovering something, or the promise of a new experience. Novelty is a critical aspect.[139] Associated to some extent with the *power motive*, discovery connects with the excitement of conquest, and the overcoming of interpersonal barriers. However, once the object of passion has been uncovered or discovered, this drive can quickly dissipate. The knowledge itself is not as exciting as the *process of acquiring* knowledge, the discovery process itself. The acquisition of knowledge is like being granted access to something new: this is why pornography involves many images. Each new image grants a momentary anticipatory excitement, but once uncovered, it loses its novelty power, and other images are sought.

This drive not only has the erotic dimension of entering unknown and perhaps forbidden territory (creating arousal), but also the stimulation and interest of 'otherness'. That is, it seeks relationship experiences that are explorative in both a sexual and non-sexual way. There is also the element of mystery and risk that contributes to sexual arousal.[140] Perel (2006) described passion or sexual excitement as deriving from the unknown, risk, and surprise. While the eroticism drive is about the desire for sexual arousal for its own sake, this drive theme has more to do with curiosity and the discovery of something new. However, curiosity, while a positive factor in learning, can lead a person into risky sexual situations. Linked with initiative and adventure, it is a drive more likely to be associated with the masculine.

Difference is a key factor ('differences attract') when it comes to discovering new experiences. To the degree that it overlaps with gender trait differences (see the *attraction to gender traits*) this is no doubt also an element in heterosexual attraction (the so-called 'exotic species' in Bem's[141] formulation). The search for difference may result in the pursuit of new situations and experiences and/or with people quite different from oneself. However, while difference can excite interest and enrich a relationship, it can also create suspicion and separateness. The inhibitory aspect of difference may arise from an inability to connect or relate to someone because of their different values, culture, language, race, religion, and so on. There is a common tendency to dislike those that disagree with us,[142] and to be afraid of or distrust those we don't understand, preventing closeness and empathy. In this regard, the drive to curiosity and discovery plays an important role in the *initiation* of sexual activity, but potentially interferes with the long-term maintenance of a sexual relationship. This drive theme may be a factor in the SDP of people involved in affairs, promiscuity, visiting prostitutes, accessing pornography, and in some homosexual or bisexual experiences, although it is a drive that seeks variety in sexual experiences in the context of conventional long-term hetero-sexual relationships as well.

The attraction to beauty

The *attraction to beauty* or physical attractiveness plays an important role in sexual attraction.[143] But this raises several conundrums: the definition of beauty; the nature of the drive towards beauty; and the role of beauty in sexual desire. Philosophers and social researchers have long sought to define beauty. Physical attractiveness may relate to body shape, facial features,[144] skin texture, clothing, posture, fragrance and other characteristics. Yet there are other qualities in a person that may influence the perception of sexual attractiveness beyond the physical, such as a sense of 'presence' or strength of character, a positive outlook, depth and humour, and a capacity to embrace life. Both physical and personality characteristics may in turn reflect a person's social status, their social awareness, and their general care and sensitivity. Beauty is furthermore influenced by cultural mores, by socialisation and media images which create meanings and associations around the idea of sexual attractive-ness,[145] and is to some extent context-dependent so that a person's attractive-ness is relative to others with whom comparison is made.[146] Another element to the judgement of beauty relates to the observer's past history. For example, certain features may associate with desirable qualities or with familiar people who have been loved and cherished in the past.

Why should beauty relate to sexual desire? It could be argued that physical attractiveness draws initial attention and interest, and so creates the motiva-tion for a relationship to begin.[147] Further, to have an attractive partner may be seen as a sign of social success, and enhances one's social status (and so associates with both the consumer drive and the drive for social acceptance). And then, as with all desire, it may have to do with wanting to 'own' the beauty in the other person, to the extent that the enjoyment of their beauty gives pleasure in its own right. Yet the equation is not a simple one. While a person's beauty might be recognised, it might also trigger a negative response in a sexual relationship sense, should a person feel inadequate by comparison — this will affect those with a poor self-image. When someone perceives themselves to be physically flawed or unattractive, they are less likely to be attracted to someone else, especially a physically attractive person, partly for fear of rejection, but partly because of self-rejection. Indeed, we often find a matching between partners in relation to perceived physical attractiveness, along the lines predicted by exchange theory.[148]

Conversely, unattractive personal features, whether perceived within oneself or perceived within another person, is an inhibitory aspect of this drive theme. As such, it may prevent initial interest in establishing a relationship with a person. This is a drive to reject the other person on the basis they have undesirable physical characteristics that may affect their social desirability, and by extension, the social status that comes from being in relationship with someone attractive. Alternatively, certain manners, habits, or personality characteristics may be deemed intrinsically unattractive, as might disfigurement from disease or injury, and so reduce sexual attraction.

The attraction to gender traits

The *attraction to gender traits* (the 'X-factor') — the inherent maleness and femaleness, and the meanings and ideas associated with gender — plays a critical role in sexual interest and attraction.[149] The gender exclusivity commonly found in both heterosexual and same-sex romantic attraction (that is, in romantic partnering, heterosexuals are generally exclusively heterosexual while homosexuals are generally exclusively homosexual) indicates that there is a quality inherent in the gender responsible for the sexual attraction. Implied in this is also the inverse: that gender traits act as much to activate as to inhibit sexual desire. That is, same-sex gender traits generally inhibit sexual desire in heterosexuals, while the reverse is true for homosexuals.

While this drive theme might be linked to the *drive to procreation* (at least, for a heterosexual person), the drive to procreation has as focus the desire for children so that fertility becomes important; while *attraction to gender traits* relates directly to desiring and enjoying features of gender-associated traits regardless of whether children are desired. There is overlap with the *drive to curiosity and discovery*, where difference is a key component;[150] but here the difference is specifically about gender. There is also overlap with the *compulsion to eroticism*, but again, here sexual desire is about attraction to gender traits rather than sexual arousal for its own sake.

As we have seen, defining 'maleness' and 'femaleness', like defining beauty, is an elusive task. Generally it reflects the attraction of a male to traits associated with 'femaleness' and the attraction of a female to traits associated with 'maleness', and is the basis for heterosexual attraction. While gender is biologically influenced, cultural norms and expectations shape the expression of gender, especially in the social roles (as distinct to traits) ascribed to gender. Nevertheless, distinction is commonly made across cultures between male and female gender traits. Maleness relates variously to robustness, strength (generally physical, but also endurance or powerfulness in a psychological sense),[151] dominance (or competitiveness), forcefulness, confidence in risky situations,[152] courage, independence (or self-reliance), assertiveness, restricted emotional expression,[153] and capacity for procreation (virility) — that is, to be able to produce the sperm that fertilises the female. Femaleness in turn, relates variously to gentleness, protectiveness, 'prettiness', nurturance, compassion, empathy, sensitivity, tolerance, caring, deference, and the capacity to generate and nurture new life from within.

It could be argued that the basis of attraction is that a man wants to have aspects of the feminine he doesn't have within himself, while the woman wants to have aspects of the masculine she doesn't have within herself. Each desires what they see in the other sex and don't have within themselves (or only to a limited degree; but also without rejecting what they have in their own sex) — it is, in a sense, a drive for completeness, an embrace of *both*. In many respects each gender complements the other. The presence of her femininity serves to accentuate his masculinity, and vice versa. If he is comfortable with his masculinity and it is well integrated with his sense of self, he is likely to be drawn to a woman simply because the inherent difference reflected in her femininity — the 'exotic' element — enhances his masculinity.[154] If, however, his sense of self does not have a strong alignment with masculinity, then her femininity does not serve to enhance his sense of masculinity. Instead, dissonance results, and her presence can add to confusion rather than clarification of his sense of self. In the heterosexual context, the sexual relationship could be seen as a celebration and embrace of *both* sexes and genders: the embrace of one's own gender, and that of one's opposite-sex partner.

Chapter 5

SDP Themes Relating to Broader Social Needs

With these drive themes the overriding need is to belong to or be recognised by the wider society, rather than that the experience of belonging or validation being restricted to the sexual partner. Furthermore, there is generally a need for the social group to *recognise our belonging together* — we generally want to belong both to our sexual partner as well as to our society. The social recognition of such belonging becomes a basis for stronger commitment and more relationship stability.[155] These drive themes have less to do with sexual desire than they do with social needs, so that the relevant drive themes reflect more indirect motives influencing sexual behaviour. It is about seeking out sexual activity that meets needs related to society: needs to be accepted, to prove something, societal position and empowerment, or needs reactive to social pressures. In this respect, a sexual relationship is viewed in terms of the social value a partner or the relationship itself might have.

In traditional society these drive themes also relate to issues of social class (traditional sociocultural sexual scripts have a strong emphasis on the social ramifications of the sexual relationship). But in contemporary society it might be understood in terms of social exchange theory. They also play an important role in adolescent sexual relationships, given the adolescent's developmental need to establish themself socially. The *drive to procreation* is included here because, while the desire to have children might be a source of self-fulfilment or reflect relationship needs, it also represents a contribution to society at large, may be responsive to societal expectations, and has many implications in regard to the parents' subsequent societal roles.

The *power motive* has played a central role in the politics of sexual relationships, and finds negative expression in coercion and aggression, issues of ongoing social concern. The sexual relationship can also be a statement of social position and power, and so is included here. Nevertheless, the *power motive* is also an intensely personal dynamic in sexual relationship, and could as easily have been listed under *relationship-need themes of the SDP*. Then again, for some the power motive has strong erotic elements (such as in BDSM situations), and so it could find its place among the *themes of pleasure and desire*. It is a theme that bridges different categories. In addition to the *drive to procreation* and the *power motive*, other SDP themes relating to broader social needs include the *need to prove oneself*, the *need for social acceptance*, the *consumer drive*, and the *desire to rebel*.

The need to prove oneself

As a *rite of passage* and need to 'prove' oneself, this drive theme is largely about entering maturity. It is about expressing adulthood, self-discovery, asserting the completion of childhood and innocence, and embracing a new sense of self in a unique way with another adult through sexual experience.[156] This means that it is a major drive theme in adolescence or young adulthood,[157] although those afraid of leaving behind the joys and securities of childhood might suppress this drive. Its ascendance in a person's SDP is generally short term, given the nature of its objective. It associates with the drive to find *social acceptance*, where acceptance in this case is found by undergoing the (sexual) rite of passage and being able to talk about sexual experience with peers as a badge of accomplishment and new-found maturity. Here sexual conquest or experience is the object: to a degree, who it involves is largely immaterial.

This need to 'prove' something might also find expression in various other sexual contexts. For example, it might involve a person trying to 'prove' his or her heterosexuality if there have been homosexual experiences or inclinations, or to 'prove' sexual desirability if there are self-esteem or body-image problems. For others, it might signify the need to 'prove' that the passion and virility of youth has not yet been lost in advancing age and may act as a drive to fend off a fear of sexual impotence or indifference, especially if this expression of masculinity or femininity is also about self-esteem and self-acceptance.

The need for social acceptance

The *need for social acceptance* is a drive theme that associates with the need to belong to a larger social or familial group. It associates with doing the 'right thing', with being seen as 'normal' and successful, and with being respected by others in the larger social circle.[158] As such, this drive theme is strongly connected with the prevailing sociocultural sexual script. The need for social acceptance may influence the type or qualities of person someone is drawn to: a person with attributes that meet the criteria of social acceptance, whether of family (especially parents), of friends, or of society at large.[159] And so the influence of the community in what is seen as morally or socially acceptable in the choice of sexual partner becomes an important factor. This drive is vulnerable to peer-pressure,[160] and also operates in the context of arranged marriages where the respective parents form the social context. It sees pressure to restrict sexual relationships and marriages to certain acceptable (similar) sociocultural or religious groups.[161] The drive to social acceptance may also result in entering a relationship with someone in order to not be left out: a fear of being 'left on the shelf', the 'fear of missing out'. In this case, the drive is not so much about being attracted to a particular person, but to conform to the social pressure to 'have someone', or to be sexually successful. Poor self-esteem is also related to the need for social acceptance, so that when other drives draws a person with low self-esteem into a sexual relationship that is not socially condoned or applauded, internal conflicts can emerge that form the basis for anxiety and depression.

Not only does the need for social acceptance influence the type of person someone might be drawn to, but it also influences the nature of the sexual activity they might engage in. An inhibitive aspect relating to the *need for social acceptance* drive theme is social prohibition, a sociocultural overlay that motivates avoidance of some sexual relationship possibilities. This is an aspect of the moral dimension,[162] and assumes the capacity not only to refrain from entering proscribed sexual relationships, but also to disallow interest in such relationship. In this case, the 'shoulds' of sexual behaviour are not so much about the other person, but about one's own behaviour, potentially inhibiting various expressions of sexuality such as the visiting of prostitutes, engaging in casual sex, sex with near relatives or 'under age' persons, and homosexual behaviour. Not all prohibitions are universal, and some are restricted to certain sociocultural contexts: these may also change with time.

The consumer drive

The *consumer drive* is the need to get the 'best deal' in a sexual relationship so to not 'miss out'.[163] This contrasts with being satisfied in a sexual relationship when essential sexual and relational needs are met, regardless of what else might be possible. As such, it is about marketplace possibilities and a preparedness to move on if a relationship is no longer deemed worthwhile or 'good enough'; or something 'better' presents itself. The sexual partner or sexual event is treated as a commodity or product: aspects of a person or relationship are measured to determine its worth. Any personal cost in the equation should not outweigh the perceived value of the product obtained. Despite the potential exploitive and dehumanising aspects, a reasonable aspect of this drive theme is the idea that each person is expected to bring into the relationship something of benefit to the other person — a 'fair market exchange' — ensuring reward value for both parties. It forms the basis of social-exchange theories of interpersonal relationships.[164] The consumer drive, however, is not simply about the *fact* of reward gained in a sexual exchange (a necessary element in the dynamic of desire and attraction), but the *basis* upon which it is obtained. If I receive something freely given, I have been rewarded. The consumer drive, however, demands not just *a* reward in the social exchange, but a good deal, or perhaps the *best* reward it can expect in the circumstances.

What might be sought in a social exchange? A person might seek in the other person complementary qualities[165] — looks, athleticism, ambition, intelligence, competence, humour, wealth, status, charm, character strengths; qualities with social value that might enhance their own status in society. Reeve (2005) observes that people 'consider first the "necessities" and then the "luxuries" in mate preferences. At the "must have" necessities level, men value physical attractiveness and women value status and resources, [while] both sexes also rate intelligence and kindness as necessities in their possible mates... then men and women... consider luxuries like a sense of humour, liveliness, creativity, and an exciting personality' (p. 98).[166] It seems that the more highly women think about their appearance, the more important it is to attract a man of high status. Similarly, the more important wealth is to a man, the more important a woman's youth and looks are to him.[167] The value of what they can expect to obtain in the sexual equation is relative to how they measure their own value.

The product or reward sought is also informed by the social context. This context includes the media, what is 'fashionable', and the perceptions of what others are enjoying in their relationships, creating expectations of what a sexual relationship or encounter should provide. In fact, the media play a potent role in the marketing of sex as if it were a commodity, reinforcing this outlook. This drive lends itself to a competitive outlook, a 'try before you buy' attitude, to be confident you are satisfied with the product, and to potentially being critical of a partner in relation to their characteristics or 'performance'.

Feeding off entitlement schemas, it can promote dissatisfaction and jealousy when comparing what one has or is experiencing with what others are perceived to have or to experience with their sexual partner. It can play a role in promiscuity and general relationship instability, as the consumer is always searching for something 'better' — in a sexual experience or in a sexual partner. In another sense, the commerce of prostitution and other market-place sexual activities relates strongly to the consumer drive.[168] This drive inhibits attraction to someone judged as not 'good enough' in terms of the expectations a person might have, but in this regard self-image is a moderating variable: a person with poor self-esteem will settle for less in the exchange than a person with good self-esteem.

The desire to rebel

The *desire to rebel* is a drive theme that appears to be the antithesis of the *need for social acceptance*, but it is in many ways reactive to non-acceptance and not having belonging needs met. It may be birthed in anger, bitterness or emotional pain in someone who feels unjustly let down or rejected by wider society, or by those that they see to represent wider society. As a result, a person may be drawn into behaviour or a relationship circumstance that is not acceptable to the prevailing social culture *because* it is not 'acceptable'.[169] 'Not belonging' is no longer a reason for distress, but becomes a point of pride. It can be a statement of heroic individuality which implicitly criticises or diminishes the community that the person doesn't feel they belong to, or by which they feel rejected.

In a somewhat different context, the pain and anger emerging from sexual betrayal by a cheating partner[170] may lead to the desire to punish the offender by sexual infidelity. Or more generally, by rebelling against any expectation that they should care about the person with whom sexual activity is entered into. In this respect this drive theme may overlap with the *power motive*: when a person feels not only angry but disempowered by their cheating partner, they may enter a sexual relationship in order to reassert their power. This may also find expression in the seduction of someone already in a relationship, because it gives the person the capacity to hurt and punish someone, just as they themselves have been hurt and feel punished.

There are other expressions of this drive theme. For example, a person may be drawn to sexually bond to someone who is not socially acceptable — one who represents the rebel, the outsider, the one who rejects social pressures. For someone who feels rejected and alienated, such a person may inspire admiration or empathy. Furthermore, the experience of joining forces with another person against a hostile world — a common enemy — also helps to forge a bond with that person.[171] In a different sense again, this drive theme associates with the desire for release from the constriction of rules and authority along with the frustrations such rules and authority might induce, so that a person, relationship, or experience is intentionally sought that does not conform to prevailing social mores. Related to this is the thrill in being different, or in doing something one ought not to do: sexual arousal can be experienced in engaging in activities regarded as taboo.

Because of the elements of non-conformity and social alienation, this drive theme may be linked to any expression of sexuality that happens not to be accepted by society at the time. It resists cultural expectations of acceptable sexual behaviours, including those related to gender stereotypes. However, rebellion against broader sociocultural rules and expectations can also generalise to rebellion against a partner's relationship expectations, including the expectation of fidelity. And so the *desire to rebel* may find expression in refusing to belong to *anyone* and may incline to relationship instability.

The power motive

The *power motive* in sexual relationships is a drive theme with many aspects. It may be characterised by coercion and aggression, or moderated by respect and care; it may or may not have erotic elements; and it may relate to social needs as a statement of dominance and power; or it may reflect a personal desire to dominate, manipulate, or control another person (or conversely, to be dominated by another person).[172] These different aspects mean that while there are social aspects to this drive theme, it could just as easily be listed under relationship-need themes or themes of pleasure and desire.

There are many ways in which sexual power can be expressed. It may be expressed in the seduction of someone into a sexual encounter, but it can equally be expressed in the denial of a desired sexual encounter to punish or control the other person. Sexual activity may be used to keep (control) a partner where there is a fear of losing that partner. The power motive can play an important part in the sexual exploitation of an existing social power imbalance, such as between a boss and employee, or a more mature and sexually experienced adult with a young and inexperienced person; and, of course, in child sexual abuse. It may find expression in establishing 'ownership' of someone.[173] The one with the need or desire to be in control or to experience power tends to initiate and define the sexual encounter: this might also happen where a person seeks out a powerful person to 'conquer' in a sexual relationship to gain a sense of empowerment. The power motive associates with the need to express strength, competence, agency, and control, and keeps vulnerability and anxiety at bay. Meanwhile, some people find security or pleasure in another person's strength and power, and choose to play a passive role and submit to the other person and the security this represents; while others are passive because of feelings of inadequacy, perhaps relating to poor self-esteem.

But there is a further dark side. Because a satisfying sexual encounter requires the cooperation of two parties, non-cooperation by one party can translate into a coercive expression of power by the other party, resulting in aggression, force and exploitation. This finds a terrible expression in rape, frequently in the context of war, where one is forcibly subjected to the stronger party as a show of victory and authority, perhaps even of revenge and punishment to the vanquished people that the raped person represents; but it can also find expression in the cruel satisfaction some experience in sadistic practices that find origin in their own anger and pain.[174] Although dominance tends to associate with the masculine and coercion is generally perpetrated by men, a woman nevertheless can also have capacity to express power in a sexual relationship. Indeed, research suggests there are no gender difference in the power motive as such; only that the power motive is more likely to find expression in males in aggression and sexual exploitation, although this tendency is moderated by the disposition to be responsible.[175]

The *power motive* can also have erotic elements. Such an erotic element can emerge from the arousal generated in the experience of power and of powerlessness. This erotic element is a feature of BDSM practices, where sexual arousal is augmented not only by power or powerlessness, dominance and submission, but also by arousal related to controlled pain or the fear of pain.[176]

Finally, this drive theme can play a role in prostitution. Some people visit prostitutes because the sexual arrangement allows them to make demands they would not otherwise make in a sexual relationship — to exercise control; conversely, some prostitutes choose this role because they feel empowered by having control of the sexual arrangement, and obtain their own financial benefits from it.[177]

The drive to procreation

The *drive to procreation* — the desire to have children — is historically a key drive and a fundamental biological reason for the sexual impulse.[178] A biological motivation for male and female to be drawn into sexual activity is that offspring may ensue. However, here our focus is on the *conscious desire* for children motivating sexual behaviour, rather than any biological imperative: indeed, for many there are also familial or social pressures to have children. This aspect has coloured the social rulings around sexual relationships historically and continues to do so in most cultures — partly with a view to the protection of children born into a relationship, as traditionally they were expected to. In many cultures, this drive also associates with the establishment of a form of social security through progeny, or the continuance of the family name. As noted earlier, it is included here because of these social aspects, but it might equally find a place in the relationship-need themes of the SDP.

This drive is susceptible to hormonal priming. This is especially so in women, in relation to their ovulation cycle, and in relation to general concerns regarding their 'body clock'. That is, they may experience a desire to have sex in order to have the child they want while they are still biologically able. This drive does not make discrimination in relation to whom I might be (sexually) attracted to except that, by definition, it will relate to someone of the opposite sex and so is instrumental in heterosexual attraction. Having said this, it might relate to the desire to find a person who would make a suitable father or mother from a cultural, social or financial perspective. It may also find expression in an attempt to stabilise an existing sexual relationship through the creation of a shared focus, interest, and sense of mutual belonging — the baby — where there is perceived insecurity within the relationship.

Although procreation is a drive theme that normally causes a person to *embrace* a sexual relationship, for some the possibility of procreation playss an active role in its *inhibition*. As such, fear of procreation could also be listed among the *SDP inhibition themes*. It may associate with the fear of having children and the associated responsibilities and loss of freedom (see the *fear of entrapment* drive theme), or perhaps the fear of being an inadequate parent. The presence of this drive as an inhibitor in sexual attraction or desire has been greatly reduced by access to contraception and safe abortion in recent decades, but it remains an issue when, for example, one partner desires children but the other doesn't.

Chapter 6

Relationship-need Themes of the SDP

S exual relationships are as much about relationships as they are about sexual behaviour. The relationship-need themes of the SDP comprise drive themes that have to do with the relationship dimension — with mate selection and pairing, the romantic aspect of a relationship, marriage, and the needs to intimacy, connecting, belonging, bonding, and love. These themes involve the qualities of the person being related to sexually, as well as the emotional needs a sexual relationship is uniquely able to meet.[179]

The strength of these themes in a SDP profile help predict what a person's goals for a sexual relationship might be, whether it be a short-term uncommitted sexual relationship or a committed relationship. A person's attachment history plays an important role in the extent to which these relationship-need themes might find expression, with a secure attachment history more likely to see these themes in ascendency, while an insecure-avoidant attachment history is more likely to see other themes in ascendency.[180] The relationship-need themes include *the need for intimacy and to belong, the need for love, the attraction to the familiar, parent-related motives,* and the *demand of practical concerns.*

Research findings consistently report gender differences in the ascendency of relationship-need themes in the SDP profile, with women more frequently focusing on relational aspects in their sexual behaviour.[181] This is true both for heterosexual and homosexual populations, mediated by attachment histories, and reflected in their stated goals for their sexual activity (for women, the goal tends to revolve around love and intimacy needs), their fantasy life (for men, fantasy is more likely to involve sexual adventure), and their attitudes to casual sex (with men having a much more permissive attitude — so long as their partner doesn't cheat on them).[182]

The need for intimacy and to belong

The need to connect and be close to someone links the need for intimacy and the need to belong. It associates with a desire for oneness or unity, for closeness (the basis for attachment), and for affiliation.[183] This of course lies at the heart of a sexual relationship, and is a key drive theme connecting sexual activity with relationship. Unsurprisingly, it is a motive for entering a sexual relationship in those with a secure attachment history, who desire to replicate earlier attachment experiences in the sexual relationship.[184] Attachment is best understood as the bond created in an intimate relationship, while the need to belong describes both a drive to establish such a bond, and the outcome of an established bond. The need to belong has to do with companionship, shared identity, having a 'place' in the relationship, and having a 'soulmate'. In a negative sense, it is a drive to escape the loneliness of disconnection and non-belonging. Similarity in attitudes[185] and shared interests and values contribute to feelings of belonging — in this regard, we see here an overlap with the *attraction to the familiar* drive.

Intimacy, however, is not only about belonging, familiarity or similarity, although it certainly normally includes these. It has the added dimension of the sharing of the body in sexual encounter, as well as the sharing of the inner self with another person. This involves a disclosure of one's feelings, to be 'known', to be acknowledged and validated in a deep sense, to become vulnerable, and feeling safe in such vulnerability with someone else. Intimacy requires certain social skills, such as the capacity to listen well, to be transparent, and to be able to articulate one's own thoughts and feelings. The desire to know and to be known by another person emotionally, cognitively, and sexually is a critical factor in achieving closeness in all its dimensions. Intimacy in turn creates the conditions for attachment — the emotional component of desiring another person so that they both feel joined together and find emotional security in each other.

The desire and expectation is that the sexual relationship is a place where it is safe to be 'uncovered', and where the experiences and the very existence of the inner self are acknowledged.[186] Over time a relationship built on such a drive theme brings increasing familiarity with each other, and the creation of a mutual sense of 'home', with the feeling of belonging this implies.[187] This experience of belonging to someone contributes to feeling valued, and to one's sense of identity and social orientation. The qualities of the sexual relationship that relate to this drive theme, including mutual trust, are by their very nature enhanced over time and critical to relationship stability. The protective instinct this drive activates (based on the idea that a person 'belongs' to me or has become 'a part of me') also becomes the basis for jealous reactions should there be a possibility of losing the partner.[188] At a dysfunctional level, this drive can lead to relationship enmeshment — a unity at the cost of personal identity.[189] At a healthy level, closeness is established while the integrity of a separate self is retained and differences are celebrated.

The desire for intimacy is more strongly associated with the feminine. Unlike the physical factors that might stimulate sexual desire in a man, a woman's sexual desire is highly responsive to emotional intimacy. Indeed, a woman's sexual motivation and behaviour reflect closeness and a desire to share with her partner more than it reflects her physiological needs.[190] And although sexual desire can certainly enhance long-term relationship intimacy, intimacy motives in turn relate to positive feelings about sex for the woman.[191] Having said this, there would appear to be no gender differences in the need to belong (and to have someone belong to us).

The need for love

The need for love is a drive theme with two critical aspects. Indeed, one could argue that two separate drives are represented here. On the one hand, it is about the desire to *express love* for someone (care-giving); on the other, it is about the need and desire to *feel loved* by someone (affirmation). Generally, both aspects exist in the same sexual relationship where love is a factor. But the trajectories for these two different aspects of the need for love can be very different in a sexual relationship, so that they could represent separate drives. These needs are also coloured by a person's attachment history.[192] There are many nuances and associations to the idea of love, and much has been written about the many kinds of love, so that it is difficult to get conceptual clarity.[193] Yet it is a critical factor in romantic relationships. We might include 'being in love' or 'falling in love' here; but this is an expression of love that represents a particular drive profile, as described by Tennov,[194] and which I will later describe. However, it is relevant to note here that 'falling in love' has both the aspect of wanting to express love, often to extreme, involving a preparedness to forfeit everything (such as money, career, and future), for the sake of a loved one; and at the same time a need to feel loved, as reflected in an overwhelming desire to be desired and wanted. In a functional relationship, a balance is normally found between both.

We begin with the first aspect, the desire to express love for someone. This involves valuing a person enough to give of oneself to a person, practically and emotionally, to want to please them and to promote their wellbeing — even to the extent forfeiting personal comforts and freedoms — generally looking for the love to be recognised and appreciated, but not necessarily repaid. The desire to express love associates with a capacity to care for and nurture someone else,[195] which has reward value in the feelings of being needed, empowered and valued. But this is different to being rewarded on the basis of exchange, where something of value is offered a person who then becomes indebted to the giver, and needs to give something in exchange, as might occur in the consumer drive. In fact, giving without external reward or even suffering for someone may increase feelings of love, at least in the short term, because such personal investment in that person increases their value to the giver — a phenomenon explained by cognitive dissonance theory.[196] The desire to give of oneself is not only about the other person's value, but also requires a sufficient level of self-esteem to believe that the giver has something of value to give. Furthermore, the desire to express love does not only occur in the passion of 'falling in love', but also in longer-term sexual relationships where investment into a relationship becomes extensive.

The second aspect is the need to feel loved by a significant other. This need includes being accepted, valued, wanted, and desired without expectation or demand, so that the one offering the love freely gives and invests into the relationship. The experience of being loved leads to feeling 'special', enhances self-esteem, promotes emotional security, and provides a sense of 'having a place' in someone's life. In this respect, it overlaps with the need to belong. The power of the felt love is affected by how highly the giver who meets such needs and desires is regarded. An idolized status of the lover makes the lover's attention particularly important, validating and rewarding. Absence of felt acceptance may be a factor in relational — and sexual — 'performance anxiety', where a person still feels a need to prove their value.[197] Poor self-esteem may also result in the conundrum where there might be a felt need to receive love, but there is difficulty in actually receiving it on the basis that the person doesn't feel 'good enough' to receive such love.

There are both erotic and non-erotic aspects in the need to be loved. The erotic aspect is the need to be accepted, valued, wanted and desired (that is, loved) *as a sexual being*, including one's gender qualities and sexual attributes. The non-erotic aspect is the need to sexually please another person in order to *be loved* (that is, accepted) by that person. This is to be distinguished from the desire to sexually please another person in order to *express* love for them. The need to please sexually to gain acceptance frequently happens for those with a history of anxious attachment.[198] Paradoxically, this need can lead to socially unacceptable sexual behaviour that is manipulative, or open to being manipulated.

Attraction to the familiar

Familiarity has to do with knowing something or someone well. Attraction to the familiar is about being attracted to what we already know, and includes a sense of belonging that results from a shared history, shared social belonging, and shared attributes. These qualities make it easier to know and understand another person and so to be validated by that person. To the degree that there are similarities of personality, values, or social history between a lover and loved one, this enhances such knowledge and understanding, which in turn enhances the feelings of being close. Similarities between a loved one and a loved parent figure can also enhance such feelings of closeness. As such, this drive theme associates with the *need for intimacy and to belong*. However, although such need remains central, here they are built on pre-existing familiarity based on similarities and shared past experiences, rather than being built over time in a new situation with unknowns. Intimacy becomes easier, because more assumptions are possible about the other person's frame of reference, social orientation and general outlook. Similarity may serve to validate our own worldview, and to improve our self-esteem.

This drive theme plays an important role in liking, in mate pairing, and in romantic relationships. The associated idea that 'similarities attract' has significant research support.[199] And so we find that the vast majority of couples are drawn to those of the same race and religion, and are generally similar in such attributes as age, socioeconomic class, educational level, intelligence, height, eye colour, and even physical attractiveness.[200] Similarities in values also play a role: if family commitment or sexual fidelity is important, a mate sharing these values will be sought over and above other qualities.[201] Other research has found that couples who are similar are more likely to be together a year later,[202] and that similarity among couples married for up to five years predicts marital adjustment.[203] Furthermore, similar personalities in spouses predicts more closeness, friendliness, marital satisfaction, and less marital conflict than those who are different,[204] although Lehmiller reminds us that while we tend to be drawn to people similar to us, the factors that attract us to someone do not necessarily promote relationship stability and success.[205] It might also be argued that the desire for understanding through similarity plays a role in some same-sex relationships, especially in lesbian relationships:[206] who better understands a woman than another woman; who better understands a man than another man?

While we might be attracted to the familiar and the similar, this is more likely to enhance emotional intimacy than sexual desire.[207] In this regard, there seems to be potential tension between liking (attraction to the familiar) and sexual desire (drive to curiosity and discovery), perhaps because in liking, we know a person for their similarities, while in sexual desire we know a person by entering their personal space and discovering their differences.

Parent-related motives

The parent-related motives theme comprises several different aspects reflecting the range of parent-child experiences that shape later interpersonal needs. A parent figure can represent different experiences for a person, and these experiences typically play an important role in the development of attachment and intimacy skills, as well as in the capacity for love and nurturance. A parent is typically the first one with whom a child experiences intimacy, and an opposite-sex parent is typically the first opposite-sex person with whom a child experiences intimacy — ideally, an emotional closeness based on trust, safety, and love. As it is the first relationship in which attachment generally develops, a mental model is created and expectations set of what a close relationship and an intimate partner will be like. And so it is not surprising that the various characteristics of a parent, both physical and psychological, can become associated with intimacy and create cues for future sexual relationships.

In the first instance, a person might wish to recreate or replace a loved parent-figure in an intimate adult relationship. The recreation of a parent-figure in a sexual partner is a drive to find someone that shares certain qualities and characteristics that are both familiar and desired (although not always beneficial or desirable), and therefore, easier to understand or connect to, and more likely to fulfil the expectations of what an intimate relationship should be. (In similar manner, a desire to recreate past intimacy experiences may occur where a person seeks a new sexual partner with characteristics similar to a loved sexual partner they have lost.) However, not everyone desires to recreate a parent-figure. Not all parent-child relationships are positive, and a person might wish their sexual partner to play the role of the parent-figure they never had. Negative memories may motivate a person to seek someone with very different qualities from parents in a fraught parent-child relationship; qualities for which they yearn. In this case, a person with the characteristics of a parent-figure associated with negative memories may be an inhibiting factor.

Another aspect related to the recreation of a parent-figure is not so much about the personality of the sexual partner, but the recreation of parent *role* in that partner. That is, a person may seek a partner that allows a degree of dependency, one who is nurturing and strong — perhaps because of unmet childhood needs for nurturance, or perhaps because the child role is comfortable and comforting. The adoption of a child role in the sexual relationship might be one of trusting dependence, seeking safety and nurturance. And then there are those who don't so much desire to be nurtured in the way parents had nurtured them; but who seek to nurture someone either in the way they were nurtured, or in the way they wish they had been nurtured. These are some variations in how childhood experiences of parental love and intimacy can colour a person's drive profile and find expression in adult sexual relationships.

The demand of practical concerns

Although this drive theme is essentially non-erotic in nature, it nevertheless influences whom someone might want enter into a sexual relationship with. And so, the demand of practical needs can play a role in mate selection.[208] There is overlap with the *consumer drive*, although the emphasis here is on the non-sexual benefits a longer-term sexual relationship might provide. There are many different practical issues that potentially play a role. For example, a primary drive may be to find economic security for oneself or one's family. This may happen in cross-cultural situations, where one party is seeking to leave an undesirable or oppressive social or economic situation. The person to whom they are drawn represents hope for a new and better life: they are well-placed economically, or they live in a region that promises opportunities and freedoms not found in the person's own place of residence. But the hope for a better life may also play a role in sexual attraction: for a person who feels trapped, for example, in a domestic situation and who cannot leave that situation without entering into a sexual relationship with someone in whom there is the promise of freedom. In a different circumstance, the practical securities of a relationship (financial or social) may prompt a person to maintain an existing sexual relationship to keep that partner satisfied, even where sexual interest or desire has faded and the sense of belonging attenuated.

Conversely, there is the factor of *propinquity* (or proximity). That is, a person is more likely to be drawn to someone who lives locally and with whom they have frequent contact, than one far away.[209] The closer people live, the greater the odds that they will meet and an attraction develop between them over time. Such circumstance makes possible a greater chance for repeated exposure, which can increase liking in and of itself, but it may also reflect shared environments or similar interests (see *attraction to the familiar*).[210] There are other aspects to the proximity and opportunity factors: for example, the limited sexual opportunities in institutions such as prisons and same-sex schools favour opportunistic same-sex sexual encounters; and the principle of scarcity — that is, the fewer the options, the more favourably those that remain might be viewed.[211] However, although propinquity might play a role in sexual relationship choice, it could reasonably be argued that it describes opportunity based on prevailing environmental conditions, rather than a drive as such.

There are other practicalities that serve to either enhance or inhibit interpersonal attraction. These include previous relationship or marriage history, age (both sexes generally prefer the man to be older), the presence of children from a previous relationship, the capacity to have children, health issues, physical and relational availability of the person, and so on. Besides these, there is one further practical concern: the perception of what is possible. Sexual interest and desire relate not only to the object of that interest or desire and what it represents to a person at a practical level; but also to its attainability. If the potential object of sexual interest or desire is perceived to be unattainable, either for practical or moral reasons, focus on that object can be quickly shut down, inhibiting interest and desire. For some, however, the opposite may be true: the challenge of trying to accomplish the unattainable may heighten interest and desire for the forbidden or unattainable thing.

Chapter 7

SDP Inhibition Themes

Sexual behaviour is not only governed by what a person is attracted to. It is also affected by what that person is *inhibited* or *repelled by*.[212] And so we consider not only subjective drive themes that might draw a person *towards* a sexual encounter or relationship, but also themes that *inhibit* such attraction, or perhaps even cause a person to be repelled by the idea. The drive themes that might variously inhibit interpersonal attraction, sexual attraction and desire, and sexual arousal, generally correlate with negative emotions, stimulating self-protective and avoidant behaviours.[213] These emotions include anxiety, fear, disgust, frustration, anger, hurt, guilt, shame, disappointment and inadequacy. And so fear or anxiety, for example, might arise from the perception that a person might be rejected or criticised by someone, motivating self-protective behaviours. Likewise, anger might arise from situations such as betrayal of trust, being rebuffed, or receiving unjustified criticism, also motivating self-protective behaviours. Sadness, on the other hand, might arise from experiences of separation or failure, leading to withdrawal; as might the feelings of guilt, shame, and depression.

Whether it is self-protection or withdrawal, such responses essentially result in disconnection in a relationship. They tend to inhibit, if not sexual behaviour itself (sexual desire and arousal may still be strong in some of these inhibition themes), the embrace of a sexual relationship more generally, especially in regard to intimacy, and in the associated sense of belonging. In this sense, inhibition themes such as *the instinct to withdrawal* and *the need for self-protection* represent drives antagonistic to relationship-need themes, especially *the need for intimacy and to belong*. A history of insecure-avoidant attachment can play a role in the activation of SDP inhibition themes, but to a degree, so would those with an insecure-anxious attachment history. Where these drives are in ascendancy, we might expect a predisposition to sexual expression outside the context of a relationship. Some drive themes inhibit sexual interest in *any* context; others are discriminatory in that a person is repelled by those that associate with certain aversive meanings and ideas.

Like the other SDP themes, because each represents themes of 'meaning clusters' rather than describing individual drive entities as such, there will be overlap between these inhibitory drive themes. And like the drive themes that contribute to interpersonal attraction, these inhibitory themes fluctuate over time. While inhibitory themes might prevent a sexual relationship from being established in the first place, their capacity to change over time means that some inhibitory themes could emerge later, leading to the fracturing of an existing relationship. Importantly, inhibitory themes can coexist with themes of sexual desire and interpersonal attraction in the SDP, creating internal tension and ambivalence. This might be the case, for example, where a person is attracted to someone who is relationally unavailable *because* they are unavailable, enjoying the excitement of sexual interest in their limited interactions with such a person, but remaining protected from feared relationship demands. Such ambivalence can also exist with people with insecure attachment styles. Nevertheless, the inhibition themes are not necessarily negative, given they can be protective and help control immoral impulses. Nor are they simply the *absence* of drive themes promoting sexual activity: inhibition drives can *actively* lower desire for sexual relationship or sexual activity.[214]

The first four themes are self-preservation themes, and the last two are repulsion themes. The self-preservation themes promote relational disconnection, potentially leading to general sexual inhibition or to withdrawal from certain kinds of sexual relationships. Lack of social skills and lack of confidence feature, as do insecure attachment styles and past relationship experiences that have been punishing or humiliating. These themes include: *social inadequacy*; *fear of entrapment*; the *instinct to social withdrawal*; and the *need for self-protection*. The repulsion drive themes are not so much about self-protection, but might be activated in situations associated with strongly negative emotions and impulses. Reeve (2005) observes that the function of disgust is rejection: '…disgust arises from our encounters with any object we deem contaminated in some way… interpersonal contaminations (physical contact with undesirable people), and moral contaminations (child abuse, incest, infidelity)' (p. 308). Because disgust is inherently an aversive emotion, we are motivated to prevent or avoid conditions that produce it. The repulsion themes include: *disgust about the person*; and *disgust about sex*.

Social inadequacy

Lack of social skills and social confidence[215] form the basis for *social inadequacy*. Formulated as a drive, however, we would talk of the *fear* of social inadequacy, or relational fear and anxiety *resulting from* social inadequacy. It is an inhibitory drive theme that associates with poor communication ability, discomfort in social situations, difficulty 'reading' others, and having poor emotional awareness of self and others. *Social inadequacy* not only affects the capacity to initiate the sexual relationship, but also the desire to do so, and the skills necessary for its maintenance. It may contribute to fear of intimacy (as might the drive *instinct to social withdrawal* — perhaps more so), especially in the context of adult sexual relationships where considerable social and communication skills are normally needed, and where a certain amount of emotional awareness and self-confidence is necessary. There may be a history of relative social isolation or neglect, of emotional immaturity, and of being the odd one out socially.[216] Although not associated with masculinity as such, this motive may be more common in men; nevertheless, here sexual activity might still occur because relational and sexual themes are often less integrated.

Poor self-esteem, social anxiety and poor assertion skills are related to *social inadequacy*. However, although fear of rejection and a sense of inadequacy are also related issues, this theme is not so much about rejection by others as it is about not coping, nor is it so much about *personal* inadequacy as it is about *social* inadequacy. Because of the particular social skills required to negotiate a relationship with the opposite sex, it may prevent a successful heterosexual relationship; it can also affect the choice of partner, with preference for a person who makes few relational demands, or perhaps who themselves lack social skills. A socially confident partner might accentuate social inadequacy. This theme associates with absence of mature sexual relationships, and so may be a contributor to asexuality, the use of pornography, accessing prostitutes, casual sex, and internet dating. Not being able to cope with the expected or perceived demands in adult sexual relationships may also be a factor in paedophilia: children make few demands socially and emotionally, and none sexually.

Fear of entrapment

A *fear of entrapment* is a drive theme that associates with a range of related fears. These include a fear of loss of personal freedoms, a fear of disempowerment or of being controlled, a fear of intimacy and relationship commitment, a fear of being 'owned' by another person, and a fear of being unable or unwilling to meet relationship expectations.[217] To the degree that sexual behaviour is linked to the expectation of a possible ongoing relationship, this drive theme inhibits such behaviour. A potential relationship is viewed as inevitably accompanying expectations and demands (real or imagined) that may be onerous to fulfil, or which may compete with personal interests, or become a threat to personal liberties. This includes fear of sharing ownership of possessions and assets, and associates with distrust of the other person's motives and future behaviour. For some, especially adolescents, the sexual relationship might signify unwanted responsibilities which they don't feel ready to provide.[218] It may also associate with fear of loss of identity where this identity is not well developed, or where competing emotional loyalties exist, and where there is poor capacity to maintain interpersonal boundaries.

On the other hand, the person with a satisfying life and a good sense of identity may fear compromising their lifestyle or fear being suffocated by the demands of an emotionally needy person. They fear no longer having 'breathing space' to be 'themselves'. This may result in whatever a person does for the needy person in the relationship becoming a duty implicitly expected of them by the needy one. The fear of being 'controlled' by the other person in the relationship may lead to insistence on 'being myself': but to 'be myself' means to do it 'my way' — doing things 'their way' may be seen as a threat to my personal identity, separateness, or autonomy.

Perfectionists who fear making a 'wrong decision' and being stuck with a less-than-perfect relationship may also fear relationship commitment. So may those who distrust their capacity to make good judgement regarding a partner, or those who are unstable in their views and desires in the long term and often change their minds, so that they distrust their own decision-making capacity. The fear of entrapment may prevent entering a relationship; or if someone *is* in a relationship, any subsequent feelings of entrapment and suffocation may be the stimulus to leave the relationship in search of a less demanding one, or of an open arrangement without commitments. The fear of entrapment seems to be a more common in men than women: perhaps there is a greater need for independence or a greater fear of loss of sexual freedom in men.

The instinct to withdrawal

The *instinct to withdrawal* relates to both emotional and social withdrawal, predisposing a person to emotional disconnection. The fear of rejection can lead to emotional withdrawal, in which case it acts as a self-protective instinct and overlaps with the *need for self-protection* drive theme. It relates to other fears too, such as a fear of being discovered as being inadequate as a person (personal inadequacy as against *social inadequacy*, although in both cases, self-esteem is generally poor).[219] As someone gets to know a person well, they are likely to uncover that person's flaws, weaknesses and failings, and might become disappointed or even disgusted with that person, leading to disinterest in, or rejection of, that person.

However, the *instinct to withdrawal* may occur for reasons other than self-protection. Such reasons might include self-blame and self-rejection, depression, shame, guilt or feelings of personal failure. The sense of personal failure may include feelings or experiences of sexual or relationship inadequacy. The fear of sexual performance failure might also relate to medical or emotional reasons, for example, the loss of libido associated with depression, or sexual performance issues related to diabetes or other medical reasons. This drive theme might also relate to feelings of inadequacy and shame relating to poor body image (see *the attraction to beauty* drive).

The *instinct to withdrawal* may be activated in someone who suffers from various psychiatric problems or general addiction problems. It not only distracts from interest in a sexual relationship and sexual behaviour more generally, but can also lead to shame and deception.[220] Self-acceptance becomes a prerequisite to acceptance by another person: if a person does not feel 'at home' with themselves, it is difficult to feel 'at home' with another person, or welcome such a person into their 'emotional home' by revealing their inner selves in the course of their sexual relating. Emotional disconnection and withdrawal may also relate to the preoccupations and distress that arise from trauma, or from survivor guilt. Finally, guilt associated with infidelity and deception may activate this inhibiting drive. Such guilt can affect an existing relationship, although it may be hidden by blaming the partner's sexual or relationship adequacy.

Another important factor is an *insecure-avoidant attachment* pattern. This predicts ambivalence, self-doubt, and expectation of rejection or of not being understood by others because of childhood experiences, predisposing a person to withdraw at any sign of conflict or perceived rejection. In the confusion arising from mixed and inconsistent responses of a parent, a person may later distort (or have difficulty interpreting) emotional or relational signals, and become anxious and quick to withdraw in later sexual relationships. Indeed, there is a strong drive to avoid intimacy.[221]

The need for self-protection

The *need for self-protection* is an inhibitory drive theme that has two aspects: a physical and an emotional one. The physical aspect has to do with health reasons: the negative side to the *drive to procreation* (avoiding pregnancy), and avoiding diseases associated with sexual activity.[222] This aspect generally receives major attention in school sex education programs, effectively equipping young people to better manage potential health risks, and thereby reducing its importance as an inhibitory theme.

The emotional aspect of the *need for self-protection* is associated with protection from humiliation and being dishonoured,[223] disrespected, and belittled, or fearing that this might happen; and with losing trust. As we have seen, this overlaps with the *instinct to withdrawal*. However, withdrawal is not the only self-protective strategy. Vigilance, controlling behaviours, limiting self-disclosure or limiting investment in a relationship, and how a mate might be selected, may all reflect the *need for self-protection* motive in the person who feels vulnerable and unsafe. Confidence in the benefits of an intimate relationship is lost, and there is an expectation that the other person will be unreliable, unsafe, and has the potential to treacherous behaviour. A personal history of short-term sexual relationships or brief sexual encounters can fuel this drive as there is a need to protect against the potential grief and distress consequent upon the expected ending of a relationship. Relationship infidelity by the other party can activate this drive, causing an immediate rejection of the offending party, and subsequent distrust in future relationships with others. In such a circumstance, self-doubt, lowered self-esteem, and emotional pain typically result, as do cynicism, distrust and anger towards the unfaithful partner, and jealousy and anger towards the one drawing the unfaithful partner away.

Early childhood experiences of abandonment or of relational instability and experiences of sexual exploitation and abuse can result in a self-protecting rejection of another person.[224] When a child has experienced a lack of appropriate adult protection, it generally develops various self-protective coping styles. We find in both anxious and avoidant attachment patterns that distrust and self-protective drives are ascendant, interfering with adult attachment processes, lowering sexual satisfaction and increasing the number of sexual problems. Research into attachment styles found that those with an *insecure-avoidant* love style were reluctant to make long-term commitment in their sexual relationships. Their avoidant attachment was reflected in aloofness, fear of rejection, distrust, ambivalence about intimacy, and pursuing sex for non-romantic reasons.[225]

This motive can result in asexual tendencies, or, if it associates with a particular sex (a woman being hurt by men, for example), withdrawal from the offending sex (all men), and attraction to the 'safe' gender (in this case, women). Alternatively, it can disconnect the sexual experience from relationship intimacy. Self-protection does not necessarily mean sexual disinterest or negative attitude towards sex itself. Self-protection is about protecting personal vulnerabilities, and relates as much to the protection of the inner self (the relational aspect) as it does to withdrawal from sexual activity as such. It prevents connection with a person, and so interferes with the relationship aspect of the sexual encounter. And so, for example, a prostitute can remain active sexually, but separate emotionally. Finally, an aspect of self-protection is related to the judged personal readiness for a sexual relationship, generally during adolescence or the early period of a new relationship.

Disgust about the person

Toates (2014) wrote: 'disgust must surely be the most reliable, irredeemable and durable of passion killers, its effects lingering long after the triggering event' (p. 205). Disgust may be triggered after a person becomes conscious of some repellent information, or it may be triggered unconsciously by some physical stimulus.[226] Disgust is generally an instinctive reaction to contamination;[227] something believed to be dirty, or which ought not to be associated with a 'clean', 'proper', or 'right' thing. However, what is regarded as 'contaminated' will vary between people and cultures, as social norms and moral sensitivities play a role. It is also relative to the existing perception of how clean or pure a thing is or should be — a person may be desensitised to 'contaminating' events.

Disgust towards the person and what they represent may result from their physical presentation, with whom they associate, or with what they have done: sociocultural mores and personal expectations may be involved. In this respect, this inhibitive drive may link with a critical attitude towards the other person. High moral, religious, or behavioural expectations may be held: this may lead to a list of 'shoulds' that if the other person fails to meet them, leads to their rejection.[228] But it may also result from infidelity, both past and current, which may be seen to 'contaminate' the relationship, compromising the sense of belonging. Disgust will quickly erode sexual attraction or desire because the instinct is repulsion, with a view to distance oneself from the source of contamination.

Active rejection and avoidance may not be limited to the particular individual who is socially 'contaminated'. It can be generalised to those deemed similar to the one in whom negative characteristics are attributed: 'all women/men are the same, and can't be trusted (that is, I don't understand them, or can't predict them)'; or: 'all men are exploitive and self-focused when it comes to sex'; or: 'all women are critical and demanding'. In this context, this drive theme could also contribute to a change in sexual orientation. A history of sexual exploitation or relationship disappointment may stimulate this drive, as might perfectionist tendencies in a person.

Disgust about sex

Not all disgust is about the personal characteristics of someone. The *idea of sex generally*, or of engaging in sex with a person of a particular sex, age, or relationship, can generate disgust. This disgust may relate to feeling contaminated because of the exchange of body fluids; the messy, primal, physical aspect of the sexual encounter.[229] Or it might relate to what sexual activity with a person represents, such as role confusion or some abhorrent or incongruous aspect regarding such sexual activity, so that a relationship becomes contaminated by having sex. For example, the sexual act might associate with negative meanings such as exploiting or dominating someone, the expression of lust or loss of self-control, or loss of innocence. Typically, this disgust reaction is one a person might have about the idea of a sexual encounter with a child or a family member. It is also a common reaction to the idea of a same-sex sexual encounter (or, for some, the idea of an opposite-sex encounter).

Less commonly, this inhibiting drive might result from the perception of a person, or of what a person represents, being somehow pure or wonderful in an asexual sense. The man who idolises his mother, for example, may idolise all women, and see in them a quality that is diminished or contaminated when they are associated with sexual behaviour. He doesn't want to entertain such an idea, as it threatens his picture of the purity and wonder of his mother and of women more generally. Just as the idea of a child losing innocence or purity repels him, so does the idea of a woman losing her innocence.

Critical changes take place once a relationship becomes sexual. Respect may be replaced with familiarity, the removal of boundaries creates vulnerability for both parties, and if sex is associated with something negative, immoral or even sordid, then the high view someone might have of a person becomes contaminated. In this respect, any sociocultural sexual scripts that present aspects of sexual behaviour as immoral, distasteful, lacking in dignity or self-control, or potentially dangerous, can colour how a person who engages in sexual behaviour that includes such aspects, is seen. People with a history of exploitive sexual encounters — in both heterosexual and homosexual circumstances — come to associate sexual desire and arousal with self-gratification and relative indifference towards the person they happen to have sex with. When these people then enter into a meaningful relationship with a person they respect, sexual desire and arousal may be inhibited should feelings of guilt, shame, or disgust relating to their earlier sexual behaviour be activated. And so this drive theme may contribute to sexual abstinence or asexuality.

Chapter 8

Sociocultural Sexual Scripts: Origins

Kelvin drove home a little recklessly, frustrated and angry after a blazing row with his girlfriend, Sana. What *was* she thinking? Why was she so difficult? He couldn't understand her. He'd been so good to her, so respectful. Yet here, three months after meeting her, she was still resisting him, even though she was clearly drawn to him, and had said she wanted to spend time to get to know him. But she was withdrawing from him, even as his desire for her had grown. Her attitude had changed as she got to know him. He wanted her for his own, but she was certainly playing hard to get. Was she scared of her parents? Had they turned her against him? Was she sexually frigid? What *was* her problem? How could she decide whether the relationship would work if she wasn't even prepared to live with him awhile? He felt unfairly judged and upset.

Kelvin was in love with Sana. She was open and seemed naive, yet available. But her mixed signals confused him. On the one hand, she liked to spend time with him and he'd been to her place frequently. Her family had seemed accepting of him. But she was rejecting his sexual advances, and he felt increasingly frustrated with her. He loved her more than his earlier girlfriends, and he wanted to show his love as he had with the others. But she'd been upset when she heard about his earlier relationships. Why should she? Wasn't it normal? It's not like he'd cheated on her, or on anyone, for that matter. He now wanted to have sex with Sana, and for her to belong to him: why was she rejecting him?

Sana, on the other hand, had become confused, distressed and jealous when she learned about his previous relationships. She wanted someone who would belong only to her, and expected that it should be so. She didn't want the shadows of past lovers in her life. She started to doubt whether the relationship would work. Although she'd been drawn to his confidence and charm, she was in conflict. She started to wonder about his motives, about what the pressure for sex really represented for him. What did he really want of her: her body? Sex? What did it all mean? Would he one day move on to someone else once he got bored with her, as he'd done before? And how would this affect her family, who had their own expectations as to the person Sana should be with?

An attractive woman, Sana was raised in a Christian family that had emigrated from Lebanon. Unlike most of her friends, and although she'd had interest in boys before, Sana was still a virgin. She still lived with her family, and believed that sex was associated with commitment to marriage, although she was aware that many of her peers thought differently. Her interest in Kelvin hadn't had a sexual focus. She liked him as a person, and fantasised about the future life he represented. He was good-looking, confident, fun to be with, and respectful towards her. Nevertheless, she found sexual interest strengthening within her as the relationship progressed. But now, three months later, tension was rising between them.

Kelvin's background could hardly have been more different from hers. He was Australian-born, and had grown up on the sports field rather than in church. His parents had divorced when he was only five, and after a subsequent failed relationship his mother had finally found stability when her boyfriend Richard moved in. Richard was a good man, and related well to Kelvin and his younger brother. Kelvin had been in a couple of relationships by the time he met Sana. His first sexual experience with a girl was at age 17, after he'd been drinking at a party. He'd then had his first 'serious' relationship with another girl for a couple of years: his family had been happy for him. But they'd drifted apart during his studies; he then lived with a third girl for a year or so. It all seemed a normal part of growing up.

The dilemma of Sana and Kelvin represents not only different backgrounds and drive profiles, but also the dilemma of conflicting sociocultural expectations. The drives that energise and direct sexual behaviour are moderated by these expectations, and need to be managed in the light of these expectations.

And there *needs* to be shared expectations for behaviour that is inherently relational, involving at least two people (those in the primary partnership), and indirectly, many more — such as children born into the relationship and the friends and family who relate to the partnership. These shared expectations form the basis for social order, contribute to social harmony, and help prevent the frustrations, distress, anxiety, and alienation that result from divergent expectations and associated misunderstandings.[230] In this way, they essentially set the *rules* for relationships. They also play a role in the activation or inhibition of various drives in a person's drive profile.

While relationship expectations may theoretically be negotiated between the couple concerned, not all have the skills or opportunity to do so. In any event, such agreements may not necessarily be understood by the family or community they represent. Moreover, relationships and alliances have wider social implications, and so the rules of relationship are of concern to the wider family and community. It is advantageous for society to develop understandings about what sexual and relationship behaviours are functional and acceptable. The shared expectations of sexual behaviours are social narratives I refer to as *sociocultural sexual scripts*.[231] These scripts play an important role in the SDP, most directly in drive themes such as the *need for social acceptance* and the *desire to rebel*; but also more generally, in the extent to which various drives might be stimulated or inhibited.

While sociocultural scripts set the expectations and rules for sexual relationships, these do not necessarily translate into practice.[232] What it *does* mean is the extent to which sexual practice varies from the script ideals is the extent to which feelings of guilt or shame might arise, a sense of failure or social alienation might result, or legal consequences might be enacted. Sana had clear ideals about what the sexual relationship should mean. However, these did not reflect Kelvin's ideas or experience. Under pressure from Kelvin, however, she might succumb to sexual activity — but feel guilty and resentful afterwards. A study of the history of sexual behaviour is thus not the same as a study of the history of sexual ideals and expectations. And so we observe that the *fact* of extramarital behaviour has always existed: however, the *attitude* toward such behaviour has varied according to the endorsed sociocultural script. Likewise, the *fact* of homosexual relationships has always existed; but the *attitude* relating to homosexual behaviour has varied according to sociocultural script. The *fact* of children being drawn into sexual behaviour has always existed; but the *attitude* towards such practices has varied across culture and time — this includes the age at which a child is regarded as a child.

Finally, sociocultural sexual scripts have both an *internal* and *external* aspect. The internal aspect has to do with the script that a person has been exposed to historically and has embraced and internalised, so that it becomes a basis for their moral decision-making. As such, it contributes to the internal orientation of the subjective self when it comes to sexual matters and their meanings. The external aspect has to do with the prevailing public acceptance and promotion of a particular script. The public sphere finds expression in politics, legislation and in the social pressures to conform, in order for individuals to belong to the society. It is this aspect that becomes the basis for shared understandings and expectations. But there is potential not only for conflicting co-existing sociocultural sexual scripts in any particular community, but also conflict between internal and prevailing external scripts, which can create psychological tension and distress.

Shared expectations, meanings, and rules

We have noted that there needs to be shared expectations for behaviour that is inherently relational. These shared expectations form the basis for social order by setting the rules for relationships. However, sexual scripts are not only about shared language and expectations; they also help establish shared *meanings*. Just as words carry meanings that are apprehended by the subjective self, so do nonverbal actions. I might signal 'no' with a shaking of the head or communicate my anger with a finger gesture. Sexual behaviour also carries meaning: we cannot separate sexual behaviour from its context and the meanings that context creates.[233] Like both verbal and non-verbal signals, these meanings can vary from one culture to another. Part of Sana's confusion was in how to interpret Kelvin's sexual advances: did this mean he loved her and would be committed to her, as she had been taught it meant — or did it mean something else?

sociocultural scripts play an important role in determining these meanings. If the perceived meaning matches the intent of the person's sexual behaviour and represents a socially acceptable expression of that intent, then the interaction is likely to go well.[234] Sexual behaviour may signal any combination of meanings (generally representing the expected drive animating that behaviour) such as love, desire, fascination, commitment, intimacy, belonging, domination, and so on — some of which might be seen as socially acceptable; some not. Where the perceived meaning does *not* match the intent (for example, I interpret your sexual behaviour to mean you love me and stick by me, when in fact, your intent is to have a good time and move on); or the intent is not acceptable according to the prevailing script (for example, using sex to control another person), problems ensue.

The platform of 'shoulds' — the assumptions about how things 'ought to be' — form the context defining potential guilt, shame, frustration, disappointment and anger. As such, these 'shoulds' receive frequent attention in relationship counselling. And this especially so in the area of sexual relationships, where a range of views about what 'should be' exists, creating no small amount of angst. This raises the inevitable question: what *is* the basis for determining the 'shoulds' of sexual behaviour? sociocultural sexual scripts derive the roles, goals and meanings of sexual behaviour from the commonly held values and ideas of that culture, which may associate with cultural traditions or religious or philosophical understandings.[235] As such, they provide a shared framework as to what 'ought to happen' morally and legally. The script sets out not only the limits of sexual activity, but also what is permissible: the parameters for guilt and pleasure. In normalising certain sexual behaviours the script also sets the conditions for belonging to that society — both to the extended family and the local community.

To argue that there should be no 'shoulds' in sexual behaviour is disingenuous. Such argument may be advanced by some adopting the secular Western script, and used to dismiss competing sociocultural scripts. But rules help regulate behaviour. Where there is no social agreement about the behaviours we can reasonably expect, social discord results. Moreover, when a person lacks sufficient judgement for decision-making, access to the accumulated wisdom of the community as contained in sociocultural scripts is very beneficial. And while a person who does not share the beliefs and ideals of the prevailing ('dominant') culture may feel 'controlled' by social expectations, it does not follow that 'controlling' the individual is the purpose of such expectations. The purpose is rather to facilitate social order and cohesion through a common basis for understanding and promoting certain behaviours.

Just as drive profiles are dynamic, prevailing sociocultural sexual scripts also change over time. For example, Western society has seen a dramatic shift in recent decades from the promotion of the traditional Christian script to adoption of what I have termed the secular Western script. Although the latter has been many years in the making, its practical outworking and normalisation is relatively recent. We have seen a foundational shift in relation to social acceptance of various sexual behaviours outside marriage, with multiple sexual partners, sex after the first date, and divorce now commonplace. Such change has been followed by equally foundational shifts in views regarding same-sex partner lifestyle.[236] The technological revolution has made its own contribution to unprecedented changes and new freedoms with different and rapid ways of making sexual contact and conducting sexual relationships.

But with sexual behaviour involving children and the associated child sex abuse scandals, the social mood has swung in the opposite direction.[237] What is the basis for the increased libertarian views in relation to the expression of consensual adult heterosexual and homosexual behaviour on the one hand; and the push for stronger legal censure in relation to sexual behaviour involving children, with its 'name and shame' campaigns and demands for longer prison terms and compensation for victims, on the other hand? It may be that this comes from better understanding and recognition of the emotional and social damage created in child sexual abuse victims, generally still seen many years after the event. Might we see a similar swing in social mood regarding some of the current libertarian views, should evidence of emotional and social difficulties associated with current common sexual practices emerge over time?

For now, we observe there are different sociocultural sexual scripts, some more broadly accepted than others, varying across time and across cultures.[238] In many societies that comprise a variety of cultural and religious traditions, different sexual scripts may be found within the one society.[239] Unfortunately, the presence of different scripts in the one society inevitably creates tension and conflict that a commonly accepted script would avoid: indeed, that it should be commonly accepted is the *point* of a sociocultural sexual script. Despite such variation, there are underlying themes that may be found across cultures and over time. I will describe what I believe to be important themes found in some of the major sociocultural scripts relevant to our Western society. The treatment is not designed to be prescriptive or exhaustive, but simply to highlight how different scripts affect the expression of sexual drives.

I describe several general scripts, although there will inevitably be variations of these suggested scripts. I have included what I term the *traditional* scripts, variations of which have been found in many cultures for thousands of years; the *traditional Christian* script, a variation of the traditional scripts that is particularly relevant to Western society; the *secular Western* script, which has emerged more recently; and several subscripts that relate to the secular Western script — the *sexual experimentation subscript*; the *individual freedoms subscript*; and the *virtual sex subscript*. In many respects, the traditional scripts emphasised the obligations and belonging of a couple in sexual relationship (generally assumed to be in marriage) in respect to the wider society; the traditional Christian script emphasised the obligations and belonging of a couple in a sexual relationship (assumed to be marriage) to each other; while the secular Western script and subscripts loosened the idea of obligation and belonging from the sexual relationship (no longer assumed to be in marriage) altogether, instead emphasising personal happiness and individual rights. Each of these different scripts legitimise different drives that might be present in a person's drive profile.

Sex and passion (including the notion of falling in love) were traditionally viewed with suspicion — as potentially irrational, problematic, and destabilising. These were best managed within the stabilising context of marriage, and were often not the basis for choice of marriage partner. But in the secular Western script, this was reversed: sex and passion often became the entry point and goal of a sexual relationship which might or might not become long term. Yet more recently, even this understanding is increasingly seen as an unnecessary precondition for sexual activity, which is becoming for some an end in itself: to 'have sex' simply because one wants to 'have sex'.

Traditional scripts

The *Traditional* sexual scripts comprise notions from ancient wisdom and practices developed in a largely male-dominated society. Such male domination was not seen as antagonistic to women, but protective: both of women and children. Nevertheless, then as now, good things can become corrupted and abused. In traditional society women and children were generally dependent on men, both economically and for their physical safety. Sexual unions had social and political ramifications. Indeed, marriage played a key role in the politics of belonging for thousands of years: empires, kingdoms and properties were united and divided on this basis, and personal identity was established this way.

The Mosaic laws of some 3,500 years ago (the basis of Judaism)[240] and the Quran, written some 1,400 years ago, are well-known examples of traditional scripts. In the Mosaic laws, for example, the tenth commandment (Exodus 20:17: 'You shall not covet your neighbour's house. You shall not covet your neighbour's wife, or his manservant or maidservant, his ox or donkey, or anything that belongs to your neighbour.') reflect the idea that a woman in sexual relationship with a man belonged to the man in the same way his property belonged to him. But the sense of belonging and unity found in a sexual relationship was already understood to be much deeper than this. From the very beginning, it was written: 'For this reason a man will leave his father and mother and be united to his wife, and they will become one flesh' (Genesis 2:24).

Coontz (2006) observes that 'for thousands of years, marriage served so many economic, political, and social functions that the individual needs and wishes of its members (especially women and children) took second place. Marriage was not about bringing two individuals together for love and intimacy, although this was a welcome side effect. Rather, the aim of marriage was to acquire useful in-laws and gain political or economic advantage' (p. 36). Traditional scripts centred on the extended family's need to care for the vulnerable as there was no other social security to protect them. When a woman belonged to a man, she enjoyed all the benefits that came with the man and the extended family he represented. The woman's identity, and that of the children she had with her husband, was defined by the family to which they belonged. This relationship normally excluded all other men, and the man was understood to have exclusive rights and responsibilities in relation to her, and she (generally) to him.

Because there were few contraceptive options, sexual behaviour carried a high risk of pregnancy. The question of who carried responsibility for children born from a sexual encounter was an important one. The need to prevent children being born into situations where they had no security or economic support necessitated tight regulation of sexual behaviour. These pragmatic issues defined traditional scripts, which tied its provisions in with divine intent, as the spiritual and practical were typically interwoven in traditional society. The concern of traditional sexual scripts was the wider relational networks and responsibilities, and the greater social good, rather than individual needs and desires.[241] Marriage represented an essential social unit and legal entity, carrying with it legal rights and obligations; and as such, its stability contributed to wider social stability. The choice of partner reflected this. Practical issues such as wealth and influence were more important than love and sex, as the future wellbeing of both the woman and her children were at stake. But the man also had an eye to his fortunes, and was more likely to seek a woman from a family that would be of economic or strategic benefit to him.

An unequal power arrangement was common. Once a sexual relationship was entered into, the woman typically became the property of the man, just as their shared property was owned by the man rather than the woman. Protection and responsibility for her passed from her father to her husband. Her husband now retained the legal rights and the leadership role both within the relationship and in any shared economic enterprise.[242] The man typically made the major decisions and was held responsible for the family. A girl might marry relatively young to an older husband, which helped reinforce his dominance. In some communities the man (if he was wealthy enough) might have more than one wife: she, however, typically did not have more than one husband.[243] Because of the social implications of marriage, it was common for marriage to be arranged between families. The actions of a couple were seen to reflect on the wider family, so that straying from the sexual script would bring dishonour to the family, potentially resulting in severe consequences.

The wife was seen to have a sexual duty towards her husband, and was expected to bear him children (and therefore, heirs to his property). If she was unable to do so, the man might find another woman to give him children: it was a pragmatic arrangement.

The personal experience of love, intimacy, or sexual attraction and desire in the marriage tended to be secondary in making the match. If they were relevant at all, they were expected to develop over time in the relationship.[244] The woman was expected to be a virgin at the time of marriage and be able to show evidence of this. This ensured that she didn't belong to anyone else (and their relevant property and obligation rights). Because she was essentially his property, she was expected to remain faithful to her husband, and it was her responsibility to ensure no interest was shown towards her by another man[245] (this was often reflected in strict dress codes), while any discreet infidelity on the part of the husband (with another woman or man) was more likely to be overlooked. Sexual expression for the woman was restricted to the marriage relationship and the desires of her husband — sexual activity was generally not based on any desires *she* might have had. In this respect, an extreme form of this script practiced in some cultures (still today) involved female circumcision, so that a woman was denied the pleasures associated with sexual intercourse.

Traditional scripts might be considered oppressive today. Traditional society certainly saw its share of abuse and discrimination within the family unit, and the social consequences for sexual transgression were at times draconian. Yet its cultural rules provided clear expectations in regard to sexual relationships, providing protection, stability and economic and social security when practised in the context of respect and goodwill. It established a clear sense of identity arising from the extended family into which the woman married. Conceiving love as an expression of fulfilling one's marital duties rather than linking it to sexual passion helped create a stable arrangement. Nothing of such enduring importance as the stability of the family system and its associated rights and obligations could be left to the vicissitudes of passing desire.

For all the importance of the marital arrangements to social stability and general human welfare in traditional society, the love of passion always existed. Extramarital liaisons, both heterosexual and homosexual, also always existed. They might involve household servants, those captured during war, or simply an attractive neighbour. There were circumstances where someone might be drawn into a sexual relationship outside the provisions of the traditional scripts — such as I will describe in the *sexual experimentation* sub-script. However, such relationship, and any children born of extramarital liaisons, typically did not attract the recognition, rights, provisions and privileges that were attached to the formal marital relationship. These sexual relationships existed on the edges of social propriety, and tolerance for such events varied from society to society. Likewise, homosexual activity always existed, although major traditional scripts generally condemned such activity.[246] Certainly, the idea of homosexual marriage — attributing marital roles and giving homosexual relationships formal legal status — was inconceivable in traditional culture.[247]

Traditional Christian script

Probably the best known and widely adopted of the traditional scripts in Western society, the *traditional Christian* script is given specific mention because of its historical importance to Western culture. This script found context in the ancient wisdom of the Mosaic laws and traditional culture. Women were normally dependent on male support and protection, and sexual behaviour needed to be regulated to prevent children being born into insecure environments. And although male dominance largely remained, various teachings of the New Testament laid the foundation for greater moral equality, emphasising love, faithfulness and unity on the part of both husband and wife as critical components of a sexual relationship. For example, Paul writes in Ephesians 5:28 that 'husbands ought to love their wives as their own bodies'. The New Testament also did not endorse the polygamy that the wealthy people practiced in the traditional societies of Old Testament times. And in more recent times, this script has accommodated the idea of romantic love as a desired basis for entering marriage.

The traditional Christian sexual script was based on Judeo-Christian values. A sexual relationship was established once a man and woman entered a covenant,[248] which was formally recognised by a marriage ceremony in which vows were exchanged before witnesses, and in the context of which the couple subsequently had children.[249] It ruled that there should be no sexual relationship outside the marriage (the term 'holy matrimony' reflected the idea of the exclusiveness of the relationship):[250] that each remained faithful to the other ('until death do us part'), and that sexual access between them was the expected right of both parties. This was based on the idea that a man and woman belonged to each other once they had entered into a sexual relationship, creating a new entity (they became 'one flesh'),[251] that sexual intercourse was a symbolic 'giving oneself to the other', and that the relationship commitments preserved the emotional and personal investment each made in the relationship. The exclusive nature of the marriage arrangement was reflected in the exchange of wedding rings, signalling the person was not available to enter a sexual or intimate relationship with anyone else. This arrangement provided the woman and children born into the relationship with relative security and protection. But its strength was also its weakness: if things went awry and a spouse became abusive, the wronged party was often trapped, caught between loyalty and fear.

In many Christian traditions, the marriage ceremony was regarded as a *sacrament.* This implied a sacred aspect: that is, it involved spiritual dimensions.[252] In all Christian traditions, divine revelation was seen as the authority underlying the provisions of the marriage relationship, forming its moral foundation. Furthermore, the sexual relationship between a man and a woman was seen as symbolic of the relationship of God with his people, which tended to underscore a dominant masculine role in the relationship. Marriage carried meanings that were regarded seriously and authoritatively, and the idea of 'honour' for those involved — that is, the weightiness or importance of the relevant meanings and proceedings — applied.[253]

While shaped around New Testament writings,[254] changes in cultural and political circumstances over the last 2,000 years saw variations in the traditional Christian script over time. Indeed, in the early history of the Christian church, sexual relationships were viewed with some suspicion by segments of the church, and led to the monastic movement. Sexual behaviour was regarded as worldly and non-spiritual (as were all bodily pleasures), so that sexual renunciation and celibacy was seen as an ideal to which to aspire.[255] These views were since challenged, especially in the Reformation of the 1500s, so that once again 'the natural, divinely ordained sexual drive needed to be recognized as a necessary, good and honourable impulse' (Mangalwadi (2011), p. 290). Nevertheless, the man's role as head of the home remained a central tenant, maintaining social order,[256] and the woman was expected to submit to him.[257] By the seventeenth century, we read (for example) of the Christian Puritan movement that '[they] devalued celibacy, glorified companionate marriage, affirmed married sex as both necessary and pure, established the ideal of romantic love, and exulted the role of wife' (Ryken (1986), p. 53).

Typically, marriage in this tradition is more recently seen as the initiative and choice of both man and woman. It is based on the idea that they are attracted to, and love each other. And although the man has historically been dominant (this dominance was seen in the legal adoption of the man's family name in a marriage, and in the term *husband,* which derived from 'master of the house', and associated with household management), there is now a greater expectation of equality between the couple. Roles have accordingly become more fluid: where in the Victorian era the woman was expected to care for the children and to manage the home while the man brought in the income and was the link to the outside world, the reverse might now sometimes be true; but more commonly, the roles are shared.

And so we see the traditional Christian script found its basis in the religious context. It was argued to be the basis for social stability and to provide optimal circumstances for the development of children born into the relationship, including the benefits derived from the respective gender strengths represented in the parents. The assumption of permanence in the sexual relationship protected the emotional and economic investments made in the relationship, enhanced the sense of belonging, created strong motivation to resolve differences, and protected children from the destabilising problem of divided loyalties, so preventing confusion about to whom they belong. But for all the idealism inherent in marriage as promoted by this script, there has never been an illusion that it provides a simple solution to the potential conflicts and difficulties inherent in sexual relationships. As Mangalwadi (2011) observes: 'The only way to make monogamy work is to value love above pleasure, to pursue holiness and humility rather than power and personal fulfilment, to find the grace to repent rather than condemn, to learn sacrifice and patience in place of indulgence and gratification' (p. 291).

Chapter 9

Sociocultural Sexual Scripts: Changing Perspectives

In traditional sexual scripts, marriage played a central role. Sexual behaviour was associated with probably the most important socially recognised rite of passage, while the ensuing family comprised the fundamental social unit: society's health was often seen to be tied to the health of the family unit. Marriage represented many things: a permanent change in social status; the social and economic responsibilities of mature adulthood; the bringing together of two extended families, along with whatever social status and economic privileges might be associated with either; legal rights that flowed from the union; a change in living arrangements to a shared abode; sexual intimacy that was restricted to the marriage partner; and the probability of having children and managing a family. No wonder weddings could be elaborate affairs.

All this changed in the Western culture. From the 1700s, traditional theologically-based thinking began to give way to secular humanism. This, in turn, accompanied a radical rethink of the rules of sexual relationships. And then, in the course of the 1900s, with increased options for birth control and the increased opportunity for women to access education and become economically independent from men, as well as the introduction of social welfare in many countries, and with the advances in science, technology, and in medicine generally, profound changes in social structure, in expectations, and in the meanings of things emerged. There were also political elements, as the feminist movement challenged the tradition of male dominance in all sectors of life, seeking social equality and balance in power, questioning prevailing power arrangements in the sexual relationship and beyond. (This push for social equality also reflected Marxist ideology.) The prevailing social scripts were seen to empower men (and this included the role of male-dominated religious institutions), and the accepted 'wisdom' of the traditional scripts was rejected. [258]

With these changes, the logic and pragmatics of the traditional sexual scripts was questioned. This was driven partly by changes in moral philosophy as a new secular morality took hold, partly by what became technically and socially possible, and partly by the feminist movement.[259] A search for other ways to understand sexual relationships and sexual behaviour began with a push for a more egalitarian arrangement between the sexes, and the promotion of individual freedom, rights, and choice. This in turn led to questioning about what should be regarded as 'normal' and acceptable, to the extent that the very idea of fixed genders came to be seen by some as an 'oppressive social construct'. Although considerable benefits emerged from these changes, including a greater respect for the female position, increased sensitivity to and honesty about exploitive dynamics in sexual relationships (and relationships more generally), more personal freedoms, greater tolerance for difference, and increased expectations as to what an intimate relationship should deliver, there were also many costs, including, paradoxically, costs to mental health, which we explore later.

The new science of psychology made its own contributions to these changes in thinking — and continues to do so.[260] Importantly, the changes were reflected in the so-called 'values-free evidence-based' approach of science and evolutionary theory,[261] and came to represent a secular viewpoint. Through the work of such people as Ellis, Kinsey, and Masters and Johnston, science found its way into the bedroom. Existing moral and sociocultural rules relating to sexual behaviour were increasingly viewed as the values of a bygone and outdated era, difficult to align with the logic of scientific thinking. These traditional values were tied to religious ideas and old social structures and so were seen as irrelevant to modern society. And so the 'progressive' *secular Western* sexual script emerged.

This script is less cohesive than the traditional scripts in that it draws from a number of different social developments and tolerates a wide range of sexual behaviours. I will also describe three subscripts that relate to the secular

Western sexual script which identify three important streams contributing to the changing expectations and meanings colouring the script. The freedoms inherent in this script make it relatively forgiving both in regard to the drives that might be expressed in sexual behaviour, and in the sexual behaviours themselves. In so doing, the conditions for shame and guilt were considerably reduced. That its appearance is relatively recent means that it continues to evolve and its longer term wider social implications have yet to be established.

Secular Western script

The *secular Western* sexual script is largely about personal freedoms. It is seen as a more honest account as to what the rules for sexual relating should be, even though the freedoms it promotes do not necessarily provide freedom from relationship failure, loneliness, or insecurity. It seeks to better match what is *actually* happening in the changing world of sexual behaviour and relationships than to promote traditional ideals. Freedom and choice has become central — this also extends to whether or not to have children. Family planning became possible as medical advances allowed couples to enjoy sexual relationships while choosing not to have children, or, alternatively, had increasing choices about having children through medical interventions where it might not otherwise have been possible. And so the idea that stability was necessary in a sexual relationship because it might produce children was no longer necessarily valid. Nevertheless, couples continue to live together and have children, and once children are involved, many revisit at least some traditional values, particularly those that recognise the importance of continuity in relationship and belonging, resulting in the adoption of an uncertain mix of sociocultural sexual scripts.

In this script roles and expectations are negotiated rather than assumed, and individual rights and the drive to personal fulfilment eclipse relationship needs and obligations. Psychotherapists John and Kris Amodeo (1986) argued for a transition from the traditional 'formal commitment', necessary for 'protection, security, and social order' to a 'process commitment', which they described as a 'more flexible, yet equally serious, commitment to the wellbeing of both ourselves and others. It reflects a consistent dedication to embody factors that reliably lead to personal growth, which provides the foundation for love and intimacy' (p. 144). Moreover, they observed that it is 'highly questionable whether it is possible to sustain [the traditional marriage vow of a life-long commitment] without sacrificing our integrity'. They added that 'clinging to a mate as an end in itself, or as a strategy to eliminate our fear of the unknown, may relieve loneliness and provide a semblance of security, but the price we pay is often one of betraying the precious calling toward the actualization of our full potential' (p. 145). Love and intimacy continued to be seen as necessary for the 'process commitment' that replaced the traditional notions of marital commitment, but the relationship also needed to provide for the ongoing personal 'growth' and 'actualization' of both parties for 'integrity' to remain: these latter were seen to be necessary for 'true' love and intimacy.

Personal preference and freedom of choice, normally with a view to securing happiness, fulfilment, and 'actualization' have become foundational values.[262] This eclipses the promotion of wider social and relational health or the recognition of divine will. As such, this script is accepting of diversity of sexual expression, so long as the relationship meets various personal needs such as intimacy, happiness, and personal fulfilment — but even this is not always necessary. The script is a loose and evolving one. The idea of romantic love — 'falling in love' — remains an ideal basis for a sexual relationship for many,[263] but there is increasingly room for other sexual arrangements: for temporary access to sex (in casual arrangements such as one-night stands, and more recently, 'friends with benefits' to fulfil 'sexual needs'),[264] or for experimentation with a sexual relationship to see what it might lead to.

In the latter part of the 20th century, couples increasingly had sexual relationships without being married, or even without intent to remain in a long-term relationship. Couples cohabited[265] without formal ceremony to mark the social and legal recognition of their relationship, and they had children outside wedlock without social censure. Children born into such a relationship were no longer 'illegitimate', although the ensuing family life differed little from that of more traditional scripts, except that there remained a greater openness to variety in sexual expression. Legislation adapted to reflect the social changes. Legal privileges once reserved for those who were married — such as tax arrangements, inheritances and property distribution should the couple separate — became available to all. Women had greater access to careers and income, and continued to push for gender equality in career opportunities and wages, and in doing so, reduced their traditional dependence on the provision of their male partner.

If couples *did* marry, there was an increasing rate of infidelity and divorce. The marriage certificate no longer promised financial and emotional security for the wife and children. It came to be cynically referred to as 'just a piece of paper'. Besides, the obligations and responsibilities that came with the marriage vows were often dishonoured. The introduction of 'no-fault' divorce made divorce easier, but further undermined the sense of obligation a marriage covenant might have assumed. Others saw couples trapped in unhappy or abusive marriages where they sought to honour their commitments, and questioned the value of doing so. As did the disillusioned children of these parents, who subsequently searched for personal happiness and greater freedom in their own sexual relationships. Marriage seemed to have lost its protective and stabilising role, and instead came to be seen as a threat to individual freedoms and to the ability to be 'fully oneself'.

The secular Western sexual script allows a couple to enter a sexual relationship with few expectations or obligations, except that they generally should not be in multiple relationships simultaneously. They still feel they 'belong' to each other, but neither party 'owns' the other; they might be loyal to one another, but neither feels any 'duty' towards the other — there is a reluctance to give up personal freedoms, and there is often the memory of previous relationship failures. Prenuptial agreements have become increasingly common, as there is potentially less security in such arrangements — after all, no promises have been made. The couple might retain their own family names, their careers and bank accounts, and negotiate their respective contributions to the daily costs of living. The terms 'husband' and 'wife' are replaced with 'partner', emphasising equality rather than difference, or male dominance. Some partners choose to enter into a relatively loose sexual arrangement where they might not even live together; each choosing to retain their respective homes and sexual freedoms. But the looser the arrangement, the less the sense of belonging. The easier it is to get out, the quicker they get in; and the quicker they get in, the easier it is to get out. And where a long-term view is no longer taken, the other person's personality, values, or circumstances matters less in the sexual arrangement, increasing the chances of a poor relational match.

Where 'falling in love' is the basis for entering a relationship, 'falling out of love' becomes a logical and acceptable basis for exiting the relationship. How such an action might affect the other partner or children often becomes secondary. Importantly, the fundamental independence and freedom of the individual is given precedence over relational obligations.[266] These expectations form some of the 'shoulds' of the script: both parties understand that if individual needs or desires aren't met, this is sufficient ground to leave and find someone else. Options are kept open. This allows no complacency in the relationship — each has to ensure the other's needs and desires are given priority for the relationship to survive, and this is of course a positive thing.[267] But where the long-term sexual relationship is based on the expectation of love and intimacy, this can be more difficult to establish in the context of past relationship failures, which leads to distrust and self-protective responses.

It has become increasingly common for partners to have been in previous long-term sexual relationships in which they had children. Of course, these might be brought into the new relationship. Such blending of families generally brings with it competing loyalties to various parent figures, and the complex family dynamics often results in the collapse of the blended family, although there might at the same time be an underlying need by the respective partners to prove 'this relationship will work', implying that the failure of the previous relationship was not due to any inadequacy on *their* part. Nevertheless, because of past experience, both parties understand that there are no guarantees regarding the relationship, and so mutual planning is often provisional.

Where marriage is still recognised, it has come to be seen as simply a public statement that a couple love each other and are committed to each other. It is a formal and legal recognition of what is already a reality — they frequently already have made home together and often already have children. This new understanding paved the way for the call for recognition of same-sex marriage. Here, too, it was to seek social acceptance and legal recognition for what was already a reality: same-sex couples already loved each other, had already made home, and sometimes already had children. In the spirit of equality, and of individual human rights, they sought the same recognition for the same existing realities.

Sexual experimentation subscript

When he was 17 years old, after a few drinks, Kelvin had built up the courage to approach Esther at an end-of-year party. She'd shown some interest in him, and, egged on by his friends, he'd slept with her that night. There had been no intention to pursue a relationship as such — he hardly knew her. But he had been able to prove he was now adult: it was a rite of passage enhancing peer acceptance and self-esteem. Although it had been an admittedly awkward experience, it also had exciting and pleasurable elements: Kelvin wasn't going to forget Esther. He enjoyed several further sexual encounters, but his subsequent discovery that she had also slept with his friend disturbed and hurt him, even though he had no expectation to stay with her. With his new-found confidence and his disillusionment to find Esther sexually available to his friend, he found another girl he might have for himself. His sexual encounter with Esther was accepted as a normal part of adolescence by his peers and parents.

The *sexual experimentation* subscript that normalised Kelvin's behaviour is one of several sexual subscripts linked with the secular Western script. Variations of this subscript have long existed in conjunction with traditional sexual scripts, but even more so with the secular Western script, wherein it has gained almost universal acceptance. This subscript is primarily about a transitional period of sexual activity during adolescence, although it is also used to account for sexual activity outside of an existing sexual relationship. It can find expression in short-term sexual encounters with multiple partners, and relates especially to the *drive to curiosity and discovery*, and the *need to prove oneself*. The subscript provides a socially accepted context and meaning for sexual behaviours that might otherwise be viewed as morally suspect because of its potential to exploit others for self-interest. This subscript also finds representation in a numerous TV reality shows, often billed as 'social experiments', where couples unknown to each other are filmed as they have sexual encounters under various circumstances to 'see what happens', and are interviewed about their experiences. Driven by financial incentives, the situations are contrived to meet the curiosity of the audience, and, although the whole arrangement might be consensual, it is exploitive in nature.

Sexual experimentation gained popularity in the 1960s, the era of 'free love'. Since then, the expectation that adolescents experiment sexually as an important part of their initiation into adulthood was supported by sex education programmes and the media. The task of adolescence was seen as entering adulthood by self-discovery and learning about sexuality through trial and error. They were provided 'values-free' information about sexual behaviour, focusing largely on how to avoid health-related problems, how to avoid pregnancy, and to ensure mutual consent existed. The assumption was that passing sexual encounters in adolescence was inevitable and normal, and that there was really no need to wait until there was sufficient maturity to make long-term relationship decisions and to have the skills and circumstances to maintain a functional sexual relationship. Because of this, less attention was given to the teaching of the management of sexual interest and desire with a view to delay entry into a sexual relationship until such time as social and emotional maturity was better established.

Early and fleeting sexual experiences were seen as simply biological events constituting a normal and harmless part of the maturation process. Indeed, the idea that a teenager remained sexually 'inexperienced' might be seen as a sign of immaturity or of suffering social or emotional problems: virginal status, a prized circumstance in traditional scripts for entry into a long-term sexual relationship, became a source of embarrassment and a sign of social or sexual failure. This subscript legitimised personal exploration of sexuality and sexual orientation issues, although this process could result in increased confusion rather than clarity: a problem we will explore later. It was seen, even in very conservative communities, as a passing phase young people (especially young men) went through before they 'settled down' to a more responsible lifestyle. In this sense, it made a distinction between sex in *relationship*, and sex for *self-discovery*, each seen as a valid expression of sexual behaviour, but for different purposes.

More traditionally, variations of this subscript were found in the (admittedly sexist) ideas 'he needs to express his sexual drive' or 'he is sowing his wild oats'. It recognised the strong sexual urges a man might experience and condoned their expression as representing a natural need for which allowances needed to be made. And so there was the historical condoning of wealthy males marrying and maintaining a wife for social reasons and as the context for family life, but keeping a lover (male or female) to meet the sexual needs his wife may not meet because she was chosen for social expediency rather than sexual desire. Such sexual urges might also traditionally find expression in homosexual activity, avoiding the risk of having children out of wedlock, or being the only avenue available for sexual expression (for example, when the man was away on a military campaign). Another context where this subscript found expression was where a woman turned a blind eye to her partner visiting a prostitute because she was unwilling or unable to satisfy him sexually, yet needed the marriage for her security — or the partner might justify such behaviour on this basis.

Of course, extramarital sexual experimentation has always existed. For the young man not yet ready to 'settle down', there has always been a recognition that a period of low social responsibility and high 'sex drive' might result in high risk sexual activity possibly leading, at least historically, to a child being born out of wedlock. But traditionally when this occurred the honourable thing was to marry the woman involved so she might get the security she needed in which to raise the child — alternatively, the baby might be delivered to the doors of a convent or orphanage. Today the risk is greatly lowered through contraception, although the high rate of abortion and increased rate of STDs remain unwanted outcomes. However, these extramarital sexual behaviours were traditionally not approved and were seen as failures in self-control, even though they might be tolerated as understandable. The secular Western script has changed social attitudes to this situation, so reducing guilt, but not without cost.

Problematically, viewing sexual experimentation as of little consequence potentially devalued the experience or the other person involved. So did the underlying message that the delay or denial of sexual gratification was unnecessary or irrelevant.[268] Furthermore, the generally short-lived nature of adolescent sexual experimentation occurring at a time of emotional instability, even when scripted as a normal part of the adolescent experience, was often painful and sometimes traumatic, and the association between sexual activity and relationship bonding was weakened. The lessons learned through such experimentation were not always helpful. For example, the idea that sexual activity is largely about personal discovery and happiness; or that failure to establish a longer-term sexual relationship reflects inadequacies in sexual performance, rather than poor relationship skills. Sexual experimentation in contexts other than adolescent experimentation could be equally problematic, such as the erosion of trust fuelling the drive to self-sufficiency and self-protective behaviours, typically at the cost of intimacy. But possibly the most disturbing aspect of sexual experimentation is that which has been made possible by modern technology, detailed in the virtual sex subscript.

Individual freedoms subscript

The *individual freedoms subscript* might also be labelled the *individual human rights* subscript.[269] Although it plays a key role in the *secular Western* script, as applied to sexual relationships it is in one sense a non-script from a sociocultural point of view, as its primary reference is the freedom to *not* conform to restrictive social expectations: its focus is on rights, rather than roles and responsibilities.[270] The idea that human rights and their associated individual freedoms are somehow inherent and natural became widely accepted as a basis for secular morality and, indeed, formed the basis for the constitutions and legislative rulings of many nations. Human rights laws also formed the basis for various antidiscrimination measures. Furthermore, it had considerable appeal in psychological research into sexual behaviours, as it provided a secular basis for a permissive non-judgemental sexual morality. Accordingly, it played a role in the changing understanding of what was and was not acceptable in sexual behaviours.

From a rights perspective, the primary function of sexual behaviour was typically seen in personal rather than relational terms. It fit in well with the secular science perspective where sexual intercourse was viewed as a natural biological event without moral dimension or meaning — the various inclinations a person had sexually were seen as points on a natural continuum of biological expression. In removing the moral dimension, the basis for some existing legal provisions was eroded. The historical, moral, and religious meanings and roles associated with sexual relationships were seen as imposed social constructs that carried social (and power) agendas. The *individual freedoms* subscript tended to be reactive to the 'dominant (conservative) culture',[271] which was seen to delegitimise sexual variation and the freedom of individual self-expression. The rights perspective essentially asserted that what a person did in private was nobody else's business, which assumed that what a person did privately affected no-one else. [272]

This subscript championed the freedom for a person to express themself sexually in whatever way they wished as a natural 'right'. This was on condition that others were respected, were not harmed, and could also pursue their own freedoms. The law should be kept out of the bedroom. [273] The shared expectations within a relationship and the sexual behaviours that might be entered into were negotiated between consenting adults. The 'shoulds' of sexual behaviour were largely restricted to the need to respect the rights of others, and the protection of children from sexual exploitation. This subscript contrasted with traditional scripts that prohibited various sexual behaviours, even when done in private between consenting adults. Moral judgements were avoided regarding the sexual and relational behaviour a person wished to embrace; indeed, it was argued that a person should do what seemed natural and good, and gave them pleasure and satisfaction, provided it was consensual. Because the focus was on personal rights rather than relational obligations, entering a sexual relationship was not necessarily seen to afford rights to one party in relation to another.

But the focus on personal rights rather than relational obligations in a sexual relationship (or indeed, in any relationship) creates its own tensions. For example, the idea of 'ownership' in a sexual relationship, arguably ratified in the traditional marriage covenant, might lead to the idea I have 'a conjugal right' to a variety of expectations about my spouse, including a 'right' to have sex with my spouse. This could lead to a competition of respective individual rights: the 'rights' of the aggrieved spouse against the 'rights' of the entitled spouse. The language of the voluntary giving of each to the other in the context of belonging to one another was replaced by the language of 'my right' to take or protect what I see to belong to me. It is easy to see how 'rights' thinking could justify domestic violence (I have a right to demand this of you), even though the same 'rights' thinking is used to condemn domestic violence (the rights of the victim is violated), which, of course, it should. Despite the intent that individual human rights laws create freedom from oppressive politics, this subscript does not necessarily prevent power politics in sexual relationships.

As widely accepted as this subscript is, inherent difficulties exist in the promotion of individual freedoms and rights as the basis for sexual morality and legislation. Unsurprisingly, it has generated much debate. [274] But a further development that legislation has had difficulty keeping abreast with, and which has thrived under the individual freedoms subscript, is the development of virtual sex, made possible by the technological revolution.

Virtual sex subscript

In separating many traditional meanings associated with sexual expression such as love, intimacy, and belonging, the *sexual experimentation* subscript provided the natural context for its extension, the *virtual sex* subscript. This subscript developed around instant gratification made possible by the technological revolution, and found expression in many forms. In many ways it represented not so much a cultural subscript as a technologically-driven phenomenon. Nevertheless, what is easily accessible and commonplace becomes normative, and what is normative sets the expectations and rules for behaviour. As a phenomenon, the emerging technology allows rapid access to what appears to be a form of intimacy or simply of sexual experience without the complications of relationship development; and in doing so, questions whether a relationship is even necessary for sexual gratification, or whether a sexual encounter needs to have anything to do with love, connection and belonging. Instead, sexual activity and experience becomes more closely aligned to entertainment, a way to have fun and discover new things, or to escape stress or boredom. As a subscript, virtual sex in its many forms promotes sex without relationships, meanings, accountability, or rules[275] — with the exception that child exploitation in cyberspace remains immoral and illegal.

Sexting, hook-ups, snap chats, online pornography,[276] chat rooms, webcam, and certain online games are some of the avenues that have become available to a new generation to explore sexual activity, often incognito. It is an (often unsupervised) avenue open to young teenagers, those at a most vulnerable stage of their sexual and relational development. Computers, iPads, and iPhones give a person ready access to many ideas, people, and situations, anywhere in the world. But without meaningful connection there is no sense of belonging, meanings are eroded more generally, and loneliness and unmet relational needs result. In some forms it is possible to develop an alter ego — an online personality based on fantasy in order to pursue imaginary relationships. In other forms, there is opportunity to expose personal intimacies (both of an emotional and physical nature) to strangers (encouraging both voyeurism and exhibitionism), or to participate in the exposure of those strangers themselves. In yet other forms, it is possible to quickly locate a stranger for a fleeting (actual) sexual encounter, no questions asked.

And so 'designer sex' has become possible. Not only can people access virtual sex through pornography depicting every possible sexual experience and act, they can specify what they want in a sexual encounter using apps such as Grindr and Tinder. This allows access to sexual experience at minimal cost and great convenience. Of course, the low cost and great convenience also devalues not only the other person involved, but the act itself. The multi-layered meanings of the sexual relationship are reduced to a brief consumer-driven 'pleasure-hit'. The added attraction to the virtual world is the degree of control it affords the participant. It appears that no-one can own or control the participant. If someone decides not to pursue a 'relationship' or sexual event, all they have to do is press 'delete'.

But the availability and apparent lack of personal cost in virtual sex is not without its problems. Not only does this devalue the relationship experience, but deleting events from the virtual world is not as simple as it seems, and the digital footprint left behind can haunt a person later. The privacy a person feels when entering the virtual world in the intimate environment of their own home or bedroom, is also virtual. In reality, they are entering a public domain, and risk the embarrassment and shame of exposure or the humiliation of put-down or deception as they discover they have less control and privacy than they had imagined. But that is the nature of the 'virtual world'. It might also contribute to disinhibition and dissociation generally; and especially in children, lead to over-sharing of images and information.[277]

Not only does the virtual world allow sexual contact and fantasy 'fulfil-ment' without the complications of relationship, it also allows rapid, if not immediate, gratification of sexual impulses. But this is a negative develop-ment, given psychological research supports the benefits of delayed gratifica-tion, an outcome of self-control. Baumeister and Tierney (2011) concluded: 'People with good self-control seemed exceptionally good at forming and maintaining secure, satisfying attachments to other people. They were better at empathising with others and considering things from other people's per-spectives. They were more stable emotionally, and less prone to anxiety, depression, paranoia, psychoticism, obsessive-compulsive behaviour, eating disorders, drinking problems, and other maladies.' (p. 12) While little research has yet explored the specific relationship outcomes of the immediate sexual gratification made possible in the virtual world, we would expect to find patterns of immediate sexual gratification compromising the establishment of secure and satisfying attachments to other people and contributing to a desta-bilisation of emotions more generally with poor mental health outcomes.

Competing scripts and moral notions

I have noted that sociocultural sexual scripts set the shared expectations, meanings and rules for sexual behaviour. But the existence of different scripts raises the question: what should be the basis for sexual morality in contemporary society, and does psychology have a role in helping determine what those moral notions should be?

We first need to make a distinction between what is *legal*, what is *moral*, and what is *wise*. What is *legal* is the domain of legislators. What is *moral* is arguably the domain of philosophers and theologians, although it is also coloured by what is commonplace or 'normal'. But what is *wise* is open to the insights of the discipline of psychology, which concerns itself with the psychological and emotional health of individuals and groups. Nevertheless, the psychologist cannot be indifferent to the moral and legal aspects; furthermore, what is and isn't 'healthy' or 'functional' in relationships generates its own debate.

Although psychological research is supposedly objective, the presence of ethics committees is a reminder that legal and moral issues remain relevant. In the field of sexual behaviour, the different moral standards espoused by competing sociocultural sexual scripts create conundrums. Psychologists and their clients will vary in their outlook. The solution is not necessarily to embrace moral relativity (a position in its own right): the point is simply there are different points of view. But therein lays the problem — if the shared meanings and expectations of a sociocultural script form the basis for social order, contribute to social harmony, and help prevent the frustrations, distress, and alienation that result from divergent expectations and associated misunderstandings, then the presence of different scripts would arguably result in the very problems a script exists to address.

Furthermore, the view a person holds contributes to the perception as to whether a sexual or relationship problem exists, and what the nature of that problem might be. A psychologist might redefine a sexual relationship problem by questioning the sociocultural script with its associated expectations that created the view a problem exists. For example, traditional scripts call for a greater subjugation of various sexual drives to accommodate social expectations, while the secular Western script might be more accommodating, seeing their expression as reflections of 'personal integrity', or of individual choice. Where a person is having difficulty with the management of their drives or with meeting sociocultural expectations, the question arises as to what extent the script itself contributes to the definition of the problem. Moreover, not all scripts necessarily promote healthy sexual relationships. Cultures don't always promote healthy lifestyles. And so part of the conversation needs to be whether a particular script promotes optimal outcomes for sexual relationships.

sociocultural scripts are transferred and adopted through various avenues — formal and informal. Parents play a significant role in the scripts to which their children are exposed and which generally become internalised, as it did for Sana and Kelvin; the parents' own sexual narratives colour the delivery of these sexual scripts. Probably the most influential culture to which the child is exposed is that within their own home. But social media, school curriculums, peer groups, religious organisations, and the internet all make substantial, if at times conflicting, contributions, creating the external context for sexual decision-making. Psychologists, sexologists, and relationship counsellors make their own contribution in promoting what is 'normative' or helpful, and in defining what is 'functional' or 'healthy'. And at a more subtle level, the very language used to discuss sexual matters, both by professionals and non-professionals, influences meanings and what comes to be regarded as normal and functional.[278]

Chapter 10

Sexual Narratives: Early Years

No behaviour occurs in a vacuum. Making sense of behaviour involves understanding the *context* in which it occurs, because drives invariably emerge from a context, interact with it, and find meaning in it. Just as there are two drive sources — biological and subjective; there are also two contextual dimensions — current and historical. With sexual behaviour, the *current* context includes the sociocultural sexual scripts adopted by the local and wider community, and the social circumstances in which a person happens to find themselves. The *historical* context includes a person's internalised sociocultural sexual scripts and their sexual and relationship history. These internalised scripts, events and experiences which comprise a person's historical context I refer to as their *individual narrative*. Such a narrative begins in infancy, and continues through the formative years, including the transition years of adolescence, shaping a person's subsequent patterns of sexual behaviour. Early and initial sexual and relational events and experiences are especially significant.[279]

Individual sexual narratives help define the meanings, moral overlays, and expectations that come to be associated with sexual relationships. These become part of a person's orienting mind map, and are reflected in their drive profile. The interrelationships between intimacy, attachment, love, and sexual expression; the expectations of happiness and fulfilment (or otherwise); the expectations of fidelity, monogamy, and heterosexuality (or otherwise); and the anticipated roles and behaviour of the partner in a sexual relationship emerge from this individual narrative. It defines the behaviours that are prohibited or allowed in a relationship, the expected trajectory of a relationship, and the anticipated rewards in a relationship. Initial relationship and sexual experiences are important in such a narrative, as is true of any initial experience, in that it shapes the expectation for subsequent experiences at a subjective level, and it establishes the associative neural networks upon which subsequent connections are built at a biological level. As Baumeister (2001) observes: 'Most people retain lifelong memories of the first time they had sex, and in at least some cases these first experiences have a lasting impact on their sexual attitudes, feelings, and behaviours' (p. 135).

A person's sexual narrative typically encompasses several key themes. These include their *attachment history*, their *interpersonal boundary* experiences, the development of their *sexual orientation and identity*, and their *sexual conditioning history*. The first two relate to patterns of connection and intimacy, and the last to patterns of sexual arousal or inhibition. The first three play a role in the shaping of subjective drive themes, the last in the shaping of biological drives. It is to these developmental themes we now turn. In this chapter I outline the critical experiences of childhood; and in the following chapter I look at the transition period of adolescent experiences. Both chapters emphasise various aspects of learned behaviours and associations that contribute to a person's sexual narrative, and influence adult sexual relating. We will also see how the drive to belong is interwoven in both the attachment dynamic and in the development of sexual orientation and identity.

I begin with attachment theory. We will see how the early attachment experiences of infants create learned behaviours that shape their relationships generally, and especially their capacity for intimacy. But, as important as attachment is in the formation of relationship behaviours, there is also the need to establish a separate self through the development of appropriate interpersonal boundaries. We consider what can happen to adult sexual relationships when such boundaries are violated in childhood, using the example narrative of the case of Alicia. We then ponder the gender aspect, how sexual awareness is first established in childhood, and what experiences contribute to emerging sexual orientation. The narratives of Charlie and Derek are used to illustrate some complexities in gender identity and orientation formation.

Childhood belonging and attachment

Attachment and sex are related. So is attachment and emotional security. We have seen how adult sexual behaviour is intertwined with the ideas of belonging and attachment. However, the dynamics of attachment are not limited to sexual behaviour; nor do the drives relating to belonging begin with the sexual awakening of adolescence.

The story begins much earlier, in infancy: it is the story of *attachment theory* which finds a connection between infant-parent[280] attachment and the attachment typically found in adult sexual relationships.[281] This connection is unsurprising. In both circumstances we find the natural needs for affection, emotional safety and protection, nurturance, acknowledgement and acceptance, and emotional closeness or intimacy. In the adult relationship, these needs are typically integrated with sexual desire and sexual behaviour. Indeed, Tolman and Diamond (2014) acknowledge the extensive research that shows a correspondence between infant-caregiver attachment and adult romantic ties, observing that these 'share the same core emotional and behavioural dynamics: heightened proximity maintenance, resistance to separation, and use of partner as a preferred target for comfort and security seeking'; and 'even more powerful evidence is provided by the voluminous animal research documenting the two types of affectional bonding [that] are mediated by the same opiod- and oxytocin-based neural circuitry' (p. 9).[282]

But we begin with childhood belonging, which exists from the beginning. Children are inherently relational. As their capacity to recognise familiar faces and voices develops in early infancy, their sense of both belonging and attachment grows. A child belongs to their parents, and the parents belong to their child. This *fact* of belonging becomes an *experience* of belonging in the course of increasing familiarity, shared life experiences, and an increasing role in family dynamics. This experience of belonging goes beyond the primary belonging to parents and the family home: in ever widening circles, it involves secondary belonging to extended family, to the social and physical neighbourhood, and to the wider culture and race. This belonging orients the inner self of the child, shaping its identity in terms of its place and role socially, just as later the sense of belonging orients a couple in a sexual relationship, creating a social identity. It is a foundational drive, and plays a critical role in a child's emerging mental health.

Attachment refers to the quality of the bond created with those to whom one belongs. It colours the perception of what it means to belong. And so, in a child a secure attachment may be observed in such behaviours as the expression of special positive emotional attraction specifically for their parent, reluctance to be separated from that parent, and delight in reunion with that parent after separation.[283] A central characteristic is the trust a child learns in their parents, assuming their goodwill, seeking safety in their company, and looking for reassurance, support and protection specifically from them. Such attachment is predicated on the sensitivity of the parent to a child's emotional state, their predictable presence, and their ability to meet their child's emotional needs.[284] Such a parent knows when to be present and when to keep distance, how to show interest and enjoyment in the relationship, how to be positive and responsive, and how communicate in an age-appropriate way with their child. Having spent time with the child and developed a connection with them, their parent knows them sufficiently well to 'read emotional signals'. At a time of profound dependence, a child is primed to bond to such a person able to meet its dependency needs. This attachment is also mediated in the neurochemistry of both parent and child, largely activated by close physical contact in the early years.[285]

Once secure attachment is established, the relationship between the child and their parents tends to be long-lasting. It remains a primary source of intimacy well after dependency has diminished. In the process, secure attachment brings with it many general and long-lasting benefits. It becomes the basis for self-esteem, trust, and ongoing capacity to keep the balance between intimacy and a sense of self. Securely attached children are more popular with peers, cope better with failure, are more curious, and are less aggressive and anxious. And as adults, secure attachment predicts emotional wellbeing, good emotional regulation, self-confidence, happy marriage (that is, a successful long-term sexual relationship), and a warm relationship with their own offspring.[286]

But while they might always *belong* to their parents, not all children form a *secure attachment* with them. Ainsworth (1973) made observations of child behaviours using the 'Strange Situation', where a stranger entered a room in which a child and parent were sitting, or where a parent would exit the room for a short period leaving the child in the room. She discovered several forms of *insecure attachment* in children. Some parents were emotionally insensitive or indifferent and aloof, and their pattern of physical contact was often limited. Their children tended to display *insecure avoidant* attachment behaviours, where indifference to their parents was seen throughout the experimental procedures, with no particular attention paid to their parents, nor delight in reunion with them after separation. Such children showed relatively little upset when a stranger entered or a parent left, and were reluctant to cling to their parent at any stage. While they belonged to their parents, they were relatively disconnected. A pattern of deactivation of the attachment system typically resulted, a self-protective avoidance of close relationships. This pattern compromised their later capacity to properly bond in intimate relationships — including intimate sexual relationships.

Another type of insecure attachment is *anxious-ambivalent* attachment. In this circumstance parents were inconsistent in their presence or behaviour. This unpredictability created wariness and anxiety in their children, who tended to cling to or hover near their parents, showing distress when they left. However, their children showed little joy or relief upon reunion with them. This pattern created an ongoing hyper-activation of the attachment system, predicting insecurity in adult intimate relationships, along with a tendency to distrust and an inclination to cling to a sexual partner, for fear of losing them. Patterns of *disorganised or insecure* attachment occurred where parents were hostile or critical, leading to agitation and stress in their children, who became disorganised, anxiety-ridden and negative. For such children, belonging did not mean closeness. The distrust and wariness they learned in their relationship with their parents meant that subsequent intimate sexual relationships were likely to be a source of stress rather than of nurturance. They had learned to feel unsafe in such relationships, which generally involved the expectation of closeness, even if only fleetingly.

But it is not only attachment patterns that are important in shaping relationship patterns in the developing child. Equally important is their capacity to maintain integrity in their interpersonal boundaries.

Childhood boundaries

Countries have boundaries. 'Home' has boundaries. So do people. Boundaries mark the limits of territory: what belongs to me and what belongs to you. We need to agree where this boundary lays. Neither must violate that boundary. We both share the responsibility to maintain the integrity of the boundary. I will defend the integrity of that boundary and I expect you to honour it.

However, sexual activity necessarily involves the crossing of such boundary, a crossing that needs to be authorised by both parties. When a boundary is systematically violated, the sense of where that boundary lays becomes uncertain, and the territory once delineated by the boundary is no longer safe. This leads to distrust and anxiety. The adventurer who loves to discover unexplored territory nevertheless needs to respect the boundary marking where the other territory begins, just as the owner of the territory needs to be clear where the boundary lays, and protect it.

Normally, I control what belongs to me, and you control what belongs to you. But when you are in my territory (and I in yours), even by agreement, who is in control? When territory is shared, how do we share control? Typically, this involves a dance of giving and taking control, a dance based on mutual respect. Governance over my territory is weakened when another person shares my territory, even when it is done by agreement. I now need to trust the other person to respect my ultimate right to control the territory that belongs to me, even as I share it with them.

The maintenance of interpersonal boundaries is critical. The drives for intimacy and belonging are balanced by the opposing drive for separateness and autonomy.[287] To develop a robust sense of self separate from others necessary for subsequent healthy intimacy patterns, a child needs to establish a sense of healthy interpersonal boundary, both physical and psychological. And just as early experiences in intimacy and attachment have ramifications for a person's later sexual behaviour, so does the ongoing integrity of a person's interpersonal boundaries — especially in relation to sexual behaviour.

The establishment of healthy interpersonal boundaries begins with a child's desire to privacy and the development of a sense of ownership over their own body. At the same time, the child learns to recognise of the ownership others have over their respective bodies. Not only does a child learn to take ownership of their own body, but also of their own ideas, perceptions and preferences. Being relatively powerless as a child, however, the establishment and maintenance of such boundaries — whether physical or psychological — depends on adult recognition, respect and support for those boundaries. Clothing a child reinforces the idea that their body is 'personal space' and belongs to them. Showing an interest in the child's point of view recognises the legitimacy of the child's perceptions and preferences, acknowledging that these, too, belong to the child. A child also typically learns that there are other points of view, which forms the basis of their *theory of mind*.[288] This understanding of the independent subjective experience of another person — a separate mind — becomes the basis for empathy, but also emphasises the need for inquiry to enter into another person's subjective world, so contributing to the capacity to develop a functional intimate relationship. And so the child learns about interpersonal connection as well as autonomy, two keys that form the basis of emerging relational skills that colour subsequent sexual behaviour.

Critical to a child's boundary management is the control of interpersonal sexual activity. Childhood attachment and intimacy experiences need to remain asexual, a need recognised in most sociocultural sexual scripts. Adult attachment and intimacy experiences, on the other hand, are very frequently sexual, involving the consensual entry into another person's physical and psychological space, which such sexual intent requires. However, adults retain control over their interpersonal boundaries, and can choose whether or not to let into their lives someone with sexual intent. Children have limited control in this respect, and rely on the adults to whom they are attached and with whom they might be intimate, to recognise sexual intent — within themselves or in others — and to honour and protect their boundaries by disallowing sexual behaviours. But interpersonal boundaries can be (and are) violated by these very people.[289] When this happens, the consequences can be devastating. One consequence is that the rules relating to the recognition and negotiating of interpersonal boundaries become unclear. Such confusion is often found in those suffering borderline personality disorder. Other consequences include confusion about the meaning of sexual behaviour, the loss of trust, and unwanted sexual conditioning.

Such was the experience of Alicia. When Alicia was nine years old, she was daddy's special girl, and she loved him. But unknown to her mother, she started receiving nocturnal visits from him. His affectionate behaviours gradually changed as he caressed and fondled an unsuspecting Alicia and eventually engaged in various sexual activities with her. No-one else knew — it was their secret. She didn't want to upset him: indeed, she'd always delighted in pleasing him, but what he did left her feeling perplexed, sick, and dirty. And so she took long showers and scrubbed herself to be clean. But she couldn't scrub the dirty feeling away. She wanted to be clean, she wanted her world to be clean — but no matter how much she cleaned, it felt dirty. She no longer wanted him to visit her at night and do sexual things with her, things she didn't understand.

But he was there all the same, uninvited, in intimate embrace. She felt violated, desired, disrespected, loved, angry, special, hurt, and frightened — all at once. She was confused. He had drawn her into an intimacy she didn't understand, and without her permission. But then, he *was* her father: he didn't need to ask permission of her; and although she didn't understand, she'd been taught to trust him. She belonged to him and was attached to him. She felt special to her father but at the same time, worthless. Because she couldn't hate her father who'd given her everything, she hated herself for being in this situation.

What she felt she couldn't articulate or make sense of. And there was no-one who could help her understand what she was feeling. Although she didn't know why, she sensed this was something she couldn't confide in her mother. Her father needed her, and she didn't want to let him down, but she didn't understand him. She felt trapped. She heard others comment on the lovely relationship he had with her: she felt guilty and complicit. She knew him more deeply than anyone could imagine, and she carried the responsibility of that knowledge. His shame — their shame — was her shame. It was pleasurable when he caressed and touched her: she could almost enjoy it, but she sensed it was illicit pleasure and it tore her apart — the desire and the loathing; her love for him and her hate for what he was doing. She felt a special closeness to her father, yet felt utterly alone and distant. He stimulated feelings in her she had never known before, feelings that both pleased and frightened her.

She felt increasingly different from everyone. She felt lonely, disconnected, experiencing things no-one knew about, that no-one could imagine might be happening to her, and about which she couldn't talk. Everybody continued to treat her as if everything was normal, as it should be — even her father did, the only one who knew. Yet things were not normal — she gradually withdrew into herself, and concentration at school become difficult. She herself did not understand — how could anyone else? And if she did, and if she was to say, what would they do? She would be betraying her father, whom she loved and to whom she felt loyalty. She didn't want him to get into trouble — she just wanted it to stop. He'd been good to her. And so he could trust her with their secret, but she couldn't trust him. She protected him, but he didn't protect her. The only one she could talk to about this was the very one she didn't want to talk to — her own father. She felt she was going crazy.

She learned to cope by setting a different kind of boundary. She gave him her body, but not herself, her soul — like a prostitute. He had her physically, but in her mind she went far away to a safe place where this wasn't happening, even as it happened. It was a place of innocence where there were no demands. She learned to disconnect herself emotionally from the mix of pleasure and pain that intruded upon her. She dissociated, separating herself from her own body — it no longer belonged to her. She felt nothing — she was able to numb herself. She was close, intimate for him, but far away nevertheless. She loved him, but she didn't love him at all. She was obedient, but resentment, fear and anger lay suppressed within her, making her feel sick, anxious, and depressed. The more she hid the truth, the more anxious and despondent she became. All the while, and unknown to her, sexual conditioning was taking place, and her hormone levels responded to the things she was experiencing, hastening her entry into womanhood.

As Alicia grew older, she began to find ways of expressing what was happening, but not explicitly. She only hinted at things for fear that her shame might be uncovered, and that something terrible might happen to her father. She ached for others to know, but at the same time she was frightened and ashamed for anyone else to know. When someone said something that hinted at the truth, she distracted them and denied there was a problem. She drew and wrote things that hinted at what was happening, but anyone who saw the pictures she drew and the stories she wrote wouldn't understand. She did and didn't want them to — it frightened and repulsed her to see what she had put down on paper.

Unwanted memories and associations were seared into Alicia's brain, and flashbacks of her father's sexual intimacies came to her regularly. She belonged to her father, and he to her — but could she now ever belong to another? How could she give to someone else what she had already given to her father? And if she did, who could she now trust? Who would protect her? Could pleasure ever be clean? Could intimacy ever be without shame and confusion? Would she ever give herself sexually to another man without seeing in him one who, though he seemed to care for her, really didn't care for her at all, but only for himself? How would she ever relate to another man when nothing was as it seemed? And what would happen should she one day have a daughter? Would the confusing and mixed messages she had experienced become confusing and mixed messages that she might then send?

Such were the questions emerging in Alicia's sexual narrative. This narrative informed her future relationships and coloured her sexual drives. It formed the basis for the meanings she attributed to sexual interest a man might show her. She learned she could use her body to satisfy other needs by disconnecting from her own body. She could become sexually aroused by a man's caress and desire for her, while at the same time any attempt to emotional intimacy inhibited her sexual arousal. She learned that she herself was of no value: her body was the only desirable commodity. She had learned how to let someone else do what they wanted with her body: it was the only way she would know acceptance.

Alicia's sexual narrative and drives were shaped around the boundary violation she had experienced with her father as a young girl. These experiences were more powerful in shaping her sexual narrative than the sociocultural scripts to which she was exposed. She became angry and bitter. And so she used her sexuality to taunt men — to give her body, but not *herself.* She exploited men as she herself had been exploited. She acted as if she cared for a man, but she didn't give a damn. She was cynical about their motives, and used them as she herself had been used. She believed no man when he said he loved her, and trusted no man to protect her, however much she yearned for this to be possible. For her, this would always be impossible: she could never be loved, never respected. Alicia craved intimacy, but she feared the inevitable rejection that came with intimacy — self-disclosure would expose her shame and guilt,[290] her dirtiness, flaws and failures; and her pain would be relived. She had learned that sexual relationships were about pleasure and power; not be about love and intimacy. If a man desired love and intimacy, she ended the relationship. She would never by trapped again. The drives that motivated her and eclipsed the drives for intimacy and love were the drives for personal power, fear of entrapment, and self-protection.

Alicia's experiences relate to childhood sexual boundary violation. But sexual boundary violation can occur in other contexts too: adolescents going through a time of self-doubt and self-discovery are equally vulnerable to sexual boundary violation as they seek closeness, reassurance, and acceptance from others, especially those of the opposite sex. The rules relating to sexual behaviour in this period are often unclear, and this creates its own problems. Alicia's childhood sexual experiences were clearly damaging. But this raises a new question: are there childhood sexual experiences that form part of a person's sexual narrative that are normal, and do not reflect boundary violation or inappropriate expressions of intimacy? We consider this next.

Childhood sexual awareness

The relationship between a child and their parents represents a child's first experience of love and intimacy. The characteristics of the resulting attachment set the pattern for intimate relationships. Parents are also responsible for setting and teaching appropriate interpersonal boundaries, helping the child develop a healthy sense of self and respect for self and others. These boundaries protect a child from behaviours with sexual intent. But while early attachment processes and early intimacies are normally asexual, and while interpersonal boundaries are protective in a sexual sense, this does not mean a child is without sexual impulses.

A child can display curiosity of a sexual nature from an early age, and periodically engage in limited sexual inquiry, exploration and play.[291] Even a baby can be sexually aroused,[292] and there are various childhood activities that might be considered 'sexual', including curiosity about seeing others undressed (especially those of the opposite sex), the excitement associated with kissing or the touching of private areas during play with other children, the comfort of physical touch and embrace, and the pleasure of masturbation (generally done as a self-soothing activity).[293] Nevertheless, sexual arousal is not the same as sexual intimacy; and sexual desire and intent play an important role in defining whether behaviour might be considered sexual in an adult sense.

Sex has different meanings for a child than it does for an adult. While sexual interest and physiological sexual responses are present in children, these generally do not carry adult meanings or motives, and any imputation of such meanings and motives by adults can be misleading. For example, sexual desire and the complexities of intimate adult sexual behaviours, including intentionally activating sexual arousal in another, is normally absent in children. Equally, exposure to and understanding of the function and purpose of sexual intercourse is not normally part of a younger child's interest, despite their awareness of, and interest in, sexual and gender differences. In other words, there is no integration of relationship needs, motives, and skills with sexual needs, motives and skills in a child. It is this lack of adult awareness that we refer to when we talk of 'childhood innocence'; not the absence of a child's limited sexual play. And it is this innocence adults seek to protect to prevent a level of sexual awareness and activity about which a child does not have the emotional or social capacity to make good judgement.[294] Moreover, when a child is exposed to things they do not understand, as we saw in the story of Alicia, these become a source of anxiety and trauma.

The typical drive profile that animates children in their relationships also looks different from that of adults. While the enduring drive themes of love, intimacy, belonging, familiarity, curiosity, discovery, and self-protection will be found, the sexual aspects with which these drives might associate in adults will be largely latent in children. Drives relating to eroticism, sexual curiosity and rite of passage are unlikely to have been activated unless children have been exposed prematurely to the events and experiences that relate to such drives; that is, sexual experiences before a child has reached sexual and relational maturity.[295]

But there are also social influences that shape children's drive profiles in relation to their sexual awareness, and especially their sexual readiness.[296] For example, Steinberg found that a girl's BDP was affected by her closeness to her mother: girls who were particularly close to their mothers were found to enter puberty later than those who were more distant. In contrast, girls growing up in single parent or step-parent families reached puberty earlier.[297] Other research found that father's prolonged absence during a girl's first seven years of life appeared to stimulate early menarche.[298] It seems that, at least for girls, the circumstances of their relationship with their parents during early development can affect the timing of their sexual maturation and readiness. But the media can also play a role in early sexualisation, especially of girls. Such early exposure to sexualised material and situations may lead to earlier heterosexual intercourse, although little is known about its general effects for the girls in childhood, or later.[299]

A child's sexual awareness and their sexual experiences and behaviours needs proper management. Adult representations and understandings of sexual behaviour, often through media exposure or in exploitive sexual situations, are difficult for a child to process, risking distorted understandings and negative associations, and potentially compromising healthy sexual development. While basic understandings of reproductive processes are more easily understood, preadolescent children are not ready to comprehend the complexities and abstract meanings, drives and intentions that associate with adult sexual behaviour and relationships. Yet some basic and concrete notions are needed to complement sexual awareness. Certainly, the teaching of general relationship principles — the conditions allowing healthy intimacy and respect for interpersonal boundaries — precedes and provides the essential context for sexual awareness and experience.

Parents play a critical and necessary role in the shaping of sexual behaviour in their children, as they do their behaviour more generally. This involves the provision of a protective and supportive environment where a child's developing sense of self is respected, so a child can experience ownership over their bodies and thoughts. And, because of the potentially long-lasting effects of initial and early sexual experiences, it involves the protection of a child from such sexual experience until they have the maturity to both to understand the meanings and drives that associate with sexual behaviour, and have the satisfactory relationship skills and the capacity for the responsibilities and judgements that associate with such events. These relationship skills also assume the general capacity to regulate one's own drives and emotions, that is, capacity for self-discipline, a measure of emotional maturity. These self-regulation skills form an important focus of a child's social learning that begins around the age of two.[300]

Early gender identity and sexual orientation

There is a further dimension to the development of sexual awareness in a child: the development of their *gender identity*. This is central in a child's emerging sexual narrative, and important for their social orientation. While sexual *intent* is an adult concept, the idea of physical sexual *differences* is learned early in childhood. The identification as male or female begins at birth with the name a baby is given and the colours and toys that are introduced into the nursery. The many and various associations with maleness and femaleness are woven into a child's awareness even as their language develops.

By around age three, a child will have a clear sense of their sexual identity. That is, they identify as a boy or girl. But it takes a little longer to appreciate gender stability and constancy, and to integrate the notion of gender identity with gender role. This might not by mastered until around age six or seven, around the time a child has typically mastered a basic ability to regulate their own drives and emotions — the basis of their socialisation.[301] Gender role becomes associated with the cultural norms and expressions of the respective genders (including how fluid the gender role is perceived to be), and are reinforced by what the child sees in the behaviour of their parents, and in the social activities and groupings that typically take place in the course of childhood, especially in the primary school years.

As a child develops and their social orbit expands, it becomes necessary to learn the social skills that allow them to negotiate with peers — in play, at school, in sports, and in other social activities such as in clubs and faith communities. These social skills are necessary to deal with the growing demands of diverse relationships, which are initially largely focused on same-sex relationships. These are generally easier for children to negotiate because of shared interests and attitudes. And so girls typically prefer to relate and play with girls, are grouped with girls, and are drawn to different activities than are boys, while an equivalent same-sex pattern is found in boys. These same-sex friendship patterns in middle childhood tend to be supported by sociocultural expectations in most communities, which set the agenda for what are seen to be gender-appropriate behaviours. These experiences and expectations emphasise a sense of belonging based on gender, and contribute to healthy gender identity development.

But belonging to one group also means *not* belonging to the other, and this identification with one or other group can result in a polarisation between sexes. Friendship patterns can create an increasing separateness from the opposite sex, so that they come to be seen as an 'exotic species'.[302] Layers of meaning develop as to what maleness and femaleness means — these meanings can also have a positive or negative valence. They emerge from the multiple experiences children have of male and female behaviour, which not only colour the identity process, reinforcing the identifying with or belonging to one or other sex, but also how the opposite sex comes to be viewed. This awareness of gender contributes to the merging SDP, and sets the scene for the subsequent development of sexual interest in the 'exotic species', potentially activating the drive to curiosity and discovery. This begins to happen after puberty, the time when a child's emerging sexual orientation begins to be established.[303] The girl becomes curious about the boy, typically her 'exotic species', while the boy begins new discoveries about the girl, his 'exotic species'. But while gender-identification helps develop sexual identity and orientation, it does little to develop the social skills and self-confidence necessary to negotiate a relationship with the opposite sex. This comes later.

Not all children follow this pattern. As we have seen, certain hormonal profiles in a mother's second trimester of pregnancy can lead to atypical gender expression, so that a boy's interests and sensitivities might be more typical of girls, while a girl's interests and sensitivities might be more typical of boys. Such a pattern generally emerges quite early (between the ages of two and four).[304] This can create alienation in same-sex friendships while retaining a comfortable relationship or even a preference to be with the opposite sex, which in turn can influence the formation of sexual orientation. Bem (2000) observed that those children born with a temperament that predisposes them to gender-atypical behaviours see themselves as different from children of the same sex. He further argued that feelings of difference evoke nonsexual physiological arousal whenever a child is near peers from whom they feel different. In such case, for example, another boy becomes the 'exotic species' a gender-atypical boy becomes curious about. Where this felt difference involves members of the same sex, it may lead to the development of homosexual orientation.

There is certainly evidence suggesting this as one pathway to homosexual orientation; indeed, probably the most common pathway. One study found two-thirds of some forty-four boys who tended towards femininity identified as homosexual or bisexual as adults.[305] Other studies report the prevalence of homosexuality in adults who as children displayed effeminate behaviour, avoided rough-and-tumble aggressive play, and were generally unassertive.[306] A common memory for many homosexual men is feeling 'different' from at least primary school years. There might be a preference to play with girls, or general social withdrawal may be remembered. This feeling of difference may be exacerbated by the active exclusion by other boys in play. They often remembered being emotionally sensitive, creative, and unassertive.[307] This may result in disconnection or alienation from same-sex peers, and a feeling of 'belonging to' the opposite sex.

Nevertheless, Isay cautions: 'One should not conclude... that most adult gay men are feminine. We can conclude that most homosexual boys are not typical boys and that they do have some traits usually associated with girls.'[308] While effeminate inclination is a recognised predisposing factor to homosexual orientation, such orientation is by no means an inevitable outcome. Charlie, for example, was bullied and excluded in primary school: the boys simply didn't want to play with him. He was sensitive, enjoyed music, but didn't read much. He wasn't competitive, was unconfident in front of groups, and clumsy at soccer — he felt different from the other boys, and didn't see himself as 'one of the boys'. However, although Charlie had more in common with girls, he didn't really feel he belonged with them either. He became a loner. Charlie's experience of feeling 'different' was reinforced by not being masculine in interest or behaviour as understood by his family. He learned to see girls as 'one of us', rather than as 'one of them' at a critical time of his development, so that they ceased to excite sexual interest, but rather allowed for the comfortable closeness one might have with a sister. This led to confusion, rather than unequivocal homosexual orientation. Although Charlie felt no sexual attraction to girls, *neither did he feel sexual attraction to boys*: he still wanted one day to marry a woman and have a family.

Peer-group identification is not the only factor in gender identity development. The relationship of a child's mother and father also models how members of different sexes relate together; and how a same-sex parent relates to their child has a bearing on their self-concept as masculine or feminine. A child will typically identify with the same-sex parent, and imitate the behaviours and attitudes of that parent. Both their identity as male or female and their intimacy skills in relation to the other sex is shaped by how each parent relates to the child, by how the parents reinforce masculine or feminine attributes in the child, and by how they relate to each other as a man and woman. These behaviours are modelled by the parents and learned by observation and social reinforcements.[309]

We finish with Derek's narrative, which highlights this process, and the confusions that can follow. Derek had a conflicted relationship with his father. Since he was a young boy, Derek remembered wanting to be masculine. He was intrigued even then by male bodies: these were symbols of strength and power that demanded respect, just as his father demanded respect from his mother. The male body encapsulated everything he wanted but didn't have. His father was critical of Derek and regularly humiliated him. Derek felt powerless, inadequate, fearful, ashamed, and worthless. No matter how much he tried to please his father and to be like him, the results were the same: he was crushed by his father's domination. His father despised weakness — the weakness that had once been his father's own experience. If only Derek had the power of an adult male body, strong, well built and impressive. Perhaps then things would be different. Perhaps then his father would love and accept him. He would be like his father. Masculine. Because his father didn't accept him, Derek was unable to accept himself. His poor self-concept, lack of ego-strength, and poor assertion skills found expression in his whispered hopelessness and wish to die.

These early experiences shaped Derek's later sexual life. Over the years these thoughts developed into a powerful fixation: Derek wanted to be like powerful men, but he saw this was impossible — he saw himself as a weakling, effeminate. He hated his body and he hated himself. The closest he could get to masculinity was to associate with other masculine bodies, to *belong* to them, to *have* them. As he progressed through school, he studied the powerful naked bodies of confident and assertive men in pornographic books and on internet pornographic sites. He desired these bodies, and became sexually aroused through his desire. He masturbated when he became aroused to the pictures and the fantasies of masculine strength. How he loved to have what they had! Later, even when girls said that they found him good-looking and masculine, he was unable to accept this: he certainly didn't *feel* masculine, and what they said didn't match his long rehearsed view of himself. The sense of masculinity now needed to come from *within*, not from things he might do or what others might say. And within he felt anything *but* masculine.

Despite his fascination with the male body, Derek had always wanted to marry a woman and have a family. But he found himself repulsed when he looked at women. He had polarised masculinity and femininity, craving one and despising the other; unable to see there was beauty in both and a place for both. In women he was disgusted by the weakness and femininity he saw, and which he despised in himself. Even though he might recognise a woman's physical attractiveness, he felt no sexual attraction to them. He didn't want what they had. Furthermore, he followed a script that said it was a sin to look lustfully at a woman's body; and he needed to be good. If he was not good enough for his father, at least he would try to be good enough for God.

And so Derek eschewed sexual thoughts about women, and never sought to look at their images in pornographic material. He had enough shame and self-hatred — he didn't need to add to it the guilt of looking lustfully at women. His thoughts needed to stay pure, non-sexual. Besides, he didn't want to spend time in the company of women: he wasn't a woman, he didn't belong to them, and he didn't want to associate with femininity. How could he be with women and not become like them? He wanted to be a man. But he battled sexual urges aroused at the sight of male bodies. His desire to identify with and 'belong' to male company would find its fullest expression in a sexual relationship he didn't want but found himself thrust towards. His sense of helplessness in the face of this urge served further to reinforce inadequacy, guilt and shame. He was caught in the cross-currents of his drives. He wanted to be married, yet didn't want to be in a woman's company. There was no solution — he felt trapped, a failure all round.

We see, then, that the experiences and decisions of early childhood set a pathway for the developing sexual identity and orientation, shaping the drive profile. For some, like Derek, it lays the foundation for later difficulty, confusion, and distress. Yet the majority of children emerge from childhood with a good capacity for attachment, a good sense of interpersonal boundaries, a good capacity to manage their drives and emotions, and a good integration of their biological sex, sexual identity, and gender role. This forms the central themes of their childhood narrative, and sets the scene for both their sense of belonging and sexual identity. It is also largely the result of good parenting that involves a sympathetic awareness of their child's emotional needs, the maintenance of respectful boundaries, consistent discipline, and good relationship modelling.

By puberty the child will have experienced and understood sexual difference and sexual arousal, but the adult concepts of sexual intent and sexual desire remain to be discovered. It is during and after puberty (from around 12 years on) that new learning experiences take place: this transition time is a time of sexual imprinting and conditioning, of the establishment of sexual orientation, and of integration of sexual behaviour and relationship belonging. We turn to this now.

Chapter 11

Sexual Narratives: Transitions

The early attachment experiences of infants shape their subsequent relationships generally, especially in relation to trust and intimacy. But they also colour the drive profile affecting later *sexual* behaviour and relationships. Birnbaum (2016) notes: 'Early interpersonal experiences determine the development of sexuality in a relationship context, including the kinds of desires adolescents seek to satisfy, the types of relationships they seek, and what they perceive to be sexually desirable in potential and current partners' (p. 465). Furthermore, research has established that adolescents with secure attachment experiences are less likely to engage in casual sex, preferring committed intimate relationships involving affection in which to express their sexual desires: indeed, they are more likely to have sex to promote emotional bonding.[310]

Critical periods and events in adolescent sexual experiences are not only affected by *past* attachment experiences, but can in turn affect *future* integration of adult attachment and sexual behaviour. Past insecure attachment patterns can be reinforced in adolescent experiences, impairing sexual functioning in subsequent close relationships. This will play out differently depending on the nature of the insecure attachment which differentially affects the drive profile.[311] There are unique drives and pressures adolescents need to manage when making decisions with regard to sexual behaviour; furthermore, their drive profile will undergo considerable fluctuations during this time.

In this time of change and new learning, are there 'right' and 'wrong' motives for sexual behaviour? Is there a 'right' and 'wrong' time to make such decisions? What might be the long-term consequences of decisions made relating to sexual activity? How does the changing drive profile (responding to different belonging needs) and emerging gender identity shape sexual desire and relationships? What we *do* know is that during this time of internal instability and compromised decision-making capacity, the external stability of the adopted sociocultural sexual script can play an important role.

Adolescence is typically the context of important sexual and relational precedents. It is a transition period of maturation and integration, a shift from parent attachment to romantic attachment, setting the foundation for adult sexual behaviour. It is a time of sexual self-discovery and of growing awareness of multiple changing drives which need to be effectively managed. The drive for belonging and intimacy changes focus and becomes coloured by sexual desire. And because sexual activity involves entering another person's interpersonal space, sexual behaviour becomes associated with intimacy, which necessarily involves relationship skills. Allen & Tan (2016) note that in adolescence the 'sexual and attachment systems both push toward the establishment of romantic relationships, characterised by sufficient intensity, shared interests, and strong affect, to begin to take over some of the functions of prior parent-child relationships' (p. 403). Nevertheless, other motives which do not necessarily promote intimacy or belonging also influence sexual behaviours and expectations and the focus of sexual desire. And initial sexual experiences can leave lasting memories, and decisions about sexual behaviour can have long-term ramifications. These issues comprise key narrative themes of this transition period, which we now consider.

The integration of the sexual and relational self

Things change during adolescence. The primary reference group defining the sense of belonging and focus of intimacy typically shifts away from the immediate family to same-sex peer groups,[312] and then to someone of the opposite sex; although there are, of course, exceptions. As the maturing child begins to navigate the changes taking place in their BDP and the extent of sexual interest and the repertoire of sexual behaviours accordingly increase, their exploratory drives begin largely centred on self-pleasure, self-discovery and curiosity.[313] However, over time, sexual interest and activity normally become more relational. That is, we begin to see the integration between sexual and relational drives necessary for mature relationships. As the two aspects of the self — the relational and the sexual — become integrated, the adolescent becomes positioned for a successful sexual relationship. Such integration takes time. It involves developing insight into and managing one's own emotions and drive profile, having a clear sense of identity and personal adequacy, maintaining effective interpersonal boundaries to retain a healthy sense of self, and having good capacity for judgement. Yet adolescence is not known for these qualities.

The early years of adolescence sees little integration. As testosterone and oestrogen levels begin their inexorable climb, adolescents are normally primed for sexual interest and desire, becoming increasingly interested in the other sex, the 'exotic species', further impelled by curiosity and social acceptance drives. For males with a tendency towards dominance, the gender differences and lack of identification with the opposite sex act to heighten the stimulation of discovery and adventure, enhancing the anticipation of sexual experience. For females, the focus may be more on being desired and protected, and on the social status connected with establishing opposite-sex relationships.[314] Either way, the anticipation of being close, intimate, and desired creates sexual anticipation and primes for the experience of mutual belonging for both emerging men and women. The young man becomes increasingly aware of his maleness and begins to desire the woman for her femaleness; and the young woman becomes increasingly aware of her femaleness and desires the man for his maleness. But other drives act simultaneously with these drives, both to activate and inhibit sexual attraction, to activate and to inhibit the desire for intimacy, coloured by conditioning experiences (such as exposure to pornography) and attachment history;[315] these drives varying from person to person and fluctuating over time, creating a complex and changing picture.[316]

If a sexual relationship is to integrate belonging and attachment, then the issue of to *whom* I belong becomes important. The expectation of belonging and attachment presuppose entry into a long-term arrangement with social and emotional obligations. This requires capacity for good judgement and a relatively stable drive profile. And so the development of an integrated sense of self becomes a critical task of adolescence — a prerequisite for entry into a functional adult sexual relationship.[317] Any associated decision to delay engaging in a sexual relationship can help reinforce a robust sense of self, and enhance self-esteem. And of course, the successful integration of sexual activity and mutual belonging also enhances self-esteem.

But these are difficult choices. The transition time is typically marked by social awkwardness as adolescents struggle with the process of individuation, with general self-understanding, and with establishing appropriate connection with the opposite sex in the face of changing drive profiles. It is a time where access to pornography and social media such as chat lines, Facebook, and various other internet products might appear to smooth the way by allowing sexual curiosity to be satisfied in the absence of the necessary social skills. Indeed, access to internet pornography has become very common, especially with adolescent males, frequently beginning around the age of 12 or 13. Studies show that boys typically report viewing pornography to get aroused and to masturbate, while girls do so out of curiosity, or because a male partner enticed them to do so.[318] But is not without hazard, given the potential for, and power of, sexual conditioning, as we will discover. The images and the context in which the images are shown become associated with sexual arousal, and will shape desires and expectations relating to later sexual relationship experiences.

On what basis does an adolescent make sexual decisions? With pressure enough to make sense of their own emerging drives, when is a person ready to factor in another person's needs and motives, also new and unfamiliar? When is someone ready to make good judgements in relation to entering a sexual relationship?[319] What does a person need to know, and what can they expect? And can or should they be protected from the pain of unsuccessful sexual relationships, given the potentially long-lasting effects of such misadventure? It is one thing to learn how to perform sexually to achieve some measure of temporary pleasure; it is altogether another thing for sexual behaviour to be effectively integrated with the relational and emotional needs of the two parties involved. We seek insights into the complexities of this integrative process by returning to the research into attachment.

Attachment and the sexual self

The rules of belonging change during a person's developmental history. Typically, it changes from belonging to parents on the basis of dependency, to belonging to the same-sex peer group on the basis of common interests and experiences, to belonging to a sexual partner on the basis of the mutual and consensual sharing of the body and inner self. In each case, there is the overlay of attachment style — concerning the emotional desire for, and security with, the other person: that is, the quality of bonding to the person concerned. In the transition years, belonging is influenced by gender roles and similarities of interest and behaviour — the *identification with*, rather than the *desire for something* that can later drive the belonging experience. But belonging and secure attachment in emerging adult sexual relationships is not easy, necessitating a well-developed sense of self to manage the demands of interpersonal differences, personal drives, sexual expression, and the various needs of the relationship itself.[320]

I noted a distinction between a child's *attachment* to their parents, and their *belonging* to them. A similar distinction can be made in sexual relationships. Attachment may develop as mutual emotional and sexual needs and desires are met and closeness and trust are established between adult partners. Belonging has more to do with the unique social orientation, the shared identity, and the perceived rights the partners have in relation to each other as a result of the relationship. In a sexual relationship, these two are generally aligned and reinforce each other to create an experience of intimacy and unity. However, it is possible in a sexual encounter to stimulate feelings of attachment mediated through biochemical release and moments of shared intense experience, which is then not supported by any sense of belonging together, as there is no accompanying social agreement about shared identity or perceived rights they have in relation to each other. This can affect the attachment style, create disconnection, and confuse the sense of belonging, destabilising the relationship.

Bowlby predicted long ago that the factors shaping attachment style may not be limited to early childhood experiences.[321] And indeed, we have noted that subsequent research has shown that secure child-parent attachment predicts secure attachment in a sexual relationship, with similar factors operating. For both infants and adults, attachment is reflected in the expression of special positive emotional attraction each has for each other, which is specific to them;[322] in their reluctance to be separated from each other; and in their delight in reunion with each other after separation. But how do preadolescent patterns of attachment and belonging — that is, the stability and quality of childhood relationships, and then those of adolescence — colour subsequent sexual behaviours and experiences?

We saw that an infant is primed to attach to those able to fulfil their dependency needs — typically their parents. During adolescence, the primary focus changes from dependency needs to emerging sexual awareness, and the interest and desire to enter an adult sexual relationship. Is it possible that, just as dependency needs primes for attachment in infancy, sexual and relational needs prime for attachment in adolescence and young adulthood? Once attached within the context of a sexual relationship, does one's partner remain the primary focus for attachment just as a parent does for their child? Nevertheless, even if there is such priming for attachment in an initial sexual relationship, not all couples in this circumstance succeed in forming a secure attachment, or establish a sense of mutual belonging. This affects subsequent patterns of sexual behaviour.

Each person has an orienting mind map or mental model of how intimate relationships function. The individual sexual narrative describes elements of that mind map. Early attachment styles shape that mind map so these attachment styles become long-lasting patterns, colouring early adult sexual relationships, which in turn contribute to subsequent love-style patterns. A person's attachment history also affects subsequent attachment patterns with that person's own children.[323] Essentially, expectations are created during the early years regarding the emotional availability of attachment figures. Adults who experienced secure attachment during infancy stand a better chance of later developing secure, trusting, and intimate relationships.[324] There is growing evidence that secure and insecure love-styles that are found in adult relationships (here 'love' and 'attachment' are used interchangeably) parallel the secure and insecure attachment patterns found in infants.[325] 'Secure love' was characterised by trust, intimate self-disclosure and comfort in being emotionally close. Couples enjoying a secure love relationship were found to have high self-esteem, to be self-confident, to see others as well-intentioned and trustworthy, to seek balance of autonomy and closeness in relationships, and to express emotional distress constructively.[326]

But what of those who had not known secure attachment in childhood? Does insecure attachment create insecurity in later sexual relationships? It seems so. Research revealed that adolescents and adults who had an insecure-anxious attachment history were later more likely to feel insecure with a romantic partner.[327] Such insecure attachment resulted in patterns of uncertainty, fear and distrust, an inherently stressful style compromising later capacity for love and connectivity. The emerging adult remained ambivalent in sexual relationships, fearing indifference or rejection, with an uncertain sense of belonging (and associated feelings of loneliness), and looking for constant reassurance. In both adolescence and adulthood, the motivation for sexual activity was frequently to secure love and acceptance, so they might engage in sexual activity they would not otherwise have been comfortable with.[328] They were also more likely to find themselves in situations involving alcohol and drugs with potentially distressing outcomes.[329] Because sex became the condition for acceptance, there was a constant fear that if they didn't perform adequately sexually (performance anxiety), they might be rejected and abandoned.[330]

The quality of sexual interaction became a measure of the quality of the relationship in general.[331] Those with insecure attachment might experience an overwhelming preoccupation with love, coupled with self-doubt and a jealous fear of being rejected or abandoned, resulting in obsessional or clinging behaviours. More generally, their self-esteem was compromised. They lacked confidence in others, seeing them as untrustworthy and undependable, and typically suppressed or denied negative emotions for fear of compromising the relationship. The confusion they experienced in infancy due to the mixed and inconsistent responses of their parent-figure might result in later difficulty with their own emotional regulation, and in misinterpreting or questioning emotional or relational signals from others, and so they would become anxious more generally. The later responses to their sexual partner might be inconsistent, unpredictable, and confusing, being influenced more by their own emotional state than that of their partner.

Adolescent and adult couples with an insecure-avoidant attachment history revealed a different pattern. They were characterised as cold, aloof, self-reliant, and superficial in their relating. Their beliefs about love were described in terms of discomfort with closeness, disappointment, and reluctance to make a long-term commitment. As infants, they typically reacted to the poor emotional sensitivities of parents by withdrawing emotionally, not seeing the parental responses as relevant or helpful. Their sense of belonging become tenuous. They later remained withdrawn emotionally, continuing to see emotional signals as largely irrelevant, and making little effort to interpret or respond to them. The expectation of rejection or of not being understood activated self-protective behaviours, so they became indifferent, and withdrew at any sign of conflict. They had low self-esteem, low confidence in self and others, believed that people have little control over their own lives, and tended to devalue the importance of closeness in sexual relationships.

Avoidant attachment essentially results from fear of closeness. It was linked to a lower frequency of sexual activity, pursuing sex for non-romantic reasons (such as self-enhancement, affirming self-worth, impressing peers, coping with negative emotions, or to manipulate a partner), and a tendency to drink or use drugs before sexual activity.[332] Not surprisingly, then, such people were more likely to be promiscuous, to be involved in one-night stands, and to have permissive attitudes regarding casual sex.[333] Men with an avoidant attachment history in particular tended to regard sex in terms of sexual conquest, to objectify women and casual partners, to use pornography, and to frequently prefer masturbation to having sex with partners.[334]

Both anxious and avoidant attachment histories have been linked to lower levels of sexual satisfaction and to a higher number of sexual problems.[335] In either case, distrust and self-protective drives are ascendant, interfering with the sense of belonging and the attachment process. Birnbaum (2016) observes: '...negative attachment experiences in childhood and the consolidation of insecure patterns of attachment are likely to impair the functioning of the sexual system in close relationships during this period and later on. ...if a person feels chronically insecure about being loved, whether this be reflected in relational worries or in being uncomfortable with intimacy, it is unlikely that this person's sexual system will function without interference' (p. 465).[336]

And so, while sexual activity plays an integral part in the development of attachment and belonging in a sexual relationship, such activity is mediated by these earlier attachment patterns. Both extremes — the equating of sex with attachment and belonging (as those with an insecure-anxious attachment history might do), and the disconnection of sex from belonging (as those with an avoidant attachment history might do), will result in a poorly integrated sexual relationship and aversive sexual experiences.[337] And so we would expect the SDP of those with secure attachment to differ from those with insecure attachment, and for this difference be reflected in the subsequent patterns of sexual activity.[338] We would predict a good balance of relationship-need themes and themes of pleasure and desire in those with a secure attachment history. However, those with an anxious-attachment history are likely to have relationship-need themes (such as the needs for intimacy and to feel loved) in strong ascendency.[339] Meanwhile, non-relationship themes — particularly inhibition themes — would be predicted in those with an avoidant attachment history.[340]

We have seen how attachment style can affect adult sexual relationships. We have seen how insecure attachment in infancy leads to insecure attachment in adult sexual relationships.[341] However, the idea of belonging and attachment being further shaped by *initial sexual relationship experience* is unclear and yet to be researched. We know that a person can *enter* a sexual relationship with insecure attachment style; but can someone develop patterns of insecure attachment as a *result* of disconnected early sexual experiences? Can the responses of a partner in an adolescent or initial sexual relationship have the same effect as the responses of caregivers in the relationship experiences of infants and children in emerging patterns of attachment and belonging? Can, for example, an initial sexual relationship with a person who is insensitive to emotional need, who betrays trust, or is indifferent or rejecting, predict later sexual relationships marked by insecure attachment style?

If, indeed, this should be the case, it has clear ramifications for the longer-term effects of early sexual relationships, especially where sexual and relational integration has not yet been achieved. Let us consider the effect of initial sexual experience on subsequent belonging and attachment as told in the story of Tim and Lucy. It is a story told not because it is unusual, but because it is a common enough experience.

Young love: Tim and Lucy's story

Both Tim and Lucy were fifteen when they got together. There was no peer pressure and there seemed nothing to prove. Tim was simply drawn to Lucy.

She was pretty and effervescent, a lot of fun to be around. In Lucy Tim saw freedom and life and joy — and he wanted this for himself. He wanted Lucy. She demanded little of Tim, accepted him for himself, and made him feel good about himself. He felt free, he felt high, and he felt great. They enjoyed sexual escapades and secrets together: out in the open air, in different places — just the two of them in freedom. He discovered himself sexually and he discovered her. She was his first. Everything was fresh and new and exciting. He didn't want the responsibility of a committed relationship, and she didn't ask this of him. He was much too young to have such responsibility, and neither was in a position to support the other in any event: they both remained in their parental home. They just wanted to enjoy the freedom of doing what they wanted when they wanted, with no-one to restrict or judge them. Tim knew he had something very special, and he enjoyed the moment with little thought for the future. Such thoughts would only weigh him down and rob him of the moment.

Their parents didn't ask questions. They believed it important the kids have the freedom to experiment and discover about sex. They didn't take this puppy love too seriously, though, and remembered their own early years when they wanted to be free to do their own thing. It didn't really matter; it wouldn't do any harm. Tim's mother had provided Tim with condoms a year earlier along with some parental advice: 'just make sure you have safe sex, and be nice to her — respect your girl'. Lucy's mother had been similarly supportive of Lucy finding her own way, arranging for her to have the pill, 'just in case'. The most important thing was that they didn't get STDs or that she fall pregnant, or that they 'did it' under the parents' roof (this would mean formally approving the relationship). Importantly, both mothers wanted their children to be happy and well-adjusted.

And they *were* happy — for a while. Then one day Tim discovered that Lucy had had sex with his best friend during a drunken episode. He was devastated, angry and confused. He felt betrayed by Lucy and by his friend. He felt protective of her. He then realised that he saw her as belonging to him. He found himself involuntarily treating the relationship seriously when he wanted it to be light. She hadn't taken their relationship all that seriously, and he was taking it more seriously than he'd expected to. Yet he knew they had been committed to each other's freedom, and that he didn't want the responsibility of commitment to the relationship — he wasn't ready for such commitment. He now felt trapped by his commitment to their freedom.

Tim hated Lucy for allowing this to happen, but he still loved her — at least, he still loved the times they were having. They had had so much fun. He didn't stop thinking about her and dreaming about her and remembering the pleasures they'd given each other. He knew that she drank far too much on the weekends, and was vulnerable. He couldn't understand why. It was then that she ended up having sex with others. She'd done it before, and would do it again. He knew, because his friends told him. But he didn't feel responsible for her, her drinking or her sexual activity, and he didn't know how to bring the subject up with her in any case. Still, he felt he needed to confront her about having sex with someone else. He didn't want to lose her.

The fact was, they'd hardly talked at all, and they really didn't know each other. He'd no idea what she thought about him. They'd just enjoyed each other, and talking too much made it all too serious and took away the fun. Talking also meant thinking and listening; and this was hard work. Lucy didn't seem to take anything too seriously. And he loved this about her — her infectious laugh, her teasing manner, her making light of things. Her relationships and her life generally just didn't seem important to her. She engaged easily, but she let go just as easily. She gave her body to him to make him happy, not to have him for herself.

But he realised that he'd become dependent upon her. Something had happened outside his awareness so that he couldn't have the same carefree attitude towards the relationship that she still seemed to have. He wanted more, even though he knew that neither was ready for this. She'd become like a pleasure-giving drug: he knew he shouldn't have her, but he couldn't do without her. Tim finally raised the subject with Lucy of her one-night stand, but she said nothing. She didn't deny or defend. She didn't know what to say. She'd had a lot of fun with Tim and then she'd had fun with someone else: what was there to say? He didn't own her! Why was he jealous and upset and trying to make her feel guilty? She'd made another boy happy. She could hardly remember what happened: it didn't mean anything. What was the big deal? Tim was confused and distressed, yet he stayed with her.

In time, Tim learned to shut out of his mind her drunken weekend adventures with other boys when he wasn't around. He kept busy, he spent time with his mates, he drank, he travelled, and he focused on other things. He decided that while he couldn't have Lucy to himself he could still enjoy his time with her during the week when he was around. He had a strong sexual appetite, one that stimulated good feelings, and he didn't want to let Lucy go. He realised he could only 'have' her if he shared her, although none of this was discussed with her, or with anyone else. Time progressed, and the nature of the relationship changed, although little was said. She was no longer his girlfriend, and this was understood by his family and friends. Nevertheless, he continued to enjoy sex with her frequently. He also felt he now had permission to do the same as Lucy did, and so had sex with other girls. These, however, were quickly forgotten one-night stands that helped him shut out his misery. The sex didn't mean anything. He wasn't emotionally attached to these girls the way he'd become attached to Lucy, and he didn't tell Lucy about them — just as Lucy shut him out of her 'other life'.

But it took its toll. Tim was hurting deeply. However much he tried to convince himself that Lucy's ongoing availability to him during the week was enough for him, however much he tried to shut out thinking about her other life, the many aspects of her that he didn't participate in, he felt incomplete, restless, and unhappy. He couldn't get her out of his mind. He dreamed about her: her gregarious, open, loving nature; her pretty looks and sparkling eyes; her unquestioning acceptance of him; her light, joyful, and undemanding presence. He wanted her so much. But he hated the fact that he wanted her, because her very openness and freedom had let others in, and he was constantly fighting feelings of jealousy, betrayal, and hatred towards her for doing this. He didn't want to want her. He knew that she could never be his — she needed to be free to find herself. All he had left were the memories and the sex itself — it became a drug he used to obliterate his pain and he took it where he could. But it left him unfulfilled.

It hurt Tim to see Lucy taken advantage of by others when she was drunk. Even though he didn't want to know, he knew what was going on, and he hated the way she was being used by others who didn't care for her at all, the way *he* cared for her. He saw in Lucy's eyes that she, too, under her bubbly surface, was confused, vulnerable, and hurting. She was looking for pleasure and acceptance and to be loved, even though she acted as if she didn't care at all.

In many ways, Lucy needed Tim as much as he needed her, but she'd lost control and didn't understand anything. She knew he hadn't been like the others, and that he'd been good to her. But she wasn't ready for any kind of responsibility in relationship. She didn't want to think and to take things seriously, because she sensed she would be overwhelmed with guilt and conflict. She too blocked it all out of her mind and didn't talk about it with anyone. How could she discuss something she didn't understand? She had no idea how she really felt, except that she felt inadequate in any relationship, and she went along with whatever she imagined the other person wanted so that they could both have fun and be momentarily accepted. She was aware that Tim was hurting, and she felt vaguely guilty and annoyed. She couldn't tell him this, so she wrote to him. Here were glimpses of the real Lucy, but the glimpses were fleeting.

Years passed. Tim tried to run away from his inner conflict, to shut his mind to the pain. But when he stopped running, depression descended. He knew that to be free of the torment he needed to let Lucy go altogether. He did so as best he could. But memories still intruded, and the mixture of pain, anger and desire for her and for what they once had continued to come and go. He entered a relationship with Erin. Although he was now older, he couldn't make a proper connection with her — Lucy was still in his head. He found it hard to trust and to be vulnerable again: he was wary now. He didn't really trust or want Erin, he felt no security or attachment with her, but he continued to want the sex and acceptance she offered him. It was a welcome antidepressant. Yet he felt guilty using her, and knew that he would hurt her when he eventually left her.

Tim felt lost, without direction or meaning in life, just drifting along, belonging nowhere. He was searching for something or running from something, but didn't know what. How would he recognise it if he found it? His sexual relationships provided him with temporary distraction, but not with fulfilment or meaningfulness — neither with Lucy nor with Erin. The pattern remained the same and his disconnection hid pain-avoidance and prevented relationship fulfilment. But, like the circumstances of his parent's separation, he adjusted to it: he expected nothing else, and he continued drifting aimlessly. Nothing had real value any more — including sexual relationships — because he wouldn't allow it to cost him as it had with Lucy. He wouldn't commit to anything. This would hurt too much. He stayed with a woman while it suited, but moved on to new adventures when it no longer suited.

Could it ever be different for Tim? Could those memories with all their associations now imprinted into his mind ever fade? Could anyone ever really replace Lucy? With the sexual relationship pattern that was now established, was it still possible for him to one day find the 'right' woman and 'settle down'? And if he did, what would he tell her about Lucy? And how would the 'right woman' respond? Might she wonder how she compared with Lucy and might she be anxious that Tim's love for Lucy might one day be reignited if he should happen upon her? Could Tim ever really trust himself to the 'right woman'? Tim didn't regret his time with Lucy, but his experiences with her coloured his later relationships, confusing his sense of belonging, and changing the meaning sex had for him.

First experiences

First sexual experiences are well-remembered and important. But there may also be a component of imprinting that is sensitive to developmental stage, with long-term ramifications. While this notion has yet to be properly researched, Bem (2001) makes some suggestive observations in relation to studies in various species of birds. He concludes from these studies that: sexual imprinting appears to occur at a 'sensitive period (roughly, equivalent to middle childhood)'; it establishes 'an attraction to an entire class of individuals well before sexual maturity'; after imprinting, 'the sexual preference is quite stable, even irreversible'; it 'follows the principle that exotic — but not too exotic — becomes erotic'; and 'physiological arousal appears to strengthen imprinting' (p. 200). If this also turns out to be true for the human experience, the timing relating to first sexual experiences may be very important. Furthermore, such timing will have implications for the likely circumstances and the prevailing drive profile that animates the sexual behaviour. What was experienced then — the sexual meanings, desires and orientation — may well set the pattern for the future.

The timing of first sexual intercourse ('coitarche') varies greatly from one person to the next. It depends on sociocultural circumstances, and will no doubt continue to change over time. Past research has suggested that most people become sexually active in their teens, while a minority remain virgins into their twenties, or even later.[342] But the early loss of virginity can affect long-term psychological wellbeing.[343] One study found the early loss of virginity predicted poor academic achievement both in boys and girls, poorer relationships with parents, less interest in religion, greater tolerance for deviant or criminal activity, and a higher need for independence.[344] No doubt the reasons for early loss of virginity play a role in these correlations. Yet we need to consider that the early loss of virginity may itself have also created difficulties. On the other hand, those who chose not to experiment sexually and remained virgins longer, showed no signs of personal unhappiness or maladjustment. Indeed, they were popular with peers, academically successful, and enjoyed good relationships with their parents. It also seems a good relationship with parents correlates with inhibition of sexual adventure. Perhaps intimacy and affection needs are still being met non-sexually, or they are simply more responsive to parental advice against premature sexual activity.

What might the drive profile during the time of first sexual experience look like? While internal drives generate increasing interest in sexual matters in the adolescent, there is often also mounting external pressure, generally by peers, to seek sexual experiences,[345] so that SDP themes relating to broader social needs are ascendant. For many, loss of virginity becomes a rite of passage into adulthood or an exercise in self-discovery (as outlined in the sexual experimentation subscript). This contrasts with the symbolic 'giving of self' to another person (implying they now belong to one another), understood in the traditional sexual scripts. In many adolescent communities the status of being a virgin may even be seen as a sign of sexual and social inadequacy or failure

— the adolescent has not been able to 'prove' him- or herself capable of negotiating a sexual experience. There is pressure to lose one's virginity.

Still, not everyone views the status of virgin negatively. Research suggests that as many men were positive as were negative about being virgins, whereas women were overwhelmingly positive about it. Neither men nor women said they abstained from sex because they lacked sexual desire: 'the primary reason for having remained virgins typically focused on not having found the right person, as well as some degree of parental influence.'[346] The notion that there must be the 'right person' with whom to engage in sexual behaviour raises the question: 'right' for what? I suspect it means 'right to have an ongoing relationship with'. If so, this suggests an intention to only engage in sexual behaviour within a relationship context — a desire to integrate sexual and relational drives. Indeed, most Australian adolescents were found to 'value committed relationships and view sexuality as a normal and natural part of relationship development.'[347] But the responsibility of relationship competes with the desire to have fun. And fun generally involves risk[348] and not being responsible. Adolescent perceptions of invulnerability can further compromise good judgement.[349]

Media messages tend to reinforce the idea of the adolescent loss of virginity being a natural rite of passage, and legitimise social pressure to seek sexual experiences (so long as sex remains 'safe' and 'respectful'). But first sexual experiences are frequently negative.[350] While research has suggested that men have more positive attitudes than women about their first experience, 'plenty of men and women reported negative feelings, anxieties, and other problems... consuming alcohol seemed to make for a less pleasant time, whereas having sex with a loving partner in a close relationship seemed to make for a better experience.'[351]

Where the need for social approval or to 'prove' oneself is the ascendant drive, it may be at cost to drives necessary for relationship success. Indeed, a common perspective is that the adolescent relationship is not meant to signify long-term intentions towards the other person: each expects to go their separate ways, often to 'experiment' with other relationships, until they are ready to 'settle down' and take a longer-term view. That is, until the drives for love, intimacy, and perhaps procreation dominate. But clinical experience suggests that participants in sexual experiences driven by social approval or for passing needs tend to devalue the significance of the experiences, which affects the meanings of sexual behaviour more generally. And the dissolution of a romantic relationship in adolescence is no less severe in its consequences than it is later; perhaps even more so because of the lack of life skills needed to cope with such a situation. In fact, a major cause of suicide among this population is the dissolution of a romantic relationship.[352]

The ascendant drive responsible for entering a sexual relationship may be relatively brief and incapable of sustaining a long-term relationship. Nevertheless, first sexual experience and first love generally leave lasting impressions, and this is not necessarily because of the 'great sex' that the couple experienced. It is partly because a bond can be created that remains long after ardour has cooled. And if the loss of virginity signifies the giving of oneself to another person, a conscious sense of belonging is added to the emotional bond. Even where this is not articulated or understood, most adolescents can relate to the feelings of jealousy, betrayal, and deep hurt when their sexual partner is discovered to be with another person — no matter how brief the relationship. These feelings betray the notion that they felt their sexual partner belonged to them, and ought not to be with someone else, as we saw in Tim and Lucy's narrative.

On falling in love

The romantic narrative demands that a sexual relationship involves 'falling in love'. This feeling state confirms this is the 'right person' with whom I should live my life. Certainly, such experience can cause a person to be reckless enough to enter a long-term sexual relationship with the utmost confidence that it is the right thing to do. But what is this mysterious thing called 'falling in love', and how can this give confidence about a sexual relationship future? And is the relationship no longer valid should a person 'fall out of love'?

Falling in love is not the same as love, nor is it the same as attachment or belonging. However, it frequently marks the *transition* into a sexual relationship marked by love, attachment and belonging. It is a state marked by intense but insecure attachment feelings that tend initially to occur outside the context of belonging to a particular person. That is, it begins with a person's strong desire that a person should belong to them who does not yet belong to them as the necessary relationship transactions have not yet taken place. It is therefore marked by hope and uncertainty driven by the desire to share a subjective 'home'. The tension of wanting but not yet securely having generates intense emotions, driving obsessional thoughts and behaviours. It marks a fundamental shift in orientation and values in life, where the love-object becomes all-consuming.[353] It is an event common in the transition years of adolescence, when the brain is primed to replace old attachments with someone new. The drive profiles are in flux: when a love-object is identified, certain drives intensify; and then, once the love-object has been securely won and a sense of mutual belonging established, the intensity of these drives gradually abates, allowing the neural system to rest.

Tennov (1999) observed that falling in love (she called it 'limerence') involves a powerful desire for someone and a desire to be desired by that person. It is exclusive in focus — this is the only person 'right for me'. (This, of course, begs the question: why this particular person? What perceived needs are being met, or what qualities in this other person create such a powerful attachment drive?) Tennov argued that falling in love is not so much about possessing the other person as it is 'merging' with them — 'a "oneness", the ecstatic bliss of mutual reciprocation' (p. 120). It seeks to erase interpersonal boundaries, physically and subjectively, so to embrace the other person's inner self and to merge with it. It is almost a recreation of a child's initial merging in dependency with a parent figure, the conditions of its initial attachment experiences. Falling in love may begin with the meeting of eye gaze, which has a capacity to bypass natural subjective barriers, a momentary exposure of the inner self, creating an awareness of being noticed and therefore the possibility of being desired. Such momentary invasion into one's personal space has erotic elements, to the extent that a person can feel both momentarily uncovered and to be the object of interest.

Such desire for merging involves vulnerability with the accompanying physiological arousal such vulnerability excites (which may be attributed to feelings of love). It also involves a joining of self to the other person, which leads to the experience of belonging and 'home'. The desired connection with another self helps validate and extend a person's experience of existence, and in such encounter creating meaning and purpose of behaviour through the powerful goal of unity. Yet falling in love remains more about the promise and expectation than it does the consummation, at which time the rules of the relationship begin to change.

In a sense, falling in love is sexual, because the love-object is desired as a sexual partner. Yet the desire for emotional intimacy and commitment outweighs the desire for physical union. Its focus is not sexual arousal or desire as such, although it primes a person for this. As recalled by one respondent in Tennov's (1999) study: '... I was in love with her — I did not think about her sexually... I did not have fantasies about what it would be like to have sex with her. I don't mean that I didn't *want* to — I did want to — but only as it would follow naturally if she was also in love with me' (p. 73). Still, that a sexual element exists is clear in that (as Tennov observes) a heterosexual person only falls in love with someone of the opposite sex, while a homosexual person only falls in love with someone of the same sex. The sexual identity of the inner self plays a critical role in the attraction: the desire for the object of love includes desire for what their gender represents.

Nevertheless, a sexual encounter is generally not the primary motive. It is secondary to a relational event wherein the sexual consummation is an expression of the mutual desire and attachment that define the relationship, the surrender to the internal desire to experience union with the love-object. The focus is desire for the other person; not sexual pleasure or release. Where the ascendant drive themes of the SDP might be of pleasure and sexual desire, we would need to conclude such a state is not 'falling in love' according to Tennov's formulation. Indeed, the focus on sexual experience or performance invites evaluation and creates emotional disconnection rather than the intimacy of 'merging' with the other person.

Falling in love is marked by great intensity and preoccupation. The mutual desire or 'acute longing' — desire for reciprocity is critical — eclipses the normal responsibilities of life and other relationships. It shifts a person's orientation and values: the love-object occupies centre stage and becomes the most important defining feature of life, around which all else now revolves: he or she becomes the basis of life's meaning. Not surprisingly, because the fear of abandonment or rejection by a person is proportional to the strength of desire for, dependency on, or bonding to, that person, fear becomes a central feature. The intense desire for the person with the accompanying fear of rejection, may result in 'heart palpitations, trembling, pallor, flushing, and general weakness... Awkwardness, stammering, and confusion predominate at the behavioural level. And shyness. When you are in love, you are fearful, apprehensive, nervous, anxious — terribly worried that your own actions may bring about disaster' (Tennov, 1999, p. 49). There is an urgency to consummate the relationship before it is lost. The intense feelings contribute to physiological arousal and the subsequent neural imprinting of the experience. And because the emotional investment is so great — I am prepared to lose all for the object of my love — the loss of love-object results in equally intense grief and disorientation, even to the point of suicide.

Although experienced as a singular drive, falling in love involves the simultaneous elevation of a number of drives — both subjective and biological. These drives include the needs for love and for intimacy and to belong; of fear of rejection; of elevated levels of hormones, dopamine and opioids; and of inhibition of the need for self-protection: a complex drive profile. The expression 'falling in love' implies a momentary loss of balance or control as other forces take over. And indeed, this seems to be case. An interactive dynamic is triggered between the BDP which I don't control, and the SDP which I *do* initially control (including the decision to submit to desire),[354] creating a powerful imperative to want a particular person. Interestingly, the ingestion of certain substances (such as amphetamines) can make its own contribution to a BDP primed for 'falling in love'.

Falling in love begins with a perception and desire whose source is the subjective self. But the subjective self expresses itself through biological processes which are activated by the motives, intentions, and emotions of the subjective self. These have a capacity to then create their own momentum. The subjective self receives and interprets signals from the body activated by the initial subjective experiences, so that these experiences are reinforced by the body's reactive neurochemistry. These two enter a circular, snowballing dynamic, the BDP aligning with and fuelling drives in the SDP, forces over which a person loses control, aligning with desires they have assented to, and resulting in the overall singular experience 'falling in love'. Differentiation between the BDP and the SDP is difficult once momentum is established. Nevertheless, the activity of the BDP is evident in the intrusive thoughts about the object of desire and the sustained alertness; the heightening of awareness, including an acute sensitivity to the other person's motivations, looking for clues of reciprocity; and effects on perception where the whole world looks different. Indeed, this distorted perception causes a person to see what they want to see, a person easily deluded, misinterpreting signals. It is an optimistic and idealistic perception, seeing only the positive, the beauty and perfection in the other person.

Powerful as it is, the passion of falling in love generally lasts only a limited period. There is need to adjust to the longer term stability of 'affectional bonding' or 'companionate love'.[355] The intensity and obsessional nature of the emotions and thoughts associated with falling in love creates emotional fatigue over time,[356] so that a person can even experience reactive depression. Such a depleted neural state can prevent the production of the neurochemicals required for the feelings of desire and pleasure associated with love, so that one might question whether they are still in love. Self-doubt and doubt about the future of the relationship grow. Was it all an illusion? Do I *really* know this person? Do I *really* want to continue to share myself with this person? Do we *really* belong together? This, of course, will create consternation and fear in the partner, who has invested so much in the relationship, who *does* feel they know the person and belong to them.

This conundrum was well described by Sacks (2015), whose falling in love experience involved both amphetamines and attachment through intense sexual activity. His initial impression of his lover Karl was muted: 'I thought him charming and civilized but did not think of him as especially attractive in sexual terms' (p.139). But amphetamines created a powerful sexual appetite, changing Sacks' perception of the relationship, even though there had been no real change in his knowledge of Karl. While high on amphetamine, Sacks 'made love ardently... But what I did not expect was that this experience would cause us to fall in love with each other.' His perception of Karl and the nature of the relationship changed, so that 'we idealized each other; we saw ourselves spending long, loving, creative lives together — Karl fulfilling himself as an artist, I as a scientist.'

But it was not possible to sustain the illusory experience, and the feelings changed. Sacks was left confused and bereft: 'We asked ourselves whether the experience we had shared was real, authentic, given the huge aphrodisiac thrust of the amphetamines. I found this question particularly humiliating — could so lofty a transport as falling in love be reduced to something purely physiological? In November, we oscillated between doubt and affirmation, thrown from one pole to the other. By December, we were out of love... In my last letter to him, I wrote, "I have memories of a fevered joy, intense, irrational... totally gone"' (pp. 140-141). While Sacks' chemistry had created sexual desire and bonding and his behaviour had enacted intimacy, the felt love was an illusion. Love and belonging had not been sufficiently established in the relationship to match the chemistry and the sexual behaviour. Sacks felt 'in love', but when the neuro-chemistry changed through its inevitable depletion and the feelings accordingly faded, two relative strangers were left in confusion about what the relationship really meant for each other.

In constructing reality, the brain simultaneously integrates information from different sources. These are both external and internal; both current and past. The mind accesses information from what is seen, heard, and felt; from emotion, 'logic', and memory. Meaning is constructed as this information is drawn together and interpreted. Where the multiple signals from the various sources are all faithfully received and integrated by the brain, the resulting reality and meaning it constructs can be a relatively accurate representation of what is going on. But where information from some sources is absent or unreliable, the brain constructs reality from what information it *does* have, creating anticipated meanings, and imposing the assumed information on the absent signals, filling the gaps. This allows a person to 'see' what is not there, and to 'hear' what is not heard: it is the basis of illusions of various sorts. A picture is built from partial information: the fewer the sources of the incoming information, the greater the risk of inaccurate interpretation.

This is also true in the experience of interpersonal and sexual attraction. There is a complex array of information involved when someone 'falls in love' with a person — visual, aural, olfactory, as well as the various meanings, expectancies, and internal signals (such as sexual arousal), which are integrated to mean 'I am in love with this person'. The brain works along associative principles, and is generally primed to associate sexual arousal or sexual desire with intimacy and belonging. The person associated with sexual arousal or desire somehow becomes mine — or should be. But not all signals may be present, and information gaps are filled so that a person may come to believe that certain attributes exist that are not necessarily there. Furthermore, signals to the brain may be artificially distorted through ingestion of a substance. Either way, a reality may be created which does not stand the test of time. As the brain responds to the gaps or distortions, an illusion can be created which is not revealed until the neural system is depleted, as Sacks discovered to his confusion and distress.

But even if the relationship does not suffer the perils of a depleted neural system and its concomitant doubts, the drive profile nevertheless changes, and other drives come to ascendency. Once the relationship is established, the drive to belong and to be desired fades as these drives are sated: I now *do* belong and *am* desired. The experience is no longer one of being 'in love', but of love for other reasons, including a growing history of mutual acknowledgement and the bond created by sexual activity and shared experiences. The drives that initiate a relationship may not be the drives necessary for long-term relationship stability.[357] When the passion abates, attachment and belonging remain — provided the factors necessary for consolidating such attachment and belonging occur, providing the basis for 'companionate' love.[358]

Chapter 12

Psychological Practice and Sexual Relationships

A s with sex, there are many motives for eating. It involves an interplay of subjective and biological drives. The current obesity crisis with all its attendant health problems is attributed in part to our poor eating habits: we eat too much, we eat for the wrong reasons, and we eat foods that are not good for us. It seems we often manage our various eating-related drives poorly. But poor management of sexual drives can equally give rise to health problems. When we engage in sexual activities for the wrong reasons, or in circumstances that are not good for us or for our relationship, mental health problems can result. Unfortunately, the prevailing sociocultural scripts do not always promote or encourage sexual behaviours that are good for us. By definition, a sexual relationship is about sexual activity in an ongoing relationship. Good integration of the sexual impulse with the need to belong will promote a secure and healthy sexual relationship. We will find that this in turn is linked to good mental health outcomes. Importantly, however, there are also sexual behaviours and experiences that are linked to poor mental health outcomes.

There are many sexual issues for which people seek psychological counselling. Sexual relationships in crisis, confusing sexual responses that raise questions of identity or orientation, intrusive and disturbing thoughts and images of past sexual experiences (traumatic or otherwise), unwanted sexual impulses and drives, and sexual performance problems are all too commonly experienced. Equally common are mental health problems such as trauma, anxiety, self-esteem problems and depression. And all too often, these two categories — problems in sexual behaviour and problems with mental health — are related. While many clients simply seek reassurance or guidance in decision-making, others desire change, either to cope better with a problem, or to resolve a problem so they might enjoy good mental health. The psychologist is approached not only as a confessor, but also as an agent of change.

But what *can* be changed and what *should* be changed? The serenity prayer famously intones 'God grant me the serenity to accept the things I cannot change, the courage to change the things I can, and the wisdom to know the difference.' Unfortunately, sometimes 'the difference' is not a matter of wisdom but of politics, and sometimes things now difficult to change were not inevitable in the beginning. Moreover, 'difficult to change' is not the same as 'cannot change'; and sometimes the temptation is to accept the things difficult to change because I don't have the courage to endure the discomfort, or the preparedness to do the hard work involved, to change those things difficult to change.

Both psychologist and their client find themselves dealing with confusing messages when it comes to sexual behaviour. There is ongoing debate and views change about how sexual behaviour should be understood, and what behaviour can or should be changed for good health outcomes. And so the psychologist is confronted not only with the question of what is *possible* to change, but also of what *should* be changed. I have described a multiple-drive model to help understand sexual behaviour and relationships, and which gives clues as to what is *possible* to change. I have also described how this is moderated by prevailing sociocultural sexual scripts, which theoretically give parameters as to what *should* be changed. With these in mind, I will try to make sense of this complex and often confusing situation, especially in relation to the psychologist. We begin with a short review of sexual behaviour, sexual relationships and mental health.

Sexual relationships and mental health

We have seen a greatly increased public awareness of the social impact of mental health problems. Considerable attention has been given in how to understand these problems and how best to respond to them. But it is only much more recently that attention is also being given to the mental health problems arising from sexual experiences: from past sexual abuse, but also from various other sexual behaviours and experiences, including sexual relationship dissolution. This coincides with an increase in unstable sexual relationships and in arguably questionable sexual behaviours made possible by the technological revolution, creating the context for psychological conflict or emotional distress.

As we have seen, sexual relationships involve a complex interplay of sexual and relational dynamics. Sexual behaviour and associated mental health similarly involve a complex interplay, with various aspects of sexual history and sexual behaviour potentially affecting mental health. Mental health problems may relate either to the relational or to the sexual aspect of the sexual relationship — or to both; or to intra-personal sexual conflicts, depending on the drive profiles involved. Where a relationship creates difficulty for a person, sex can be negatively affected by this difficulty. But sex can equally become a form of release or distraction from such difficulty. For some, sexual performance problems can put negative pressure on the relationship, while for others the relationship allows a safe environment to work through such problems. And just as certain sexual behaviours can give rise to poor mental health, the reverse is also true: mental health problems can negatively affect sexual behaviour.

Meaningful research into the relationship between sexual relationships and mental health is difficult. Treating sexual behaviour as a single construct rather than the varied expression of diverse drive profiles makes research difficult to interpret. Furthermore, where mental health is compromised as a result of sexual relationship problems, the nature of the mental health difficulties will vary. The timing of their expression will also vary, with some mental health difficulties becoming quickly apparent, and other difficulties not emerging until much later. And so the link between existing mental health problems and past sexual relationship problems is not always obvious. Furthermore, these effects are difficult to measure, and not only because mental health problems may emerge long after problematic events have occurred.

Although research often lacks the sensitivity to the complex variables involved to return consistent and meaningful results, that sexual relationship problems can affect mental health in various ways is a familiar experience for the psychologist. We have already seen examples of this in several narratives. We saw how traumatised Alicia became after her sexual abuse experiences, and the impact it had on her later sexual relationships. We saw how Tim became depressed and struggled with alcohol after Lucy's teenage infidelities. I could give many examples of social and relational alienation resulting from pornography, feelings of unresolved guilt and anger related to relationship dissolution, internal conflicts relating to conditioned sexual responses at variance with romantic attraction, and invasion of interpersonal boundaries in sexual abuse situations leading to loss of self-esteem and confidence, and resulting in complex trauma. Indeed, trauma symptoms, anxiety, and depression not uncommonly find origin in sexual experiences and relationships of one sort or another; and equally, sexual experience and relationships are affected by trauma, anxiety, and depression.

But sexual behaviour can also promote good mental health. When does it do so? Put simply: when things are as they ought to be. A sexual relationship potentially meets a number of important psychological needs, and so can play a critical role in overall good mental health. Research reveals that satisfying romantic and sexual relationships are vital components of psychological and physical health.[359] Successful relationships contribute to the sense of identity, belonging, to being valued, to self-efficacy, and to good self-esteem. When subjective and biological drives are managed well, so that their expression in behaviour matches healthy internal and external expectations in a successful relationship, subjective wellbeing, positive self-worth and a well-integrated identity (both socially and sexually) will be experienced. When the psychological 'home' a person belongs to (both within themself, and in relationship) is a place of order, safety and wellbeing, good mental health is more likely to prevail. More generally, good mental health depends on proper alignment of the various prevailing drives with each other and with internal expectations to create internal harmony and order.

But where things are not as they ought to be, problems will result. Where there is a lack of internal order and harmony, or a poor fit between my subjective needs and capacities, and external demands, mental health problems generally result. Just as social disorder results in social malaise, so internal disorder results in mental health problems. When a person's psychological 'home' is a place of tension, violation, or threat, their mental health will be compromised. And if a sexual relationship fails to meet critical needs — especially the needs for love, intimacy, or to belong[360] — or if sexual behaviour creates unresolved psychological conflicts or emotional disturbance, we might expect identity issues, loss of self-esteem, and anxiety and/or depression. Negative emotions — anger, grief, fear, shame, guilt, self-hate, feelings of inadequacy, distrust, confusion, loneliness — can result to disturb a person. When these feelings overwhelm that person, or the person is in conflict because of them, anxiety can overtake them. And when they don't find timely resolution, depression can result. When someone adapts poorly to the demands and expectations of the sexual relationship itself, or to the expectations and demands of the prevailing culture, they might struggle with feelings of not fitting in, or of feeling disgraced, rejected or inadequate. These can find expression in distrust and later relationship problems, in unresolved grief, in addiction, and in mood disorders such as depression and anxiety.

These things we know from clinical experience. But let us see what psychological research has found thus far. We will look at good mental health that generally results in the context of belonging and attachment, and poor mental health that generally results from relationship dissolution. We will then look at poor mental health outcomes from boundary violation in sexual abuse, but also from internal and external conflicts associated with sexual identity and orientation issues. We look at mental health outcomes of sexual behaviour outside of sexual relationships, and then we finish by looking at the reverse relationship: the effects of poor mental health (depression and anxiety) on sexual behaviour and relationships.

We begin with the relationship of mental health with belonging and attachment. In general, a strong sense of belonging and connectivity enhances mental health, while good mental health in turn enhances the capacity for secure attachment. Research consistently shows that the experience of belonging and of secure attachment associates with good mental health, allowing us to conclude that a sexual relationship with these characteristics should promote good mental health. There is an association between relationship satisfaction and sexual satisfaction,[361] while insecure patterns of attachment are generally associated with lower levels of sexual satisfaction.[362] Long-term relationships (characterised by belonging and attachment) lead to better physical and psychological health, especially for men (perhaps because women have more social and emotional support outside their primary relationship).[363] People function better, are more resilient to stress, and report fewer psychological difficulties when their interpersonal relationships support their need for relatedness.[364] And when a person's need for relatedness is satisfied, vitality and wellbeing is promoted and loneliness and depression is lessened.[365] In its absence, sadness, depression, jealousy and loneliness may emerge.[366] But it is not only ongoing relatedness that makes for good mental health. The trust and self-esteem which results from the relationship experiences of acceptance, respect, transparency, loyalty, being valued, consistency, and respect for each other's interpersonal boundaries also contribute to good mental health.

Where belonging and bonding are ruptured, mental health problems can follow. Both cheating on a partner and relationship dissolution are associated with such problems: one study reported that 'around 50% of romantic unions end in dissolution, increasing the risk for psychological and physical health problems in both partners.'[367] Infidelity is a common reason for relationship dissolution, and is a major source of distress, frequently leading to depression and other psychological health problems for the betrayed partner.[368]

Relationship dissolution involves the rupturing of the sense of belonging and adjusting to the loss of the object of attachment — depending, of course, on the extent that belonging and attachment had been established in the first place. Such loss will typically trigger grief with its associated pain, disorientation and emptiness, along with agitation, poor sleep, poor concentration, loss of self-esteem, a range of other negative emotions and cognitions, depression,[369] and even suicidal ideation.[370] To the extent that meaningfulness is a function of connectedness, a loss of sense of meaning may accompany the disconnection of relationship dissolution. And, depending on the circumstances of the dissolution, significant jealousy and anger may be created by cheating partners, who themselves may suffer anxiety and guilt.[371] But jealousy and distrust can also emerge from a past history of relationship failure. Inadequate processing of these issues may lead to depression, and other complications may also emerge, such as distress about how children are affected.

A second area of research concerns the effects of violated sexual and psychological boundaries on mental health. Not surprisingly, child sexual abuse has consistently been linked with poor mental health outcomes in the longer term. Depression and substance abuse are the most common long-term sequelae,[372] but many other effects have been noted, including fear, anxiety, anger and hostility, aggression, sexualised behaviour in the shorter term; and self-destructive behaviour, anxiety, feelings of isolation and stigma, poor self-esteem, distrust, substance abuse, and sexual maladjustment in the longer term.[373] Childhood sexual abuse in women is also associated with an 'unresolved attachment state of mind' in adolescence that may lead to dissociative thought problems.[374] There is evidence that women with childhood sexual abuse history have a greater likelihood of sexual disturbance or dysfunction and of homosexual experiences in adolescence or adulthood, on top of the ubiquitous depression;[375] and substance abuse and suicidal behaviour are commonly reported.[376] One meta-analytical study identified PTSD, depression, suicide, and sexual promiscuity as long-term outcomes of child sexual abuse, with no significant differences in mediating variables such as gender, nature of abuse, or relationship to the perpetrator.[377] These mental health problems are in turn detrimental to subsequent sexual relationships.

But sexual and relationship abuse is not limited to children. Not surprisingly, sexual abuse and the abuse of power and control in adult sexual relationships also result in mental health problems — typically in depression and substance abuse — for both men and women.[378] Where distorted perceptions of belonging and ownership result in coercive sexual activity (generally perpetrated by men), the victim can experience depression, anxiety, and post-traumatic stress disorder — even more so where there was a relationship with the perpetrator.[379]

A third area of research concerns mental health problems in those dealing with conflicts relating to sexual orientation and identity. Such conflicts may be internal or between the expression of homosexual or transsexual behaviours and prevailing sociocultural expectations. For example, homosexuals are at greater risk of major depression, inclination to suicide, substance abuse, and anxiety disorders.[380] Both bisexual and lesbian undergraduate women reported having poor mental health status (as compared to heterosexual women), with greater anxiety, anger, depression, self-harm, and suicidal ideation and attempts.[381] Gay, lesbian, bisexual, and 'unsure' students reported more mental health issues (often compromising academic performance) than heterosexuals.[382] Lesbian, gay, bisexual and transsexual individuals were found to have greater levels than heterosexuals of psychological distress and depression, to be more likely to smoke and binge drink, and to report unmet mental healthcare needs. They also reported greater discrimination, although research suggests that the discrimination itself was not necessarily responsible for increased mental health problems.[383] There is evidence that it is the internal conflict resulting from viewing one's own homosexuality negatively rather than the fact of homosexual orientation, in homosexual men at least, that is associated with major depression.[384] Moreover, when compared with lesbians, gays and bisexuals, transgender men and women have even higher rates of depression and suicidal ideation.[385]

A fourth area of research that has barely begun concerns the effects of sex outside of established sexual relationships on mental health. This includes casual sex, cyber-sex, internet pornography, and other new developments in sexual experience and behaviour. We would expect issues to include the loss of effective interpersonal boundaries, the depersonalisation of the sexual experience, the disconnection between sex and belonging, the rewarding of impulsive sexual urges, the addiction of pornography, and the loss of control of personal sexual information may all potentially compromise mental health. Certainly, there is already research evidence of the negative effects of 'short-term sexual strategies'. Zeifman & Hazan (2016) note 'extensive clinical literature on the harmful effects of emotional loneliness, breakups, divorce, and sexual infidelity' already exists, and has implications for such strategies.[386] However, there is as yet very little research on the mental health effects of casual sex, cyber-sex, and so on, although psychologists regularly hear stories about distressing situations that are encountered. Nevertheless, there is some research that shows that college students having sexual intercourse in 'hook-ups' (casual sexual encounters with relative strangers) frequently had lower self-esteem or suffered depression.[387] However, the results were mixed. Those who were lonely and depressed to begin with appeared to find some initial comfort from the experience. On the other hand, those who were not depressed or lonely were more likely to become depressed and lonely, and where there was a degree of coercion or regret, depression was also a more likely outcome. No doubt many factors were at play, such as the prevailing drive profiles and the internalised sociocultural sexual scripts. And once again, the measurement of mental health outcomes remains a challenge.

Finally, and more generally, we look at the reverse effect: that of poor mental health on sexual relationships. There is considerable research that links mental health problems with sexual relationship and sexual performance problems,[388] but often the links are not well-defined. The relationship between mental health and sexual behaviour is complex, making interpretation of research findings difficult. Correlational studies give little insight into causal mechanisms between sexual relationship problems and mental health problems. Of course, in many situations the dynamic will be a circular one, with sexual relationship problems contributing to mental health problems, which in turn contributes to sexual relationship problems. Because poor mental health is frequently experienced as depression, which typically lowers libido and associates with social withdrawal, its negative effect on a sexual relationship is unsurprising. Research may also generate apparently contradictory outcomes, or outcomes suggesting poor links between sexual behaviour and mental health, because too many disparate circumstances and dynamics are grouped together for research purposes.

Keeping these issues in mind, we find that depressive mood and symptoms are associated with decreased sexual activity (and vice versa),[389] although sometimes there is *increased* sexual activity during depressive episodes — no doubt where pleasure and recreation is used to combat depression.[390] Generally, mild depression may be associated with increased sexual activity and risk-taking, while severe depression is associated with decreased sexual activity, partly reflecting loss of libido.[391] While there is evidence that people with sexual disorders get depressed, the reverse relationship gets more attention: that is, depressed people are more likely to have problems with sexual desire, arousal and orgasm;[392] although it appears that this relationship is stronger in women.[393] A further complication is that treatment with antidepressants negatively affects sexual functioning in many people — where serotonin levels are increased, libido is lowered.

When we turn to the relationship of anxiety to sexual issues, things get a little more confusing. Importantly, the focus is generally on the effects of anxiety on sexual performance, rather than the effects of a troubled sexual relationship on anxiety. With the former, the nature and triggers for anxiety play a role in whether sexual interest and performance is affected, as does the coping methods used to manage anxiety. Indeed, the increased arousal associated with anxiety (as found in heightened state anxiety) may serve to *increase* sexual responsiveness. It is a question of the extent of arousal, and whether self-protective responses have been triggered, and whether or not a person copes with anxiety by withdrawal. Barlow hypothesised that anxiety can amplify sexual arousal for sexually functional individuals, but interfere with arousal in sexually dysfunctional individuals. In the latter, anxiety about performance demands distract from adequate cognitive processing of erotic cues.[394] Gender differences are also commonly found. For example, studies linked high trait anxiety with premature ejaculation in men, while linking it with problems in desire, arousal, and orgasm in women.[395] Social phobia, on the other hand, causes men to be less sexually active — but not women.[396] Obsessive Compulsive Disorder, Panic Disorder, and Post-Traumatic Stress Disorder are all associated with various sexual performance problems.

These are but a few of the links between sexual behaviour and mental health that research studies have identified. No doubt more links and increased understanding about these links will emerge over the coming years. Meanwhile, psychologists are faced with a complex presentation of mental health issues that are often linked to sex-related experiences of one sort or another. How are these issues to be managed in the therapeutic context?

On therapeutic goals

Psychological therapy can serve many goals. Frequently it is about making sense of the client's experience: of the complex interaction of motives, bodily reactions, memory fragments, and emotions. Or it might be the validation of the client's experience: giving the client time and a safe place to think things through. For some it is about the amelioration of suffering, which might involve the resolution of disturbing emotions. Or it might be a client's desire to change certain behaviour patterns, to manage situations better. This may involve supporting the client in doing new and initially uncomfortable things necessary to achieve what they want to achieve.

But I think it is fair to say that an underlying goal always is to promote a client's mental health. Yet what this actually means for clinical practice is not necessarily evident, especially when the links between behaviour — in this case, sexual behaviour — and mental health is not always clear or well-documented. It is an easy trap for the psychologist to uncritically support a client's view about their sexual behaviour (validating their experience) even when that behaviour does not necessarily promote their good long-term mental health. We would expect a good doctor to challenge a patient whose behaviour will have eventual poor health outcomes (for example, in what that patient eats, drinks, or smokes). Should a good psychologist not similarly challenge a client whose sexual behaviour has a good chance of resulting in poor mental health in the longer term? What principles should guide the goal for psychological intervention, apart from the basic principle that it be in the best interests of the client?

The question of appropriate goals in sexual relationship counselling can be a vexed one as the values and perceptions of both psychologist and client are involved. And although it is often said that a psychologist should be 'values-neutral' and 'evidence-based', and should work with the client's values as well as the research 'evidence', the psychologist inevitably plays a role in the inter-pretation of experiences recounted by the client as well as in how research is interpreted.[397] The psychologist potentially influences the perceptions and understandings of their client, so contributing to shaping their values. But, besides client contact, the psychologist also contributes to the shaping of the sociocultural sexual script in the academic literature and specific submissions and recommendations made to government bodies on behalf of psychological organisations. These are not values-neutral, and the 'science' involved often open to interpretation and debate, yet they can carry significant weight in the community at large.

There is wide agreement that some sexual behaviour is not acceptable, and here goals for intervention will be clear. For example, there is agreement that neither children nor adults should be sexually abused and exploited — and I suggest this is not limited to 'non-consensual' behaviours. Adolescents and adults can give in to pressure to enter sexual situations to which they 'consent', but which remain essentially exploitative. Nevertheless grey areas remain, and therapy goals might be unclear. At what age is someone ready to engage in a sexual relationship with another person? Should casual sex be discouraged? When is access to internet pornography a good idea? And when should the psychologist challenge their client? For example, it is generally agreed that infidelity is unacceptable and has mental health consequences. Yet in their reluctance to make 'value judgements', some psychologists may implicitly endorse their client's infidelity, perhaps on the grounds of 'personal integrity' or the search for 'personal happiness'.

There are many areas in relation to sexual behaviour which do not enjoy wide agreement about what is acceptable, or, for that matter, helpful.[398] Dramatic changes have been seen in recent decades in what is defined as dys-functional or acceptable in sexual behaviours and relationships. These changing goalposts highlight the problem of defining dysfunction or determining what is 'acceptable' in sexual behaviour and relationships. Added to this are the difficulties in making clear links between many sexual behaviours and experiences and mental health outcomes, so that it is frequently hard to find agreement in what is helpful and what should be discouraged. This affects not only psychologists, but also parents of children and adolescents. These changing goalposts relate to many different areas of sexual expression, including sexual identity, orientation, and whether sex is best expressed in a relationship.

And so, for example, until very recently the gender confusion potentially leading to sex change was seen as pathological: now we talk of 'gender indeterminate' and personal options. A person in such circumstance now has freedom to adopt the gender identity they feel most comfortable with and to express their sexuality accordingly. Indeed, children are now encouraged to think of gender as indeterminate. Not long ago homosexual behaviour was seen as a pathological expression of a natural sexual impulse. Now it is seen as an expression of diversity and homosexual relationships are celebrated. Children are taught that this is how it should be. And it was not long ago that extramarital sex was seen as a sign of poor self-control and therefore of bad character; now it is regarded with indifference, or even in some cases a sign of personal courage or integrity. Along similar lines, it was not long ago that it was generally held that a person established their love for someone before engaging in sexual activity; now sexual activity commonly occurs where a person is hardly known at all — that is, outside a relational context. Is it the case that these changing social views reflect changing but valid alternatives in how functional behaviour is defined? Is functional sexual expression necessarily relative to prevailing but ever-changing ideas? How does the psychologist determine what is functional and healthy and wise in regard to sexual behaviour, so that appropriate goals in counsel and intervention might be pursued?

A review of psychological literature reveals that psychological thinking tends to reflect the prevailing social views, and indeed, has contributed to the formulation of such views. But it generally also embraces a reductionist philosophy of science, and this has played a considerable role in how the sexual relationship is understood and how functional sexual behaviour is defined. If it is true that sexual activity has no meaning apart from the sating of biological drives and the provision of mutual pleasure and perhaps for reproduction (consistent with a reductionist view), and that sexual activity has no enduring consequence for either party (unless someone happens to fall pregnant), and that moral values are relative to prevailing sentiments, an appropriate psychological goal might simply be to promote the conditions for a 'satisfying' sexual experience free of internal or external conflict. It would follow that personal fulfilment and sexual release may validly be seen as the primary functions of sexual activity and the measure of good mental health.

Following this reasoning, it would make good sense for a psychologist to promote the use of sex workers to provide pleasure and release for a client prevented from finding a sexual partner for whatever reason. It would equally be a good strategy for the psychologist to utilise pornography as an avenue to enrich sexual experience or to enhance sexual arousal in a client experiencing difficulty in this regard. Furthermore, it would be perfectly reasonable for the psychologist to recommend sexual exploration with different partners of different sex to gain clarity about a person's sexual orientation, and to seek relationship solutions that align with a person's current sexual inclinations — if indeed, a relationship is needed at all. But does psychological research really support these strategies for intervention, and are these approaches really the best ones for the person's longer-term mental health?

I have argued that sexual behaviour is imbued with various meanings that differ from one person to another, and that it represents the expression of multiple drives. But I have also argued for some universal meanings in sexual behaviour: one being that the establishment of both belonging and attachment serve important functions for sexual behaviour. Furthermore, I have argued that sexual experience has consequence: both in its propensity to conditioning; and in its contribution to the shaping of meanings associated with that experience. This will have consequences for the intervention strategies a psychologist might follow. And so, for example, Karl's experiences with the prostitute raises questions about the therapeutic value of the use of sex workers in psychological intervention. We will also see how Liam's struggle with his mental health after sexual arousal was conditioned to certain pornographic images highlights potential problems in utilising pornography as an aid to enrich sexual experience, or to enhance sexual arousal in a client.

A common therapeutic goal is freedom from internal (psychological) or external (relational or social) conflict.[399] In many respects this is an admirable goal. However, in the multiple-drive model that I have described it is clear that both internal and external conflicts are inevitable. I propose that good mental health does not require *freedom* from such conflict, but rather its effective *management*.[400] The *very nature* of a fluctuating multiple-drive profile means that periodic conflict — internal and external — is inevitable and normal, even if it is uncomfortable and demands attention of some sort. I believe a better therapeutic goal might be to understand what the prevailing conflict represents, to learn to effectively manage that conflict, and to cope with discomfort. The experience of short-term discomfort is not the same as poor mental health, nor should it adversely affect self-esteem.[401] It may be argued that intrapsychic harmony promotes an individual's positive self-image. I would certainly agree with this. But I see this as harmony between a person's values and behaviour, rather than between conflicting drives. Certainly, there is no question that the psychologist should promote such harmony, so to enhance respect and love between the client and their partner. But the solution to 'intrapsychic conflict' is not the acceptance of any particular prevailing internal drive as 'inherent' or justified simply because it is there, nor is it to aligning behaviour and relationship decisions with those drives without reference to other values.[402] Inevitably, other conflicts will then emerge.

Unfortunately, conflicts relating to sexual behaviour and relationships are common. Indeed, internal conflicts arising from competing drives in one's drive profile are to be anticipated. But there are no simple solutions. Whether we are talking of addictions, the effects of classical conditioning, or the inclinations of temperament, there may be things I have a strong and ongoing desire to do, but I shouldn't (for personal or social reasons); and there may be things I do not want to do (for personal or social reasons), but struggle to prevent myself doing. Certain drives are not necessarily welcome. Competing drives in my drive profile ('intrapsychic' conflict), or conflict between my drives and prevailing social mores (external conflict), are not necessarily resolved by simply giving in to the most powerful drives. Indeed, we have seen that this can contribute to *low* self-esteem, rather than good self-esteem, if it means forfeiting control of my own impulses.[403]

While the goals of a well-integrated personality and positive self-image (aspects of good mental health) are accepted as a general principle, its accomplishment has more to do with understanding one's drive profile and making wise decisions in relation to those internal forces. It is not the presence of conflicted drives that create psychological problems and lead to poor mental health so much as it is conflicted decision-making. We cannot decide to embrace conflicting drives simultaneously. Choices need to be made. No-one can serve two masters at the same time. However, given the primary role of attachment and belonging in a functional sexual relationship, and given the long-term mental health benefits of such relationship, I propose that this should be a defining drive and a guiding principle in the establishment of our therapeutic goal.

To that end, I suggest an additional rule to Peterson's popular *12 Rules For Life: an antidote to chaos*: 'Only have sex when you also belong to the person.' This rule is based on ancient wisdom as well as current research, and a further antidote to chaos. I believe the psychologist will promote good mental health by integrating such a principle into the therapeutic goal.

Some therapy principles

If by now you have concluded that antecedents and consequences of sexual behaviour and relationships are complicated, you would be right. Therapeutic intervention in the area accordingly has its challenges. And the ongoing debate as to what appropriate therapeutic gaols for sexual behaviour should be means that therapeutic principles can be difficult to clarify. Nevertheless, there are issues and principles that can usefully be identified even if it be at a more abstract level. Here I highlight a few principles useful for the therapy process and associated psycho-education. These principles include: sexual experience and behaviour is difficult to interpret; over time, it becomes increasingly difficult to change sexual behavioural patterns; giving expression to a drive can increase the drive; a person's drive profile remains dynamic over time; sexual behaviour should always be considered in the social context; and a person both had and has the power of choice in sexual behaviour. Let me elaborate on each principle.

A first principle is that *sexual experience and behaviour is difficult to interpret*. Tread with care! The psychologist needs to allow that a person's interpretation of past events is frequently not accurate. We have seen, for example, how sexual arousal can be confused with sexual desire. We have also seen how multiple motives (of which the person may be unaware or only partially aware) may operate in any one behavioural sequence. A person's interpretation of their own behaviour or experience can be distorted,[404] so that they may attribute motives to sexual experience that do not reflect the SDP at the time it occurred (or reflects only part of the SDP), in favour of one more personally or socially acceptable (that is, aligned with the internalised sociocultural sexual script, or the prevailing external script). Motives are generally determined through introspection, and their identification will be affected by concerns about social acceptability. This difficulty in determining one's own motivations — that is, accurate self-knowledge — is the burden of the psychoanalytic approach.

Furthermore, the brain is shaped by past experience and the prevailing drive profile. The resulting orientation of the subjective self colours the interpretation of both past and current events and experiences so that internal consistency is maintained. Current expectations are influenced by how past experiences are interpreted, and incoming information is screened to retain harmony with those interpretations.[405] Likewise, meanings are retrospectively attributed to past events to retain consistency with current perceptions and decisions. This means that focus on both past and current events is selective: only those things that make sense in regard to overall current subjective orientation is attended to. Of course, the psychologist necessarily works with the perceptual world of the person and with what the person chooses to report, but this cannot be divorced from external realities. The psychologist needs to interpret a person's perception with caution.

Related to the first principle, a second principle is that, *over time, it becomes increasingly difficult to change sexual behavioural patterns*.[406] This is because the brain is shaped by life events and remains consistent with the memories and decisions of the past. It is seen in the feedback loop of *Figure 2.2* earlier. I become the decisions I have made. What I rehearse I become familiar with, good at, and I think and do these things increasingly naturally. Behaviours that have been conditioned by past events become automatic responses. What I have become I am likely to remain. And so a consolidation of orientation and relational identity occurs (in this case, in my sexual relationship) that integrates and rationalises that subjective orientation, perpetuating the way I interpret things. This orientation is self-sustaining by my selective focus and memory, by the behaviours I practice, and by the friends I choose, who are likely to support my interpretations and perceptions.

Difficulty in change, therefore, does not necessarily mean that certain sexual inclinations, perceptions, or behaviour patterns are somehow 'inherent'; but rather that it reflects the shaping of my brain over time. It means that, assuming change is desired, a complex process of learning to think differently, learning to attribute different meanings, practicing different behaviours, and even establishing a new personal conditioning history will be required. Difficult though it may be, our growing understanding of brain plasticity gives confidence that change remains possible. However, because new behaviours are by definition unfamiliar, the process will inevitably feel unnatural at first, and this can create further resistance to change as a person might fear they are compromising of their personal integrity. A further corollary of the way the brain shapes itself around its own history is that early sexual experiences and decisions have a disproportional effect on sexual relationships in the longer term, and should be treated accordingly.

A third principle is that *giving expression to a drive can increase the drive*. Don't feed a hungry crocodile: it will only want more, and it now knows how to get it! Many sex-related drives are not sated in the longer term by their expression in the shorter term. Instead, they can grow in strength. The temporary sating of such drives as the drive to recreation, curiosity, power, and so on will cause them to increase in strength, and the related behaviour patterns are reinforced. This relates to the conditioning principle — that which is immediately rewarding, I will want to do again. That which sexually aroused me before, will arouse me again. The desire to engage in the behaviour again will be triggered by the circumstances in which it occurred to begin with. Looking at pornography increases the desire for more. Experiencing power in a relationship increases the desire for more. Experiencing sexual arousal in exhibitionist behaviour or covert spying fuels the need to do it again. While this loop is more likely to happen outside sexual relationship where sexual integration is poor, it can nevertheless interfere with an existing relationship. Here is a reason to inhibit or at least properly manage a drive when it is first experienced.

Difficulty in the change process and the power of first experiences notwithstanding, a fourth principle is that *the drive profile remains dynamic over time.* People change. Needs change. Circumstances change. This is especially so in the early years and during the transition years of adolescence. And even though there is normally increasing stability and predictability in the drive profile with time, fluctuations continue to occur over the years because of physiological changes, changes in relational circumstances, and changes in a person's subjective needs, as we have seen. This capacity for change in part underscores the notion of sexual fluidity. Because of the dynamic nature of the drive profile, there should always be caution in any projections made regarding patterns of sexual experience, inclination, and behaviour. Whether we are talking about the dynamics of sexual attraction and desire, sexual orientation, or even sexual identity,[407] these can and do change — sometimes with, and sometimes without, psychological intervention. A corollary of this is that sexual labelling, which locks a person into a set of expectations attached to the label, is best avoided. When explaining behaviour, it is preferable to reference the individual's prevailing unique and changing drive profile than to formulate intervention on the basis of one or other assumed or proposed label.

A fifth principle is that *sexual behaviour should always be considered in the social context.* This context includes the needs and expectations of the relevant community of which I am a part. We may be born with certain predispositions, we may have little choice in regard to our early relationship history, we may have had certain relationship behaviours modelled to us, and we may typically struggle with certain hormonal imperatives at one point or another. However, despite those predispositions, early experiences, and prevailing hormonal activity, I cannot behave without reference to sociocultural and interpersonal expectations of sexual behaviour. Nor can I interpret behaviour outside such context. Although highly personal and private, my various sexual activities are nevertheless typically social events with potentially significant social ramifications, and are (and should be) the concern of others and of society in general. And so a fifth principle in establishing therapeutic goals is that the psychologist needs to consider not only the person's own desires, perceptions, and dilemmas; but also how these may affect the community in which that person lives. In this respect, a person's capacity to adjust to prevailing social norms and expectations forms part of the definition of good psychological adjustment.

A final principle is that *a person both had and has the power of choice in sexual behaviour*. The model is not a deterministic one. Even if choice is limited or judgement impaired because of previous choices made, habits practiced, natural inclinations, and prevailing circumstances, choice is still possible. Whatever sexual inclinations, desires and fantasies a person might have, they have the capacity to choose which inclinations, desires or fantasies they might embrace, if any. This capacity for choice is a function of the inner self and the basis for human dignity. It is also the basis of human existential freedom. When a person's behaviour is reduced to the inevitable outcome of various prevailing drives, they have lost both freedom and responsibility — their essential humanity.

While we might be born with a propensity to certain drives, we are not born with decisions already made or experiences already had. This is especially true of sexual behaviour, which is a function of individual maturity. It takes time to develop readiness for adult sexual behaviour. Furthermore, no individual drive — whether biological or subjective in origin — completely explains sexual behaviour. As we have seen, it is a complex profile that reflects life experiences, learned behaviours, individual perceptions and interpretations of events, internalised sociocultural scripts, past decisions made, and inherent predispositions. Any simplistic position that I was 'born this way', or 'that's just the way I am' as a basis for accepting what I suppose I cannot change (or manage) — however difficult it might be — undermines human dignity and responsibility.[408] We all need to manage our drives and impulses, even though giving in to them is easier in the short term. However, we saw that the capacity to make well-informed decisions in this regard varies according to circumstance. Brain changes during adolescence, because of changes in the BDP during prolonged sexual arousal, or under the influence of alcohol, typically compromise good judgement. There are times where external support and direction in decision-making is protective of the person making the decision.

The maintenance and dissolution of a sexual relationship

The good things we might want are not necessarily easy to get. We have seen that long-term satisfying sexual relationships characterised by belonging and secure attachment promote good mental health, while the dissolution of a relationship is associated with distress and poor mental health. Clearly, a stable and satisfying long-term sexual relationship is a goal to be promoted. But, wonderful as the ideal is, and good as it might be for mental health, maintaining a long-term sexual relationship is far from easy. Indeed, some no longer even try.

Sharing and enjoying psychological space with someone else in the long run is difficult. It is difficult enough to enjoy one's own psychological space consistently. Remaining positive towards another person who shares our psychological home, and effectively regulating the relationship needs creates further challenges. The only legitimate control I have is only over myself, not the other person who shares my space with me. And so I need to focus on making myself liveable with, and to manage my drives accordingly. While also looking out for my spouse's (partner's) wellbeing, I ensure that I am good to live with for that person. Perhaps I could start by asking: do *I* like to live with *me*? But it also requires both a commitment to *want* to live with my spouse (partner), so that our attachment and belonging needs are met, and a commitment to manage my own impulses so I do not stimulate inhibition or self-protective drives in the other person. In this I should take responsibility for my contribution to making the relationship work, rather than to blame the other person for failing in theirs.

Of course, this is not only true for sexual relationships: it is a template for all relationships. The subjugation of my impulses and drives for the sake of the other person is necessary for the maintenance of a relationship. The capacity to sacrifice immediate pleasure — my rights notwithstanding — for the long-term benefits and wellbeing both of myself and the other person is a measure of emotional maturity as much as it is a basis for relational stability and long-term success. But the need for such sacrifice is often not understood, and it can be difficult to make.

It is easy to see how things can quickly go wrong. And when one or other party is no longer committed to the sexual relationship, they will cease to do the hard work or make the sacrifices necessary for it to succeed, so that in time it unravels. What does this hard work require? Problematically, the drive profiles of both parties in a relationship will fluctuate over time, as we have seen happens with the hormonal profile, but as is equally true with the various subjective drives that change as life circumstances change. This potentially affects the degree to which the relationship meets the sexual and relational needs and satisfaction of each party at any particular time.

Moreover, the drive profile that might *launch* a sexual relationship is typically different from that required to *maintain* it.[409] The beginning of a sexual relationship often finds the ascendant drive themes of pleasure and desire (especially for the male), strong hormonal imperatives of the BDP, or drive themes relating to broader social needs, rather than the relationship-need drive themes that better serve to provide relationship stability. Should a couple fall in love, insecure attachment patterns may dominate, and although this may go some way to meet the need for mutual love and intimacy, it is not necessarily matched by the stabilising presence of the fulfilled need for mutual belonging. Moreover, as we have seen, it is not possible to maintain the intensity that typically accompanies 'falling in love' from a neuro-physiological point of view. The key to maintaining a satisfying and successful sexual relationship is the capacity to properly integrate the sexual and relational aspects of a relationship — and this will involve the decision to inhibit co-existing drives that energise sexual behaviour antagonistic to relationship.

Given that long-term sexual relationships are better served by some drives than others, the question is whether a relationship is necessarily compromised by the inevitable fluctuations of the drive profile, or whether these can be managed and influenced by the parties themselves. I have argued that such management *is* possible and necessary, but requires a conscious desire and decision to do so; that is, both parties need to be committed to the maintenance of the relationship. This allows the creation of shared plans and expectations, which help to shape drive profiles accordingly. In the absence of such agreement, the fluctuating drive profiles may find expression outside the existing relationship so that it remains vulnerable to dissolution. Such a decision will find support in traditional scripts, but not necessarily in other scripts, so that social support for such commitment may vary. Maintaining a sexual relationship requires not only the ability to manage the drive profile in keeping with decisions made, but also the ability to maintain the boundaries to protect the relationship and the ability to meet the ongoing needs — including sexual needs — required by the relationship. Where a couple is successful in maintaining a sexual relationship in this way, self-efficacy, self-esteem and good mental health are promoted.

But the maintenance of a long-term sexual relationship has its challenges, and there are many ways a relationship can dissolve. Consider Alan, a company manager and happily married man. Alan found himself in the all-too-common circumstance of falling in love with his assistant, Stephanie. He loved his wife and was committed to his family, but against his own judgement and intent, he found himself attracted to Stephanie. He worked with her every day, and saw in her an attractive, warm, responsive and intelligent girl, who was a tremendous asset to the company. No doubt she was lovely at home too. He found himself thinking about her a lot, and wondering and fantasising about her, and how great it would be to be with her. He knew it was wrong. And although logic told him that pursuing a relationship with her would be costly in every way — it would destroy his marriage and family life, it could be bad for his career, and it would deplete his bank balance — yet he could not get her out of his mind. It was not even about sexual attraction — although he *was* sexually attracted to her — but it was more a fantasy of mutual desire, the recreation of old passions, and the magic of an imagined deep connection.

Alan obsessed about wanting Stephanie to notice him as a person, not just a work colleague. He wanted her to know how much he appreciated her, hoping she would in like manner appreciate him, even though he knew she could never belong to him. Every time she was around, he felt good but vigilant, looking for even the smallest signal that she, too, desired him, and understood and approved of his desire for her. It was an intoxicating feeling, yet he wanted the obsession to stop: it was a distraction affecting his concentration and his work performance. He knew it was illogical and felt guilty about it. But the impossibility of it all and the knowledge this could never be consummated did nothing to quench his desire and preoccupation with her.

Alan struggled with his own poorly understood drive profile: what set this unwanted desire in motion; what were the prevailing conditions? The desire did not in itself justify its consummation. It was a personal desire looking for relational expression, an individual obsession looking for social recognition. The latter would be disastrous. His internal conflict could not and should not be resolved by enacting his desires. Psychologically, the goal, as indeed Alan himself wanted, would be to deal with the drive without its consummation. He did not see the fulfilment of his fantasy as an expression of 'being true to himself', or the road to happiness. He wasn't unhappy. In fact, his fantasy competed with all that he believed in, was committed to, and had made him happy.

Alan recognised that this impulse needed to be dealt with so that he might remain true to his wife and children and peers and extended family: he belonged to them all. He was not living a lie in continuing to be sexually faithful to his wife; it was not a self-deception to fight his own impulses as if these impulses should somehow define his real self. Yet where once the fight against the impulse to embrace or pursue a forbidden sexual relationship was seen as a right and noble one, such a position may now be less convincing. It might now even be seen as unrealistic or unnatural, or a denial of a person's inherent right and freedom to pursue 'true love', as dictated by a fluctuating drive profile. Nevertheless, you and I might still agree that Alan should 'deal' with his impulses and remain true to his wife and family. But would we continue to take the same position if Alan should have fallen in love with a male colleague? Do the rules then change? Should he now pursue a sexual relationship with the man to remain 'true' to himself? How are such judgements to be made?

There may be fifty ways to leave your lover, but what are the reasons one might *want* to? Let us look at some typical ways a relationship might fail. A lover can be *pushed* away, *pulled* away, or simply find no room in the relationship. Lack of social support can also contribute to relationship failure and to general dissatisfaction in the relationship,[410] and inhibition drive themes can play a role, although such drives are more likely to interfere with the establishment of a sexual relationship in the first place than its subsequent dissolution. And importantly, the lack of decision by either party to commit to a sexual relationship in the first place — now common in many loose cohabitation arrangements — makes it vulnerable to dissolution.[411]

A lover might be pushed away if their partner becomes unsafe or unsavoury — they are critical, rejecting, or resentful towards the lover. Such resentment may be the consequences of unfulfilled expectations, reasonable or otherwise. But insecurities in the relationship resulting in jealousies and over-involvement (with attendant accusations and distrust) can also play a role in being pushed away.[412] A lover might be *pulled* away if they are unfulfilled or unsatisfied in the relationship. This might be because of unmet expectations; boredom; differences in interests, background, or intelligence; desire to be independent; living apart too long; making comparisons with others; or lack of drive fulfilment where drives are better met elsewhere. Or they might be seduced — drawn away by an affair and the promise of wonderful experiences.[413] Third, a lover may find no room in a relationship where their partner is self-sufficient and independent, or always 'right' so that there is no room for another point of view,[414] or the partner has relationships with family or friends that take the time and energy necessary to maintain the relationship with the lover. These other relationships become the primary external influences so that there is no room for the lover to negotiate shared views, goals, and values. Each of these represents a failure in the proper maintenance of connection, attachment, and belonging in the relationship; a focus on personal wants, rather than a failure in sexual arousal, desire, or attraction — although the latter also no doubt has the capacity to contribute to the dissolution of a sexual relationship.

And if we should choose to end the relationship, how do we return what we have given each other emotionally and sexually? What we now 'own' of each other, we cannot give back. How does the loss of the other person, with whom I have developed a sense of 'shared self', affect my ongoing sense of self?[415] Even though I might end my sexual relationship and enter a sexual relationship with someone else, what was transacted with the first person can remain even in the new relationship. Furthermore, the memories and transactions of the previous relationship has coloured the nature of the self entering the new relationship and will now colour the new one. But most importantly — and no doubt the reason why ending a sexual relationship is so often linked with poor mental health — is the multiple meanings and implications that relationship dissolution can associate with: perceived personal failure and loss of self-esteem; the anger of betrayal, rejection of self, and loss of trust; and the grief of loss of companionship and shared future, and economic loss. These meanings do not readily dissipate, and can result in longer-term anxiety and depression.

This is all the more reason to promote the therapeutic goal of maintaining the existing sexual relationship in the face of a changing drive profile: to preserve all that has been invested into it as much as to maintain the integrity of belonging.

Chapter 13

Some Stories to Finish With

W e finish with some narratives about sexual experiences and relationships which help highlight the complexities involved. These narratives are in fact narrative fragments, in that they do not give a
comprehensive history of attachments, conditioning, or values formation.
Nevertheless, each provides insights as much as they might stimulate further
questions for the psychologist. They cover a range of sexual experiences, and
each narrative tells something about the dynamic drive profile that energises
and directs the experience and relationship, and how past decisions and experiences colour current events. An important theme is the internal conflicts that
regularly appear. Each story includes internal conflict that emerges from a
complex drive profile. One's past history can interfere with current dynamics,
sexual desire and arousal can become confused, and attachments may occur
where belonging is not the goal. Where such conflict or misalignment occurs,
mental health can be compromised. Each narrative also tells us something
about the role of belonging in the experience and the relationship.

The contamination of association

I have earlier proposed that, consistent with the principles of classical learning
theory, the circumstances and cues that relate to early sexual experiences lay

the foundation for subsequent patterns of sexual response. Putting flesh on theoretical bones, I begin with two narratives that highlight the power of this aspect of the drive profile in the transition period. These narratives show how sexual conditioning has the potential to create confusion for an adolescent in the process of discovering their sexual self, including confusion about sexual orientation, because of the autonomous nature of the conditioned sexual response. But we also see how such sexual conditioning establishes long-term response patterns that shape a person's sexual self-image, and that are difficult to change. I begin with the story of Liam.

Social life at school had been difficult for Liam. His confidence was poor, and he often felt miserable. By age ten, Liam discovered porn, which provided a new and fascinating distraction for him. It helped him feel good. He desired more, and the images he accessed become more confronting. But it also fed his curiosity. He started to feel more grown up, more empowered. By around the age of twelve,[416] he was regularly surfing the net, easy access to the world of sex in the intimacy of his bedroom, no questions asked. He felt excited and guilty about taking part in an adult world of strange intimacies, seeing things he hadn't thought about before, things of which he tried to make sense. He shared his discoveries with friends who would come to his place. It gave him kudos and helped gain him acceptance. When he felt tired and flat after school, masturbating to the porn helped him to feel better. This might also happen when friends were there. He knew this was just experimentation and fun — it had nothing to do with romantic attraction. No-one took it seriously — not as they would have if girls and romance had been involved. It was just messing around. But the sexual arousal associated with the porn also became associated with his mates.

What started off as interesting and fun began to create anxiety. At first Liam only pursued images of heterosexual activity. He became sexually aroused, but the images left him feeling guilty. He thought of the people he knew and felt a bit strange about what he was doing. Then he discovered lesbian porn, and after this, gay porn. Oddly, the latter didn't seem so bad. Perhaps he found it harder to relate these images to people he knew. Even though he was driven more by curiosity than sexual desire, he became sexually aroused. He found that all sexually explicit scenes aroused him, regardless of the gender involved. Over time he saw a lot of porn: it distracted him when he was feeling low, angry or alone. He would feel momentarily better, although he felt a bit disconnected from people afterwards. He didn't understand this effect on him — the intensity of his experiences, the overwhelming desire to do something that felt so good in the doing, and yet the feeling of emptiness and disconnection that came afterwards.[417]

Liam had no romantic inclinations to men, yet he become sexually aroused to gay images and thoughts. This was confusing. What if he really *was* gay? He became tormented with self-doubt. To try and figure out what his sexual orientation really was, he'd ask himself: do I prefer to kiss a guy or a girl? These uncertainties remained, haunting him into early adulthood. When homosexual thoughts and images intruded and aroused him, he would ask himself: am I really gay or bisexual? The fear that he might be gay made him feel guilty for being homophobic. What if he decided he wasn't gay, but twenty years from now he discovered that he really *was* gay? The images and fantasies that had conditioned his sexual responses now tormented him. He became increasingly anxious and depressed. When he wasn't busy, intrusive and arousing homosexual thoughts destabilised his sense of self, and his mood would spiral downwards. He was constantly evaluating and questioning himself, monitoring his own reactions when he saw various people. What aroused him sexually? To whom was he *really* attracted? Who was he sexually?

To cope with the stress, he turned to porn again. Watching *any* porn aroused him — lesbian, gay, or straight — creating further confusion and self-doubt. The images would stay with him; states of hyper-arousal would destabilise him. He found it very difficult to shut the images and thoughts out, to refocus, and to get control of things again. He became preoccupied with the thoughts and found himself dreaming about gay sex; seeing gay friends exacerbated his confusion. He regularly masturbated to these thoughts and images, even as he began to realise this had contributed to his confusing arousal patterns. His mood depended upon what his sexual focus was, on whether he had viewed porn, and who had had been with.

Then one day Liam fell in love with Jess. They had sex. Regularly. Whatever insecurity and self-doubt he might have struggled with earlier evaporated in the heat of intense passion. He felt accepted and desired. He could think of nothing else but being with Jess and abandoning himself to sexual pleasure. But soon his love for her became confounded with his love of sex with her. He felt charged up, sexualised, strong and confident, in control, and masculine. His desire for sex eclipsed everything else. Importantly, here was proof that he wasn't gay: he experienced both sexual desire and arousal with her.

But the intensity of their passion was unsustainable. As the months passed, he became emotionally exhausted. His libido diminished and he started to withdraw. Jess reacted to his withdrawal by becoming critical of him. This reactivated Liam's school memories of inadequacy and he became more withdrawn. His experience of dominance, of being empowered and in charge of the relationship had generated feelings of sexual desire and arousal. But he was now starting to become aware of her as a person, and she was exposing his vulnerability. As interpersonal awareness replaced sexual passion, sexual desire for Jess faded. It was very confusing.

Once again he turned porn to feel better. He became aroused again, but this fed self-doubt: had he enjoyed sex with Jess because she was a woman, or simply because it was sex? What was the relationship without sex? Would it have made a difference if she had been someone else, or even if she wasn't a woman? Could the passion have been the same with a man? What had been his real motive? Yet he thought he was in love with her, and they had had times of amazing sex. Now he wondered: 'Am I still in love with Jess? I'm no longer feeling the way I think I should or the way I *want* to feel towards her. It freaks me out when I now see her and feel nothing. What does it mean?'

Fears returned that he might one day discover he really *was* gay. The more he evaluated his relationship with Jess, the more disconnected he became. After the relationship ended, he noticed that he might feel attracted to and have sexual desire for other girls, but anxious memories and self-doubt prevented sexual arousal, adding to his confusion. In the end, he found it easier to stay away from sexual relationships altogether — at least for now.

•　　•　　•

Liam's history of masturbating to gay and transsexual porn left him confused. Sexual arousal was conditioned to a range of sexual images, but there had been no integration of his sexual and relational self. With Gerald, there were similarities — but also important differences. Like Liam, Gerald struggled with his sexuality. Like Liam, conditioned sexual arousal played a role in the confusion of Gerald's transition years and interfered with the integration of his sexual and relational self. The circumstances, however, were quite different. Here is his story.

Gerald was an excellent student: competitive, ambitious, and well-liked at school. He wasn't one to question his superiors. On the contrary, he was keen to please his teachers as this enhanced his chances being successful. He understood authority, and his housemaster represented supreme authority. He had the ability to make or break the future of the students. So when the housemaster invited Gerald into his room at night after lights out, Gerald obliged. He thought it odd, and didn't understand what was happening. Yet, being a good student, getting special attention wasn't surprising. Besides, there wasn't anyone he could ask about this odd request. But the unexpected sexual activities that took place that night unsettled him — the subsequent memories kept him awake as he struggled to make sense of it.

Then, a few nights later, it happened again. It became a regular event. The nocturnal visits to the housemaster's room were embarrassing and uncomfortable, but he learned to shut these feelings out. It was just one of those things one has to endure to get ahead, a rite of passage known only to him and his housemaster. Nothing was forced upon him. If he'd chosen to, he might have stopped it. But his social standing might then be compromised. Gerald himself had no sexual interest, even though he was a teenager. His focus had been on his studies, his sport, and on social recognition. Nevertheless, these experiences awakened sexual awareness, and he began to fantasise and to dream about having sex with men. Despite his growing awareness and familiarity with sexual behaviour, he remained largely indifferent to sexual experiences and meanings even as he accommodated the housemaster. He sought to disconnect himself from the sexual arousal that the housemaster stimulated in him. He put up with it to get ahead, and in doing so, became accustomed to sexual intimacy in the absence of sexual desire, love and commitment. Sexual intimacy had other purposes.

In fact, the experience gave Gerald an unexpected feeling of power and a doorway into adulthood. In some ways he had become equal to the housemaster. He had a relationship that he believed no other student had. He had a secret that made him more important than other students, one that gave him an invisible status, one that not only made *him* vulnerable, but also the housemaster. Moreover, the favours he granted the housemaster might be returned to him in academic and social status. While the night ritual was unwanted and the sexual activity distasteful, it was also the ultimate test in obedience and recognition by someone important — it was an opportunity to prove himself. And so he tacitly agreed to the activity, compromising objectivity and the ability to make moral judgements, and thus removing the basis for anger or disgust towards the housemaster. If he were to blame anyone, he'd have to blame himself also. The housemaster and he both benefitted from the encounters. They'd become partners in promoting each other's agendas: the housemaster, his sexual pleasure; and Gerald, social status creating an open door to his future.

But Gerald emerged compromised and confused. His familiarity with homosexual behaviour made him a target for other men seeking homosexual encounters. He discovered that homosexual porn and fantasy aroused him, even though he had no romantic desire for men. But he did have romantic interest in women, although he didn't fantasise about them sexually. He subsequently discovered he had sexual desire for women, although the conditioned sexual arousal to gay thoughts and images persisted. He became uncomfortable with his own nakedness as it associated with shame: he became disconnected from his body and emotions.

Gerald wanted to start afresh. He wanted to marry a woman and have a sexual relationship in the context of love and commitment, and put behind him his sexual confusion. And so he found a girl and married her, proving he was a family man capable of a heterosexual relationship. But his marriage didn't last. Although he sought to be a good husband and sexually desired his wife, he was unable to be emotionally present for her. His emotional absence had helped him to survive the attention of his housemaster and kept at bay the shameful memories associated with sexual activity, but it now prevented emotional intimacy with his wife. There were many secrets he wished to keep from her, leaving him feeling guilty and self-critical. Furthermore, he had come to understand relationships essentially in terms of power, status, and control. Now he was the one whose power and authority should be respected, and she should acquiesce to his sexual desires and initiatives. But this wasn't the language his wife accepted and it wasn't how she understood a marriage relationship. She left Gerald.

Gerald despaired. His social standing had been damaged, and his commitment to 'doing the right thing' left him wounded. Moreover, Gerald found his non-sexual relationships with men continued to be a source of tension and disquiet. Sexual fantasies and dreams involving other men continued to play on his mind, a long-term reminder of adolescent experiences. He fantasised sexual encounters with men, but was repulsed by them at the same time. He wanted to have normal friendships with men, to go to the beach for a swim or to go to the gym with mates. He wanted to be able to greet them with a hug, as they did with each other. But it was difficult to touch a man or to see his naked body without it becoming sexualised, and this distressed him. Although popular, he nevertheless felt isolated and alone, different from others for whom relationships appeared straightforward and clean. It was a feeling that never really left him.

•　　•　　•

Both Gerald and Liam experienced the effects of positive sexual conditioning: that is, certain contexts served to stimulate sexual arousal. Repeated early experiences of sexual arousal in the presence of homosexual stimuli, unwanted by Gerald, and sought after by Liam, resulted in ongoing arousal to homosexual stimuli, *even in the absence of sexual attraction or desire.*

Generally we envisage the classical conditioning process as an involuntary physiological response to an *external* or environmental cue, such as Pavlov was famous for describing. And so the external cue of a woman in revealing clothes might trigger an involuntary sexual arousal response in a man. However, an involuntary sexual arousal response may also be triggered by *internal* cues such as memories, thoughts and images which associate with sexual behaviour. Simply remembering or envisaging a circumstance associated with a sexual experience may be enough to trigger involuntary sexual arousal. Importantly, these conditioned responses can be created in the course of early sexual experiences, shaping the drive profile of adulthood. First sexual experiences (including simple exposure to porn and masturbating to porn) and fantasies of varied description[418] generally occur in adolescence, and these can play a role in conditioning the sexual arousal response.

A story about Gender Dysphoria

This is a story that highlights confusions and the fluidity in self-perception that can occur when the gender embraced and the biological sex one is assigned don't align. This circumstance can take someone on a journey from Gender Dysphoria to identifying as transsexual, or to same-sex orientation, or to an asexual position and lifestyle.

Kim wanted to be a girl. He didn't really know why: it wasn't that he felt like a girl in a boy's body, or that he was aware of being effeminate. He didn't even know what it was about being a girl that he wanted. He just wanted to be a girl. Perhaps it was something in his mother he identified with, or perhaps it would give him permission to say or feel or do things he now felt inhibited from saying, feeling, or doing. Perhaps he was frightened of the social demands and expectations he associated with being male: to be tough and dominant. Whatever the reason, as an adolescent he would regularly indulge in fantasies about being a girl — what it would be like for the rest of his life — or just for a year, or for a day even. He rather hoped that magically it might happen. But when his magical thinking didn't come true, he pushed his thoughts away.

His home hadn't been a happy one. His father was strict and his mother permissive. They had been in constant conflict. Kim had withdrawn, but conflict had remained within. He wanted to be what he wasn't, and didn't understand why. Did this internal conflict mirror the external conflict he witnessed between his parents? Kim began to experiment with masturbation. His experimentation involved both male and female friends — experiences which provided him with passing distraction, pleasure and relief, yet only confusing him more. He masturbated frequently, and then had a fumbling sexual encounter with a man. Although he'd never had desire for intimacy with another man, he enjoyed the experience, and found that he was sexually aroused by it. When he was later massaged by a male without being distracted by emotional talk, he again became sexually aroused.

But it was the opposite with girls. He'd had a girlfriend, but didn't have sex with her. He liked her, and was emotionally intimate with her, but she had her own difficulties. He identified with her conflicts and wanted to help her. Perhaps he knew that sex wasn't on her mind: there was too much else going on for her. Perhaps he felt inadequate, or overwhelmed by the complexities of having a relationship with her. Perhaps he didn't want to exploit her vulnerability by having sex with her. In any event, he didn't feel sexually aroused by her. He noticed that although women could be attractive, he didn't think of them sexually. When his friends thoughtfully shouted him to a brothel to help him along the road to masculinity, instead of having sex, he had a long chat with the girl. He wasn't aroused. He liked her, wanted to get to know her, and liked to talk about himself.

Kim decided he must be gay, and 'came out' in his late teens. But his family didn't understand or didn't want to understand what was happening for him, and his internal conflicts found no acknowledgement or resolution. And he still wanted to be a woman. His confusion and self-rejection found expression in drinking and drugs — partly because he hated himself, partly as an attempt to escape his situation. He had arguments with his family. He became suicidal. He felt isolated and misunderstood, and eventually felt nothing anymore. His emotions seemed frozen in his body, in the tightness of his muscles. He continued to see other men. Yet he never experienced romantic attachment to any of them. It was just sex — a 'safe' avenue for sexual release. He always chose dominant males, and he chose the role of submissive partner. He liked to be treated as female. But as much as he wanted to be a girl, he also wanted to be punished for wanting to be a girl.

It felt like there were two Kims at war within: a weak, submissive Kim — the girl Kim; and a dominant, tough Kim — the boy Kim. The tough Kim had little time for the submissive Kim, criticising him for his sensitivity and vulnerability, and strongly disapproving of his having sex with men. Yet the tough Kim was also protective. He could stop others taking advantage of him, and could push him to do things he wouldn't otherwise have done. He wanted to get rid of the tough Kim because he was afraid of the demands this might make of him, but couldn't get rid of him without getting rid of himself. The temptation to kill himself didn't leave him: it would stop the never-ending dialogue in his head. The opposing forces within him — sexual arousal without emotional intimacy (associated with men), and emotional intimacy without sexual arousal (associated with women) — found no integration and left him confused. It also left him without a sexual relationship. He had sex with those with whom he had no relationship, and he had relationship with those with whom he had no sex.

Kim's narrative describes a lack of integration occurring at two levels — masculine with feminine, and sexual with relational — ultimately preventing the formation of a successful sexual relationship, and resulting in significant mental health problems. Kim failed to integrate his feminine (his submissive, emotional, vulnerable self) and his masculine (his dominant, tough, protective self). This interfered with the integration of relational intimacy with sexual desire and arousal. Although the meanings that associate with masculine and feminine vary from person to person, some form of integration needs to be achieved. This requires an embrace of both masculine and feminine aspects within oneself, but also an embrace of one's sexual identity to confidently express oneself sexually in relationship.

A story about porn

Seduction does not always come in the form of an attractive personal assistant or personal trainer: pornographic images or active fantasy can do just as affec- tive a job. Mostly, we might battle against *actual* sexual history where it competes with a current sexual relationship. However, a virtual sexual history centred on *fantasy* (personal fantasy or cyberspace; romantic or explicitly erotic) can be just as powerful. Fantasy creates ideals and expectations about sexual performance or romantic behaviours which, in turn, can result in rela- tionship frustrations and disappointments. And eventual alienation. Hidden 'expectation traps' can snare a spouse or partner.

Shirley struggled with her self-image and with maintaining sexual desire as she negotiated the years of menopause. Nevertheless, she felt confident and secure in her marriage. It had been a fairytale marriage in many respects. Married when young to Don who adored her, she could remember many good years as they shared parenting and supported each other in the ups and downs of life. There was a strong sense of belonging to each other. In many respects, Don was her 'home'. She felt connected and happy and fortunate to have such a good man who'd provided well for the family. And she, in her turn, had loved and nurtured him during difficult times, and had felt solid in the warmth of his company. There'd never been a question that their sexual life had been less than satisfactory. It had been a long and pleasant summer of love and intimacy. Now more than ever, as the children left home, they had each other to enjoy.

But then a cold wind began to blow through the relationship. Don started to become increasingly distant from her. Shirley didn't at first connect it to the increasing time he was spending on his laptop and iPhone, looking at images of women. When she asked him what he was doing, Don said he was just 'looking'. She didn't argue, but felt increasing disquiet. She couldn't understand why he wanted to do this. Wasn't she good enough for him? How had she failed him? She felt her confidence dropping, and felt increasingly vulnerable. The porn that his curiosity had let into their relationship was like a stranger let into their shared space — the territory that was once theirs alone. Their sexual experiences had once belonged to them as a couple, and to no-one else. Now there were sexual experiences and ideas that entered their space that didn't belong to her, and she felt violated. She was competing for his attention and sexual pleasure with images of young and seductive women in poses and activities alien to her. She was competing with whatever fantasies these might stimulate in Don. And she was losing.

'I'm not doing anything wrong,' Don would reassure her and himself. He thought: 'Of *course* I love her: I wouldn't expect her to understand that this is normal for a man, and it doesn't do any harm. It's not like I'm having an affair, and I don't intend leaving her. Now, *that* would be wrong. She's a woman, and thinks differently, but I can't let her naive and sheltered views stop me. I'm a man, and want to enjoy myself — I don't want to miss out. There *are* other women, after all, and I'm just curious. It stimulates and arouses me: I feel more masculine. I must admit though that the stuff I see arouses me more than Shirley does now, and I'm starting to get annoyed about her negativity. If only she was open to joining me, and experimenting and doing the stuff I see the girls do on the screen.'

Shirley didn't know how to respond, but she knew that what the girls were doing on the screen wasn't her way to express her love for Don. She noticed how little attention he now paid her, making it even harder to feel close. She would say things, but he wouldn't hear. He no longer asked how she was or what she was doing. He seemed irritable. He no longer seemed to care — he was much more attentive to the images than he was to her. Don didn't want to admit it at first, but he'd become unsettled in his otherwise secure world. His eyes started to appreciate other women when he and Shirley went out, and he started to wonder if they might be more adventurous than Shirley. Shirley noticed too.

The cold wind turned to ice when one day he told Shirley he no longer felt the same way about her. He finally voiced what she'd feared. He'd become a stranger to her, and she'd ceased to be interesting and desirable to him. The safety and trust and security that she'd rested in for many years evaporated. She no longer felt welcome in the home they'd shared: she felt shut out, and instinctively shut him out. She felt that she was intruding on space that had become *his* space and was no longer *their* space. She no longer belonged. Whatever warmth she might have felt towards him had now gone. All she could feel was coldness. Then she knew the relationship was finished, even though there'd hardly been an angry word spoken between them, and there was no woman who'd seduced her husband, and they'd had such a long and stable history together. Pornographic images and fantasy had stolen her husband.

The debate around pornography tends to be either a debate about censorship, or whether pornography promotes sexual violence. However, the capacity for porn to intrude upon or replace an existing sexual relationship tends to be overlooked.[419] Clinical experience shows that through its capacity to condition arousal responses to new and different sexual images, it can interfere with existing sexual relationship patterns. The focus is on the pornographic image; not the partner. The focus is on eroticism and sexual performance, not the integration of relationship needs with sexual needs. It feeds the drives of pleasure and desire, not relationship needs. Furthermore, indulging drives of adventure and curiosity and pleasure in this way returns a powerful but temporary reward, which in the long term *increases* the drives through dopamine activation, rather than sating them. The trigger for sexual arousal becomes boredom (hence the desire for adventure), stress (a form of escapism), or seeing someone sexy (to aid sexual fantasy), rather than the sexual desire for a person *as a person*.

Stories about ghosts of the past

We earlier saw how Liam and Gerald were affected by ghosts of the past in the form of conditioned sexual arousal patterns. But ghosts from the past involving earlier sexual experiences can appear in many shapes and disguises — sometimes seducing, sometimes tormenting the lover in a relationship. Even where a couple believe they have achieved good integration of sexual and relational drives, where love and intimacy have been established and the relationship appears otherwise healthy, these ghosts can haunt and fracture a relationship. Nikki Gemmel, author of the erotic novel *The Bride Stripped Bare*, once wrote: 'That dangerous allure of first love: why is it that an early, defining passion can whisper through our blood our entire lives, becoming the standard of intensity by which all other partnerships are measured?'[420] She observes that this first love experience often occurs at an age when we are 'at our most insecure and vulnerable'. And because of this, the openness and vulnerability, the naive hope and trust, the joy of being discovered and loved, of giving oneself fully to another person, a profound imprinting can be created that 'can whisper through our blood our entire lives'. In so doing, the experiences of first sexual encounters or first love can beckon a couple back to one another long after each has entered new relationships.

Julie was one such person who discovered the lingering power of first love. After several early relationships, Julie had settled and married a loving and attentive man. She couldn't fault his love and tenderness and enjoyed his devotion to her and their children for years. But she was aware of a restlessness that remained with her that she couldn't understand. One day, she happened upon a chance encounter with the man who'd been her first love when she was a young woman, and who himself had also long since married and had a family. She'd never forgotten him, nor the moments of discovery and intense pleasure they'd known together as they explored love for the first time. Nor had he forgotten her. Although she wasn't conscious of comparing her husband with this first love, there remained a bond and shared memories that time hadn't erased. The encounter awakened a deep desire to return to her first love, the first man to whom she'd given and joined herself. She wanted to relive her first passion. Against her own better judgement, she left her astonished and devastated husband, abandoned the stable life she had with him and their children, and embarked on a passionate reunion with her childhood sweetheart.

Julie's experience has been made more common through Facebook, which facilitates the remaking of old connections. The ghosts of Julie's past had seduced her into recreating the remembered passions of the past. But ghosts of the past can also be of a different kind, a source of torment and distress: both the ghosts of a person's own past, and those of their sexual partner. Such ghosts can condition unwanted responses.

Helen was married to James. She loved him and felt sexual desire for him. Yet when they sought sexual intimacy, she found that, despite her conscious desire for James, her body refused to allow him sexual entry. It seemed that somehow sexual intimacy had become associated with conflict, disempowerment, shame, and guilt, and that her body was setting its own protective agenda. Her subjective self said 'I want James', but her bodily responses rejected him, creating a confusion and frustration that left her with no desire for sexual intimacy at all. Where was this confusion coming from?

It transpired that a ghost of past sexual experiences was haunting Helen. Helen had been taught that sex was only to be enjoyed in the context of marriage, and that a woman should be submissive to her husband. And so, when she was still unmarried and in a relationship with a partner pushing for sexual intercourse, she was in a dilemma. She didn't want to lose him, but neither did she want to betray the values she'd been taught. Should she submit to him? She negotiated a compromise: she would consent to oral sex to keep him. In doing so, she believed she was 'submitting' to his sexual desires yet retaining her virginity for marriage. Nevertheless, the level of sexual intimacy and behaviour she submitted to exceeded what she really wanted and felt right about. Helen had surrendered considerable control: the only control she retained was refusing vaginal sex.

Although Helen honoured the compromise she'd negotiated, she nevertheless felt disempowered, violated, and guilty. Their consensual sexual activities were not nearly as consensual as she imaged. She hated what she was doing, and yet acted as if she was a willing partner. She was sexually aroused and wanted to respond, but actively inhibited her responses to retain some sort of control. She wanted him and largely submitted to him, but resented the position he'd put her in. The relationship eventually finished, but the ghosts of her experiences (in this case, the negative emotions conditioned to sexual arousal) remained to haunt her in her marriage to James, where the same pattern of simultaneous sexual desire and sexual inhibition re-emerged.

A different kind of conflict rooted in past sexual experiences haunted Joe. Even before he was teenager, he'd been attracted to young girls, and this attraction would revisit him repeatedly, eventually disrupting his marriage to Annette. He'd always seen girls as pretty, accepting, innocent, trusting, open, 'uncomplicated', and vulnerable. He was sensitive and unsure about himself, but with them he felt strong, wanted, magnanimous, and empowered — a man of the world they could look up to and feel safe with. He could look after such a girl, be important, and protect her. And so through his teenage years he often fantasised about such relationships, and at times, these fantasies would merge into sexual ones. Of course, the imagined mutual pleasuring would always be consensual: acceptance and admiration of him on their part was an important part of the experience.

He was first drawn to adolescent Annette because of her vulnerability and perceived need of him. She was struggling for acceptance and for someone to take care of her. But it was some years before he finally married her, and in that time she'd been drawn into a wild world of drug-taking and 'consensual' sexual exploitation, looking for love and acceptance. Joe knew about this: it made him all the more important as a rescuer and protector of the vulnerable girl. But she'd already lost her innocence, and it was innocence he had wanted: a childlike dependence, acceptance and need for him. And so, he not only had to rescue her, but he also had to be magnanimous about her past — to forgive her for her lost innocence. He loved Annette, and was confident that her past would be put behind them. But it failed to do so. As the years passed, the ghosts of her early sexual experiences began to haunt him. He hadn't been able to protect her from these. What was worse, she didn't appear to regret what had happened, or to appreciate his role as her rescuer. She had become strong and hard and self-protective. She needed him less than he imagined.

Joe became increasingly bitter and resentful. He felt he was competing with her past lovers. He smoked pot after they married — trying to imitate what she'd known, to be part of her world, to try to match what she'd experienced; but also to numb his emotions. But he couldn't stop the feeling he was competing with her past sexual experiences, and with her past 'loves'. Was she comparing him with them? Or was it his imagination? He wanted to forgive and forget, but instead became frustrated with her and increasingly jealous that she'd lost her virginity to someone else. Joe felt she had connection and intimacy with the one she lost her virginity to rather than with him. She shared memories and a special connection — physical, spiritual, and emotional — with this person, rather than with him. He knew that in their own way these men had loved her, and she them. He had to share Annette with men from the past. Even though Joe and Annette were now married, did she really belong to him? He was competing with her first loves, trying to get closer, to be the one that belonged to her, and she to him. He pressed her for details about her past, and she told him what he wanted to know. But it only made it worse: it created more images of a girl he didn't really know and who didn't belong to him alone. Annette was upset about his anger and jealousy, and told him she felt more accepted and loved by the men that had had sex with her in her drug-filled youth than by Joe.

This only antagonised Joe more and drove him to despair. Their relationship deteriorated into regular alcohol-fuelled arguments, each reacting to the other. He saw her as closed, untrustworthy, ungrateful, and unpredictable. She saw him as judgemental, without love or affection, not trusting, and controlling. Nevertheless, they continued to have sexual intimacy, searching for connection and mutual acceptance. But things didn't change. If only Annette would admit guilt and shame about her past and share vulnerability with Joe, he might be restored to the role of a rescuer that she was indebted to. Joe found himself returning to earlier fantasies of young adolescent girls who would belong to him, accepting and understanding and needing him and preserving their virginity for him — all that Annette hadn't been or done. He would feel safe, and not be competing with anyone. He knew this was wrong, and felt guilty and in great turmoil. But he was unable to resolve his inner struggles. The thoughts and desires wouldn't go away, and the conflict continued until eventually Annette left him. Ghosts haunting their past had destroyed their future.

A final story about sex and not belonging

We finally come to a story that highlights how attachment establishes in an ongoing sexual relationship, despite a stated commitment to not belong.

Dayna had left her marriage of many years because she'd felt trapped. Her life had become defined by her husband's career. Belonging to him meant losing her sense of self. She'd always tried to do the right thing — even as a little girl. But doing the right thing was to gain another's approval, often at cost of her sense of self. In the end, she still had difficulty accepting herself, feeling like a little girl seeking approval, never being 'good enough'. But now, having left her husband, she was no longer under pressure to do the 'right thing' to gain acceptance. She finally felt free, and intended to remain so.

She met Adam. Adam was charming. He enjoyed and wanted Dayna, and she felt good around him. He always complimented her. She found it hard to believe that he should want to be with her, and was careful not to disappoint him. The times they had together were great. He sent text messages continuously. They regularly had meals. She slept with him. Sex was exciting, passionate. Increasingly, she looked forward to her time with him. The more sex she had with him, the more she wanted. There were no expectations: each remained free to do whatever they wanted. Still, she didn't want to lose him. She would do anything to keep him, even if it meant giving him all the freedom he wanted. At the same time, she didn't want to lose her own hard-won freedom, and was pleased he granted her hers. It seemed a good deal.

Adam needed his freedom. No entanglements. No obligations. No contract. No questions. Such unquestioning acceptance felt good: it was what Dayna also wanted. She had nothing to prove to Adam: he desired her as she was. And so the relationship developed, a relationship of freedom. Adam contacted her regularly, yet revealed nothing of himself. She knew he would only continue stay if he was forever free to do what he wanted. But she also realised she mustn't become attached to him. What little she knew of him was that he'd never made a lasting commitment to anyone, and she was fine with that. They committed to making no commitments. They would never belong to each other.

Yet, perversely, the more sex they had, the more Dayna's feelings for Adam deepened and her expectations of the relationship increased, as did her fear that she might one day lose him, despite the agreement that there was no agreement. There was never talk of the future, or of each other. They simply enjoyed the moment. They were sexually obsessed with each other. Despite herself, she wanted him to belong to her — yet all he was prepared to offer her was to be 'good friends'. They were close, but not really — the not knowing kept her aroused and interested. The desire to have but not having was somehow exciting, an ongoing hope never consummated. She was falling in love. Attachment without belonging. But she began to question herself. Was she really good enough for him? Would he one day move on? She found herself looking to interpret every nuance of his behaviour, trying to work out meanings, to understand and know him, second-guessing his intentions, looking for clues as to what he felt and wanted and whether he might really love her. It was a game. She fought her growing attachment to him. She didn't *want* to be attached to him. In her love for him, she wanted him to be free, to maintain an 'open relationship'. She was hurting, but couldn't show it: if he should think she was becoming attached to him, he'd stop seeing her. But she was becoming a wreck.

Eventually Dayna couldn't do it anymore. She had given herself to Adam, but had gained nothing — no security, no reassurance. And so she told Adam she loved him and that she wanted him. He reminded her: 'I didn't want a committed relationship — I'm just not good at it'. He encouraged her to get a 'proper boyfriend', but kept in touch with her all the same. They'd given each other total freedom, and yet she felt trapped: trapped by her love for him, by her promise to ask no questions and make no demands, by her promise to leave him free. She felt she'd be cheating on him if she saw someone else. Nevertheless, she tried. It went nowhere. She fought jealousy and insecurity. Was he seeing other women? Were they younger, better than she? Although they loved their times together and had some kind of bond, she did not belong to him; neither did he belong to her. He said 'I'm not in love with you, but I love the way we have sex together.' She was his friend and sex partner — but that was all.

She suspected he was seeing someone else. She forced herself to say this was fine — but it wasn't. There were secrets — many of them. He was mysterious, and there were many things he wouldn't say. This at the same time excited and alienated her. When he finally admitted to dating others, he said he wanted to see her still. But it only confused her. She was jealous and hurt and depressed, even though he'd only been true to the arrangement. She felt humiliated, mixed up — she wanted him but didn't. She loved him but felt used. Adam continued to flirt with Dayna — and she continued to love his sexual advances, the sexual play, the sexual encounters. But she hoped for more, even though she knew now there were others. Perhaps she was the one he wanted the most, perhaps she could draw him away from the others, perhaps she could be enough for him.

But the frequency of their contact diminished. It confirmed what Dayna had feared all along: that he didn't want her because she wasn't good enough. Her self-esteem plummeted. She wanted him — but knew this would never happen. He didn't want to be owned, and nor did she. That's why she'd left her marriage. Yet even with no demand or expectation, he'd controlled the relationship and got what he wanted. He might not have 'owned her' and she might not have 'belonged' to him, yet she'd done whatever he'd asked, just like a little girl looking for approval. She had remained under his spell — she'd been his mistress. He'd enjoyed the chase. She'd enjoyed being desired. They'd somehow become addicted to each other, but she realised she didn't want this. She felt out of control, helpless, and used. She hated herself, she was in pain, she became depressed. Dayna realised that, after all, somehow, she really *did* want to belong to Adam and she wanted him to belong to her, and so to exclude all others. But it was too late.

In this final story we observe the powerful nature of the drive to attach and belong that emerges in a sexual relationship, even where both parties had been committed to each other's freedom. Although there was possibly a fear of entrapment present in Adam inhibiting the drive, it proved to be a source of torment for Dayna. When Adam was sexually intimate with Dayna, she felt his body belonged to her as much as her body belonged to him — it became shared territory — despite their agreed non-belonging. Furthermore, how could she give her body without giving herself? If she gave her body without giving herself, she needed to be disconnected from her body. Having given of herself to Adam, she couldn't remain separate and autonomous from him, as he now knew her and had something of her. Moreover, each time they had sex, Dayna's attachment to Adam grew as neurochemicals creating bonding and desire for him were released, despite the secret life he kept from her.

Attempts to override the basic drives of attachment and belonging in arrangements such as in open marriage and in casual sex relationships have a poor history of genuine success. In 'open marriage' a couple have a partner to whom they belong, yet retain the freedom to have sexual encounters with others — but not to become too involved with the others as to destroy the marriage. But research into open relationships reveals underlying tensions. Tennov noted: 'Sociologist Mirra Komarovsky's study of the emotional and sexual life of college youth supports the tendency for the majority to require fidelity and exclusivity in their mates despite the rationality of "free" relationships. She reported that in open relationships, the less-involved partner in fact gained the degree of freedom because the more-involved individual accepted it "as the price of continuing or renewing the relationship.""[421] Tennov concluded that a problem with 'open marriage' is that both people do not feel the same way at the same time.

But even in casual sexual encounters with mutual consent where no relationship is intended, and where there is insufficient shared experience to begin developing a meaningful relationship, each partner nevertheless tends to treat the body of the other person in that moment as if it belonged to them. And because the body belongs to the inner self of the person, both body and inner self are normally 'given' to the other person through the sexual encounter, even where this might not be the intent, and where the preservation of separateness and autonomy is sought. Where there is no intent to 'give' of oneself to the other person, each nevertheless takes from the other. This being so, casual sex violates a key purpose of the sexual encounter to the degree that the encounter is an avenue to interpersonal discovery, attachment, and belonging.

The individual freedom retained in casual sex becomes associated with self-protection, distrust, and fear of rejection. Entering into different casual relationships means repeated risk-taking behaviour which perversely can enhance the sexual experience: fear associated with risk contributes to sexual arousal. Such mutual risk-taking can also contribute to a form of intimacy — but it is an intimacy based on shared risk, not trust, and certainly not on any sense of belonging. The sexual chemistry is different, and a different appetite is developed. The brain becomes conditioned to risk as part of the sexual experience, yet in time each person still yearns for intimacy and belonging and 'home', after the adventure and risks of youth fade. And if this is not found in a sexual relationship, it will be sought in other ways in other contexts. But when the inner self and the body are in proper relationship, one self voluntarily encounters another in a sexual relationship; each self gives something of itself and its body to the other; memories are shared and futures mesh; and each self is changed by the other, enhancing the sense of attachment and belonging over time. The self is shaped by the sexual encounter in ways unseen, but ever present.

Chapter Endnotes

Chapter 1

1 Cretella (2016) observes: 'The norm for human design is to be conceived either male or female. Sex chromosome pairs "XY" and "XX" are genetic markers of sex, male and female, respectively... Human sexuality is binary by design with the purpose being the reproduction of our species' (p. 51). While sex might be indeterminate (for example, because of genetic abnormalities), or while there might be confusion between gender identity and biological sex, there is no third sex or gender.

2 'Maleness' and 'femaleness', or masculinity and femininity, is generally understood as *gender identity* — that is, the sex the inner self identifies with. However, gender *identity* is coloured by gender *expression* or *role*. Gender roles are culturally formed and accepted ways in which 'maleness' and 'femaleness' find expression. While gender *roles* are cultural constructs, inherent maleness and femaleness are not. The psychological aspects of maleness and femaleness is affected by the intrauterine hormonal environment during the second semester — it is not a simple function of physical sexual characteristics or social constructs as such, although normally it will align with both. A further conundrum is whether maleness and femaleness are mutually exclusive categories, as the dilemma of the person suffering Gender Dysphoria implies ('I am physically male, but subjectively female'), or whether they exist as poles on a continuum,

as gender roles and behaviours do. I would argue that while gender *roles* might occur on a continuum, gender *identity* does not, reflecting as it normally does the binary nature of physical sexual characteristics. Nevertheless, a few children may suffer Gender Dysphoria where there is lack of alignment between the physical sex characteristics and gender identity. Fortunately, for most of these children, this dysphoria resolves naturally over time (Cretella (2016)) — while for some, this resolution involves embrace of homosexual orientation (see, for example, Singh (2012)).

3   Such experienced dysphoria may also relate to latent homosexual impulses (homosexual transexuals), reflecting possible self-rejection or rejection of a particular gender role; or it may reflect an erotic desire to embrace or own the perceived characteristics or role of the other sex — or even to *become* the other sex (autogynephilic transexuals) — rather than that it represent the 'wrong' sex being in the 'wrong' body (see, for example, Bailey & Triea (2007)). Either way, the binary nature of gender is evident.

4   For more on the notion of the brain and body as expressions of the inner self or 'I', see Schneider (2013); see also Tolman, Bowman, & Fahs (2014), pp. 759-804.

5   This approach is not without hazard, given the current gender debate: see Tolman, Bowman, & Fahs (2014), p. 759. However, alternative approaches are not suggested in the literature. This approach builds on the 'essentialist' view, which emphasizes sexuality as innate, rather than learned: genes, hormones and biological processes are seen as the key players (see, for example, Buss (1994), and Symons (1979)). The brain abstracts meaning from such innate biological events, and these meanings form the basis of shared understandings upon which behaviour and language depends. The social constructionists (building on the work of Berger and Luckman (1967)), however, argue that social processes (including language and shared understandings) define sexual experience and behaviour, suggesting an inherent relativity in its definition (a particular society 'constructs' the notions, based on its own agendas). However, such relativity in definition is problematic: it ignores biological imperatives. There needs to be integration.

6   Research suggests women have greater difficulty differentiating between desire and arousal, while men generally experience sexual desire and arousal as separate events. Indeed, there appears to be limited overlap between actual genital response and the experience of sexual desire and arousal in women (Brotto & Smith (2014), pp. 210-211).

7   We see evidence in the male predisposition to adventure, curiosity, and disconnection between sexual experience and emotional intimacy, in their more permissive attitudes towards casual sex (Oliver & Hyde (2001)), in their reported greater enjoyment with casual sex (hook-ups and one-night stands), and in citing sex rather than intimacy as their primary motivation in casual sexual arrangements (such as 'friends with benefits') (Lehmiller (2014), p. 203). Men

become more easily sexually aroused by stimuli outside the relationship, take pleasure in the arousal itself (and so we see a greater incidence of masturbation (Oliver & Hyde (2001), p. 36) and paraphilia in males (Baumeister (2001), p. 293)), and admit to cheating more than women do, suggesting a greater tendency to seek sexual adventure.

8   Mazur & Booth (1997) found that endogenous testosterone encouraged competitive, status-enhancing, dominating behaviours that could lead to aggressive or antisocial (rebellious) expression. Regarding territoriality, two studies found that footballers demonstrate a testosterone surge before a home game compared with before a training session or an away game; this home surge being particularly apparent when playing a team perceived as being a 'bitter' rival (Neave & Wolfson (2003)). In animals, territorial behaviour in males is common, and it has been established that the acquisition and defence of territories (especially by males) is at least partly mediated by surges in testosterone (Wingfield, et al. (1990)). Testosterone also seems to play a role in the regulation of the fight-or-flight response when under dominance challenge (Mehta & Josephs (2006) and Mehta, et al. (2008); see also Mansfield (2006)).

9   Van Anders, Goldey, & Kuo (2011) associate testosterone with two kinds of aggression, each with a different hormonal profile: one they called *antagonistic*, being oriented around gaining territory, status, mates, or dominance; the other *protective*, being oriented around safeguarding close social partners. The latter is linked with vasopressin release, which occurs at the time of sexual intercourse. In this way testosterone appears to affect both sexual interest and relationship dynamics: the two are not unrelated.

10   Research suggests men are more likely to be jealous about their partner becoming physically involved with someone else than if they were emotionally so involved, while women objected more strongly should their partner might become emotionally involved with someone else, than they did to the sex act per se (Buss, et al. (2001)).

11   In relation to forcefulness, men are inclined to aggress in direct and physical ways, while women are inclined to aggress in indirect and verbal ways (Hess & Hagan (2006)).

12   We see that a woman's focus is more on the integration of intimacy and sex, while a man tends to separate the two. For example, in the 'friends with benefits' arrangement (or FWB — an arrangement between friends to allow regular access to sex) men were more likely to cite access to sex as their primary motivation, while women reported seeking an 'emotional connection' as their primary motivation. And so women generally wanted such an arrangement to either revert to 'just friends' (without sex), or to become romantically involved — FWB was a concession or avenue towards a more interdependent and committed relationship (Lehmiller (2014), p. 203).

13   Women tend to be more trusting and compliant, although they experience more anxiety and negative affect than men in their sexual relationships (Costa, Terracciano, & McCrae (2001), and Feingold (1994)).

14   Women are better than men in decoding the emotion behind facial expressions (Hall & Matsumoto (2004)).

15   Now that condoms can catch sperm and the pill can prevent new life, the power of the equation between the biology and the meanings of 'maleness' and 'femaleness' becomes muted. But the essence remains.

16   Social construction theory overstates this, arguing that sexual meanings, motivations and identity are determined by social forces only — see, for example, Agocha, et al. (2014), pp. 202-203.

17   The capacity to differentiate between sexual arousal and sexual attraction or desire is different between men and women, with women having greater difficulty differentiating between desire and arousal, and men generally experiencing sexual desire and arousal as separate events. Indeed, there appears to be limited overlap between actual genital response and the feelings of sexual desire and arousal in women (Brotto & Smith (2014), pp. 210-211). This may reflect differences in the biology of the sexual response, but has implications for the attributional process: how should I interpret my experiences? Testosterone seems more related to sexual desire than arousal, the latter involving complex neuro-endocrine processes. Masturbation can release the sexual tension built through the arousal process; but sexual desire is not so easily sated. Furthermore, the distinction between sexual arousal and sexual desire may reflect the autonomic nature of genital responding to sexual stimuli, so that sexual arousal may occur even when the stimulus responsible is not perceived as desired or arousing by the woman. This has implications for sexual abuse, both in males and females, where it is possible for a victim to become sexually aroused against their will (including rape situations), and without sexual desire. This also affects the meanings, associations and conditioned responses relating to subsequent sexual experience and behaviour in those subjected to such circumstances, along with potential confusion.

18   Brotto & Smith (2014) observe that 'genital response may occur in situations that are not at all associated with desire... subjective desire and physiological arousal may be experienced separately' (p. 211).

19   This is especially prevalent for males, who have a more permissive attitude towards casual sex (Oliver & Hyde (2001), pp. 29-43), and report greater enjoyment with casual sex, seeing sex rather than intimacy as their primary motivation (Lehmiller (2014), p. 203). A man becomes more easily sexually aroused by stimuli outside the relationship, and takes pleasure in the arousal itself — and so we see a greater incidence of masturbation.

20 Byers and Rehman (2014), p. 321, citing Lawrence & Byers (1995). See also MacNeil & Byers (2005, 2009), and Purnine & Carey (1997).

21 See, for example, Birnbaum (2010, 2016), who argues that sexual acts and emotional attachments are governed by separate motivational systems. Nevertheless, 'joint involvement of the sexual and attachment systems is typical of ongoing romantic relationships in which intimates function as both attachment figures and sexual partners' (Birnbaum (2016), p. 464). It is recognised that some psychological parameters (such as belonging and attachment) are relevant for *all* relationships, sexual or otherwise; likewise, some sexual motives hold for *all* sexual activity, whether in relationship or not. It would be cumbersome to regularly make these qualifiers, so the observation is made here.

22 Baumeister & Leary (1995) add: 'If psychology has erred with regard to the need to belong, in our view, the error has not been to deny the existence of such a motive so much as to under-appreciate it' (p. 522). See also, however, Guisinger & Blatt (1949), and Ryan (1991).

23 Reeve (2005), pp. 121-122 and Koball, et al. (2010).

24 Williams & Solano (1983), and Cohen (2004).

25 See my discussion on connection and meaningfulness in Schneider (2013).

26 Reproduction and survival of a species is often quoted as an 'obvious' evolutionary 'function' of sexual behaviour: certainly few would dispute that the *biological* function of sexual behaviour is reproduction. I will argue that the primary *psychological* functions of a sexual relationship are belonging (or affiliation) and attachment (or bonding). This function has also been argued as having an evolutionary basis (see e.g. Eastwick (2009), and Ziefman & Hazan (2016)). The notion of the 'function' of a sexual relationship is, however, not without controversy. On what basis might function be determined? 'Function' might mean 'purpose', which we normally understand to imply intent. Yet clearly there are people for whom it is not the intent to have children with the person with whom they might be in sexual relationship. Nevertheless, we maintain that the biological function of sexual behaviour is reproduction. 'Function' might mean the *socially agreed role or purpose* of behaviour; in which case the socio-cultural context becomes relevant — is there indeed social agreement that the functions of a sexual relationship include procreation, bonding, and belonging? We will find that this varies from one community to another. The 'function' of behaviour might be seen as the role that behaviour naturally plays, or is suited for, in the wider scheme of things, and in its more enduring outcomes (such as its capacity to meet critical personal or social needs). But behaviour can have more than one function. I make the distinction between primary and secondary functions to reflect the relative judged importance of the various functions.

27   In earlier times there was also the possibility of an involuntary belonging: 'I belong to this person because they bought me (as a slave), and so they have authority over me.' It might still happen today in some cultures in the context of arranged marriages, or in the context of sex slavery, which tragically is still prevalent. This sense of belonging or ownership, however, is not my focus here.

28   The 'inner self' is the existential dimension, referred to as *I*, in Schneider (2013), but which may be understood as the spirit or soul in contrast to the physical dimension of the body and brain.

29   Just as the inner self is expressed through the body, so also the vulnerable inner self covers and hides itself like the body (in the wearing of clothes) to protect it from invasion and exploitation. When the inner selves of two people choose to intimately reveal each to the other, this also finds parallel in the taking off of clothes, revealing those parts of the body that relate to sexual union. The boundaries are removed to make connection possible at every level. When the body is exposed to another person without the concomitant revealing of the inner self, a degree of disconnect between the self and the body may result because at that point the body is not properly reflecting the intent of the self.

30   That said, I remain part of something bigger than just myself, so that in some senses my mind and body do not only belong to me. Peterson (2018) notes: '...you do not simply belong to yourself. You are not simply your own possession to torture and mistreat. This is partly because your Being is inexorably tied in with that of others, and your mistreatment of yourself can have catastrophic consequences for others'; and: '...you have the spark of the divine in you, which belongs not to you, but to God' (p. 60).

31   Tolman and Bowman (2014) observe: 'The body is at once our own, something we share with others, and also something that is important to and shaped by the social world. Almost everything about sex is also about the body; sexuality is an intrinsic part of the embodied self' (p. 759). See also Aron, Mashek, & Aron (2004) who develop the theme that 'in a close relationship the other is, to some extent, part of the self — that closeness *is* including other in the self' (p. 27).

32   This sharing of the inner self goes beyond the sexual event, of course. There is also the overlay of shared thinking, memories, perceptions, and emotions — all aspects of the inner self — that develop as a relationship develops. See, for example, Baumeister & Leary (1995). Hazan & Zeifman (1994) further suggest that the face-to-face and belly-to-belly contact typical in human sexual encounter enhances the emotional connection between partners. And, of course, there is also the sharing of our *time* together. Time is no longer my own to make decisions about; it becomes a shared commodity about which we make joint decisions, both in relation to sexual activity itself, but also more generally.

33   Tolman & Diamond (2014), p. 324.

34 Fromm (1962), for example, argued that sex involved not only the desire for physical release and pleasure, but also, and more importantly, the desire for union.

35 See Anderson, et al. (1995). The basis of the jealousy may be a little different for men than women, although Impett, et al. (2014) observe 'when they are not forced to choose between emotional and sexual infidelity, men and women alike tend to rate both types of infidelity as jealousy provoking, suggesting that both can be distressing for men and women' (p. 300), quoting research by DeSteno, et al. (2002), and Lishner, et al. (2008).

36 Davis, et al. (2004). This is especially true for those with a history of insecure anxious attachment.

37 More than 94% of sexual relationships demand sexual exclusiveness. Nevertheless, infidelity occurs regularly enough, but often at the cost of the relationship (see, for example, Træen & Martinussen (2008), Treas & Giesen (2000), Whisman, et al. (2007), and Whisman & Snider (2007).

38 Impett, et al. (2014), p. 299.

39 See, for example, Davis, et al. (2003); and Spielmann, et al. (2013).

40 See Buss, et al. (2001). We see also the peak of testosterone release in males coincides with the break from one primary belonging (parents) to establish belonging with another (sexual partner). In other research, Impett, et al. (2014) (citing Burchell & Ward (2011)) note: 'Previous experience with sexual infidelity and higher levels of avoidant attachment [compromising belonging] predict increased sexual jealousy for men' (p. 300). Traditional scripts had a better appreciation of the role of belonging, and why it was considered that marriage should be a fundamental unit in social structure.

41 The need for belonging shapes cognitive processing: the more important the relationship, the more important and complex the information associated with that relationship becomes (Baumeister & Leary (1995)). Furthermore, there is an interactive aspect where information is jointly remembered and processed: see for example, Wegner's (1986, 1991) *Transactive Memory Processes*, which is described as a 'shared system for encoding, storing and retrieving information' (Wegner, et al. (1991), p. 923).

42 Birnbaum (2016) cites a telling study by Gillath, et al. (2008), providing some evidence for a 'causal pathway from activation of the sexual system to attachment formation and maintenance.' They found that 'subliminal exposure to sexually arousing stimuli ...increases willingness both to self-disclose intimate information to a potential new partner and to engage in relationship-promoting behaviours with current partners' (p. 475).

Chapter 2

43 See especially the drive theories built on the work, first of Freud, and then of Hull (1943). This was an attempt to wed psychological thinking with 'scientific reasoning': that is, restricting the explanation of behaviour to natural laws that apply to the biological self. However, my conceptualisation of a drive follows Reeve's assertion that it is a psychological rather than biological construct, even where the source of such drives might be biological (Reeve (2005) p. 75).

44 At the same time, there were alternative conceptualisations of drive theory, such as that espoused by functionalists like Woodworth, who argued for principles of motivation playing a central role in dynamic psychology (see Hilgard & Bower; 1966; and Snyder & Cantor, 1994).

45 For behavioural intervention in the area of sexuality; see, for example, Rimm & Masters, 1979; and Fischer & Gochros, 1977.

46 See Murray, 1937; Miller, 1959; and Reeve, 2005. Reeve observes that the role of motivation in explanatory theories remains central in psychodynamic psychology, and in clinical work more generally.

47 The problem of objective measurement remains, so that they have little attraction to scientific reasoning, but the centrality of 'motive' and 'drive' in legal and social spheres, and its utility in clinical work and in the sphere of sexual relationships (with its social and legal dimensions) argues for a re-instatement of these notions in explanatory mechanisms.

48 Regarding the biological basis for drives, Reeve (2005) observes that 'drive is a psychological, not a biological, term. It is the conscious manifestation of an underlying unconscious biological need. Drive, not the underlying physiological needs per se, have motivational properties. For instance, appetite (psychological drive), not low blood sugar or shrunken fat cells (physiological need), energizes and directs behaviour' (p. 75). Although Reeve uses the term 'drive' here to represent a conscious desire (described as 'appetite') produced by an underlying unconscious physiological need state, this same psychological drive (that is, 'appetite') may also be induced by signals independent of the physiological need state, such as the sight or aroma of a favourite food, or even of other subjective states such as boredom, loneliness, or depression. Furthermore, appetite can be induced by classical conditioning, as Pavlov famously discovered.

49 There is a further parallel here in instances where self-perception and physical reality don't match. The person suffering anorexia nervosa has a self-perception they are obese, when in fact they aren't. Nevertheless, they are motivated to lose weight based on that self-perception rather than change the perception itself. Similarly, a person suffering Gender Dysphoria may have a self-perception of being of one sex, when in fact their body clearly is of the other. Nevertheless,

they are often motivated to change their body based on that self-perception, rather than change the perception itself.

50   I have chosen the term 'drive', rather than 'motive' or 'reason' in the drive model because it better captures the energising aspect of the motive or 'reason for,' rather than limiting the idea to the goal only. Furthermore, it provides it with the same status as a motivational force, whether its source is biological or subjective. Nevertheless, it relates to subjective reasons for doing something, rather than being simply an impersonal, irresistible, causative force. Toates (2014) uses the term *incentive motivation* because it better describes being 'pulled by external stimuli, thoughts about them and their associations' (p.103) as against the view of drive as being 'pushed by something arising from the tissues of the body' (p.103). My view is that the idea of 'drive' as a motivating urge does not assume the latter and comfortably accommodates the former. For example, a man 'driven to succeed' is pulled by the idea of future reward, not pushed by internal physiological forces.

51   Toates (2014) writes 'The *combination* of desires might well very greatly exceed the strength of any component. It is hard to see how such complexity of intentions could be understood in terms of a unitary notion of "sex drive". Desire can be very much situation-dependent, reflecting different triggers, something missed by the unitary notion of a sex drive' (p. 103).

52   This relates to *Cognitive Dissonance Theory* — see Festinger, (1957).

53   See Young et al., (2003).

54   See, for example, Murray's (1938) 'universal needs' and Maslow's (1943) 'hierarchy of needs', which encompasses both physiological drives and ideas-based motivations.

55   See Tolman & Diamond (2014) pp. 3-27.

56   What a 'dual' source means is conceptualised differently by different researchers, but there is recognition that there is a complexity in the drivers of sexual behaviour that requires recognition of both biological and subjective components. For example, for Pfaus et al. the two sources distinguish between biological and environmental/contextual, while I distinguish between biological and subjective perception. Pfaus et al. note that 'context and biology interact at the level of the brain for behaviour to be modified by experience, allowing even animals to learn about sex' (Pfaus et al. (2014) p. 145, citing Li, (2003) and Tiefer, (2004)). 'Context' alludes to environmental parameters for animals; but in humans, it will also include cultural, political, and social parameters and subjective interpretations of events. 'Biology' includes unconditioned neurobiological and endocrine processes in both animals and humans. Pfaus et al. argue that it is important to study the neurological aspects of sexual behaviour in the context of both the body's biology and the sociocultural environment, as each contributes to 'priming the brain' towards (or away from) sexual arousal and

desire. The interaction of the two is governed by classical and operant conditioning and other associative principles. A mix of biological and subjective dimensions are described in Pfaus' (1999) model, which involves three stages of an 'incentive sequence' for sexual behaviour: *appetitive*, *precopulatory*, and *consummatory*. Under *appetitive*, fantasy is included as a part of sexual desire, a subjective dimension that helps prime for the biological processes that occur in the *precopulatory*, and *consummatory* stages.

57   This affects experimental research design decisions in psychology: the best research designs such as the double-blind design assume the cause-and-effect dynamic of natural laws not moderated by the subjective self.

58   In reflecting on traumatic brain injury, Carrington (2012) describes how emotions of a person (mediated by the hypothalamus) directly influences their hormonal profile (through the links of the hypothalamus with the pituitary gland) as much as it does the other way: 'Regulatory molecules from the hypothalamus "tell" the pituitary how much of its own hormones and hormone releasing factors to produce. And the hypothalamus, as part of the brain itself, receives constant *neurological inputs* from all over the body, creating a host of feedback loops. It is those feedback loops that maintain a steady balance between extreme biochemical states. That connection between the brain's hypothalamus and the endocrine system's pituitary is called *endocrine* function' (p. 1).

59   Mischel (1971) concludes: '…motivating arousal states are induced in human beings not just by visceral stimuli and biological factors, but also by information and cognitive changes' (p. 263). Although the neurochemical system as a drive source is important, the drive profile emerging from the perceptions of the subjective self play a much larger role. Brotto & Smith (2014), citing Dennerstein et al. (1999), write: 'Using structural equation modelling to examine the relative effects of a variety of psychosocial factors and hormones on libido, "feelings for partner" was a much stronger predictor than were any of the hormones, including oestrogen and testosterone' (pp. 223-224). They also quote studies that question the contribution of biology in aspects of sexual behaviour, especially in women. For example, it was found that for women who lacked sexual desire, developmental history, psychiatric history (especially), and psychosexual history were more important than the hormonal profile.

60   In Schneider (2013) I describe a *mind map* (or mental map) carried by the neural system that is developed over time and contains explicit and implicit memory systems, which help to make meaning of incoming signals. These incoming signals are sourced both in the external environment and the internal biological environment. The mind map provides the orientation within which the subjective self make interpretations and decisions, which is in turn expressed in various observable behaviours.

61 Because the brain works by association, conflation — the fusing or merging of different elements (in this case, drives) — will routinely occur. In other words, one drive can prime or stimulate another drive, so that both may be experienced simultaneously. This is especially true for meanings, and is inherent in the study of subjective experience. It becomes a problem in objective scientific study, which seeks to isolate and control variables which are connected in subjective experience. Which elements and meanings are associated or merged will vary from one person to another.

62 Authors such as Tomkins (1962, 1963, & 1984) and Izard (1991) argue that emotions underlie the primary motivational system.

63 Berry & Hansen1(996).

64 Dutton & Aron (1976), and White & Knight (1984).

65 Reeve (2005), citing Buck (1988) wrote: 'Emotions also provide a readout of the person's ever-changing motivational states and personal adaption status' (p. 296). Reeve (2005) further observed: '…emotions are not necessarily motives in the same way that needs and cognitions are but, instead, reflect the satisfied versus frustrated status of motives. Consider sexual motivation and how emotion provides an on-going progress report that facilitates some behaviours and inhibits others. During attempts at sexual gratification, positive emotions such as interest and joy signal that all is well and facilitate further sexual conduct. Negative emotion such as disgust, anger, and guilt signal that all is not well and inhibit further sexual conduct' (pp. 296-297).

66 A different mix of emotions (reflecting different drive profiles — such as fear, powerlessness, adventure, and desire; or curiosity, being 'naughty', proving oneself, and desire; or affection, love, being desired and desire; and so on) represents a different sexual experience (just as food carries different combinations of flavours), and a person learns to be familiar with and enjoy one or other 'flavour' combination.

67 Drives are separate from, and precede the behaviour. For example, Patrick & Lee (2010) conclude that their study illustrated that 'motivations precede behaviours, such that initial levels of motivation and motivational changes are evident for a group of individuals who transition from abstinence to sexual activity' (pg. 678).

Chapter 3

68 Having said this, social experience and context have been found to influence sexual behaviour in nonhuman primates, both in early development and in adulthood: see Wallen (2001).

69 'Hormones are chemical products of the endocrine system and encompass either steroid or steroid-like hormones (e.g., androgens and oestrogens), such

as those produced by the gonads, or protein, peptide, or glycol-protein hormones, such as oxytocin and vasopressin' (O'Sullivan & Thompson (2014), p. 435, citing Halpern (2006)).

70 See, for example, Walum, et al. (2008).

71 Miller, et al. (2004).

72 Turchik, et al. (2010).

73 Markey & Markey (2007).

74 Geen (1997) and Garcia, et al. (2010).

75 Garcia, et al. (2010).

76 Gullette & Lyons (2005).

77 Rosario & Schrimshaw (2014), p. 568, 579.

78 Feminine behaviour in boys as a predictor of homosexuality is at around 75%-90% (Bailey and Zucker (1995)), while the likelihood of being homosexual when having an identical twin who is homosexual is at the greatest 52% (Bailey and Pillard (1991) and Bailey, et al. (1993)).

79 Katz-Wise & Hyde (2014), pp. 50-52. However, they suggest that sexual fluidity may simply operate differently in men than in women, with women more likely to experience person-based attractions.

80 See the clinical experiences of Carnes (1992, 2001), and see Toates (2014).

81 See Schneider (2013), p. 88; and Toates (2014).

82 Guo, et al. (2007).

83 Brotto & Smith (2014), p. 222.

84 Laan & Both (2008).

85 Hille (2005), Birnbaum (2016), p. 474. The role of oxytocin and vasopressin in sexual experience forms the basis of *Attachment (and Steroid-Peptide) Theory,* which views sexuality as 'a pair-bonding system that integrates sexual desire and behaviour with the processes of seeking protection and security from and providing it to a pair-bonded reproductive partner' (Tolman & Diamond (2014), p. 8).

86 See also see the animal research of Gimpl & Fahrenholz (2001).

87 In their steroid-peptide theory, van Anders, et al. (2011) suggest that there are two types of intimacy — sexual and nurturant — both of which are associated with high levels of oxytocin which enhances social bonding, but the former also has higher levels of testosterone (which essentially makes the relationship a sexual one, but contributes to inhibition of social bonding, and enhances the potential for aggression which relate to territorial and protective behaviours).

Van Anders et el. distinguish between *antagonistic aggression*, oriented around gaining territory, status, mates, or dominance, and *protective aggression*, oriented around protecting and safeguarding close social partners, especially family members. This latter involves vasopressin, supposedly absent in the former.

88 Kringelbach (2005).

89 Forbes & Grafman (2010) and Lou, et al. (2010).

90 Pfaus, et al. (2014), p. 175.

91 Rodrìguez-Manzo & Fernández-Guasti (1995).

92 Pfaus, et al. (2014), p. 150. See also Toates (2014), pp. 200-201, who identifies various physiological processes that may contribute to inhibition: increased levels of prolactin and oxytocin have been suggested, as well as the decrease in dopamine following orgasm, and feedback systems from the genitals. There are also sex differences in the way inhibitions occur.

93 Pfaus, et al. (2014), p. 178.

94 Ibid: p. 184.

95 Perelman (2006), p. 1007.

96 Chivers, et al. (2014), pp. 108-109.

97 For example, variations in body fat, medications and other ingested substances such as nicotine affect testosterone levels. Stress-induced cortisol release also changes the profile, as do various neuroendocrine disorders.

98 Wallen (2001).

99 Ziegler (2007).

100 Rosario & Schrimshaw (2014), pp. 568-569.

101 Dörner, et al.(1975). See also Bell & Weinberg (1978), Friedman (1988), and Wilson & Rahman (2005).

102 Berenbaum & Snyder (1995). But see also the following: Bem (1985, 1996, 1998), Doerr, et al. (1976), Dörner (1988), Gladue (1988), Gladue (1994), LeVay (1991), and Meyer-Bahlberg, et al. (1995).

103 See Breedlove (1994) and Meyer-Bahlburg, et al. (1995).

104 Isay (2009), p. 18; see also the work of Bem (1996).

105 See Garnets & Kimmel (1991) and Gladue (1988), cited in Weiten (2001), p. 305.

106 See Herdt & McClintock (2000) and Savin-Williams & Diamond (2000).

107 It is the hypothalamus that controls the pituitary gland and the endocrine system more generally, through which cortisol, adrenaline and noradrenaline are released, as well as the hormones regulating drives such as appetite and sexual desire. The hypothalamus also releases dopamine so that a person experiences, or *expects* to experience something 'nice' or pleasurable, like food, sex, or drugs: it leads to desire, anticipation, and excitement. When it is not activating the fight-or-flight response, hypothalamus regulates basic biological drives: hunger, thirst, and sexual desire (Guyton (1981), p. 1001).

108 O'Sullivan & Thompson (2014), p. 435.

109 See Udry, Talbert, & Morris (1986) and Halpern, Udry, & Uchindran (1998).

110 Homosexual orientation and behaviour may be shaped by various contexts, different drive profiles, and different scripts, and the diversity of these contexts, profiles and scripts need to be kept in mind. Rosario & Schrimshaw (2014) note 'there are multiple homosexualities and multiple pathways to homosexuality in both sexes' (p. 563).

111 Gangestad, et al. (2005) and Little, et al. (2007), cited in Chivers, et al. (2014), p.109.

112 Gangestad, et al. (2005).

113 Diamond & Wallen (2011).

114 See Giles (2008) and Jones, et al. (2010).

115 Kraemer, et al. (1976).

116 Gray, et al. (2004a, 2004b).

117 Hirschenhauser, et al. (2002).

118 Booth, et al. (1999), Dabbs (1993); and van Anders, et al. (2007).

119 Marazziti & Canale (2004).

120 Either married or in a committed relationship: see van Anders & Watson (2006); and Booth, et al. (1999).

121 Berg & Wynne-Edwards (2001).

122 See Pirke, et al. (1974) and Hellhammer, et al. (1985).

123 Roney, et al. (2003).

124 James, et al. (2006).

125 Pfaus, et al. (2014), p. 178.

126 Marquis (1978).

127 Rimm & Masters (1979).

128 Pfaus et al. (2012), cited in Tolman & Diamond (2014), p. 11.

129 Baumeister (2001), pp. 200-201.

Chapter 4

130 As noted earlier, the associative nature and the inevitable overlapping of meanings, as well as the simultaneous presence of multiple subjective drives makes their differentiation and measurement very difficult, despite various attempts to do so (e.g., Stephenson, et al. (2011) and Meston & Buss (2007)). Measurement of such motives depends on the items chosen, the sample of respondents and their particular histories, and on the respondent's self-aware-ness and capacity to distinguish their own motives. Psychologists are only too aware of such problems. Difficulties in measurement does not, however, mean that the conceptualisation of such systems is invalid; only that the measureable 'evidence' science seeks is hard to come by. Meston and Buss (2007) described thirteen categories of motives for 'why people have sex', under four headings: physical reasons; goal attainment; emotional; and insecurity. Our first five themes would come under their category *physical reasons*, in which they included stress reduction, pleasure, physical desirability, experience seeking. Cooper, et al. (2006) describe a two dimensional model for understanding motives of sexual behaviour that give rise to four classes of motives: *appetitive self-focused motives* (having sex to enhance physical or emotional pleasure); *aversive self-focused motives* (having sex to cope with threats to self-esteem or to minimise negative emotions); *appetitive social motives* (having sex to bond with socially significant others); and *aversive social motives* (having sex to avoid social censure or to gain another's approval) (p. 251). The first one, *appetitive self-focused motives*, is relevant here.

131 Birnbaum (2016) notes: '...men are relatively more motivated by sexual release and tend to adopt a more individualistic-recreational orientation towards sexu-ality... they are more likely to be active, to take the initiator role... and to be concerned with experiencing sexual variety' (p. 468).

132 This drive associates with Murray's (1938) *sex* or *erotic* drive, which references the sensual aspect of an erotic relationship.

133 Fromm likens the orgiastic experience to the use of alcohol and drugs: 'But in many individuals in whom separateness is not relieved in other ways, the search for the sexual orgasm assumes a function which makes it not very different from alcoholism and drug addiction' (Fromm (1962), p.16).

134 There are also other factors that can increase ANS arousal, such as feelings of guilt and fear: these, too, can play a part in the erotic experience. See, for example, Bem (1996).

135 This is especially true for men with a history of insecure attachment, who tend to substitute pornography for intimacy to enable self-gratification without risking rejection. Not surprisingly, this drive associates with sexual dissatisfaction and poor relationship quality (Szymanski & Stewart-Richardson (2014) and Birnbaum (2016).

136 This theme associates with Murray's (1938) *play* motive, and Meston & Buss' (2007) *stress reduction* motive. The play motive relates to relieving tension, having fun, and relaxing. It also associates with Hill & Preston's (1996) third dispositional sexual motive, *obtaining relief from stress*, and seventh dispositional sexual motive, *experiencing pleasure*. Both Cooper, et al.'s (2006) *appetitive* and *aversive self-focused* motives would probably be included in *the desire for recreation*.

137 See, for example, the *Insufficient Self-Control/Self-Discipline* schema of Young, et al. (2003).

138 This drive theme associates with Murray's (1938) *understanding* or *cognizance* drive: the desire to analyse and experience, and to seek knowledge, and Meston & Buss' (2007) *experience-seeking* motive.

139 See Toates (2014), pp.188-198.

140 See Stoller (1979) and Foster, et al. (1998).

141 Bem (1996).

142 See, for example, Griffitt (1974).

143 See Meston & Buss' (2007) *physical desirability* motive.

144 This is called the study of *facial metrics*: see for example, the work of Cunningham, (1986).

145 See, for example, Graziano, et al. (1993); and Mahoney, (1983).

146 Kenrick, et al. (1993).

147 See, for example, Brislin & Lewis (1968).

148 This is the basis of Murstein's (1972) theory, which argues that we choose marital partners whose physical attractiveness is comparable to our own.

149 Fromm (1962) describes the drive thus: '…above the universal, existential need for union rises a more specific, biological one: the desire for union between the masculine and feminine poles' (p. 29). He explains the polarity further: 'There is masculinity and femininity in *character* as well as *sexual function*. The masculine character can be defined as having the qualities of penetration, guidance, activity, discipline and adventurousness; the feminine character by the qualities of productive receptiveness, protection, realism, endurance, motherliness' (p. 32).

150 See the accounts given by Tripp (1975) and Bell (1982), cited in Bem (2001): '...a necessary ingredient for romantic attachment is one's perception of a loved one as essentially different from oneself in terms of gender-related attributes' (p. 196).

151 Here I mean the sense of power that becomes a source of a person's ability to protect another, to inspire confidence in another, and to be an effective provider for another, not the sense of power that might be used to overcome or disempower another person as identified in the *power drive* theme.

152 See Mansfield (2006).

153 This may find expression in sexual activity that is largely disconnected from emotional factors.

154 Bem argued that when a child feels 'different' to another child in terms of gender, psychological arousal results. Later, this psychological arousal would lead to sexual arousal towards the gender seen as different — the 'exotic' gender. He theorised that this dynamic might lead to homosexual behaviours in gender-nonconforming children (Bem, et al. (2000)).

Chapter 5

155 There is both *primary* and *secondary* belonging. Primary belonging involves the parents when a person is young and the sexual partner when they come to maturity. Secondary (or remote) belonging relates to the matrix of relationships to which the parent or sexual partner belongs — the extended family, but also the tribe, race or religion the parent or partner belongs to, and represents, and to which the child or lover becomes united. And so the uniting with a sexual partner becomes the doorway to belonging to the wider connections of the partner. To connect and belong is critical in the development both of identity and purpose, and *by definition* is a goal of relationship.

156 This drive theme also associates with Murray's (1938) *achievement* drive — the capacity to overcome obstacles and to succeed.

157 See Tolman & Diamond (2014), p. 446, regarding the adolescents' greater focus on these social needs in their drive profile.

158 This drive theme associates with Murray's (1938) *recognition* drive (to gain approval and social status), and with Meston & Buss' (2007) social status and duty/pressure motives. Cooper, et al.'s (2006) *aversive social motives* would relate to this theme.

159 A lack of social acceptance, or social disapproval (for reasons of race, ethnicity, religion, social class, age, gender, sexuality, or relationship status) by family, friends, society at large, links to less commitment (Lehmiller & Agnew (2006)); are more likely to break up (Lehmiller & Agnew (2007)); and lead to worse

physical and psychological health outcomes: 'Lacking relationship acceptance and approval may be destructive to both the health of the partners and their romance' (Lehmiller (2014), p. 159).

160 See, for example, Peterson (2004), pp. 428-429.

161 This is a factor in the traditionally low rate of interracial and interreligious relationships: see, for example, Lehmiller (2014), pp. 178-179.

162 Patrick & Lee (2010) identify *morals* as one of the three major motivations for inhibition of sexual behaviour.

163 This drive theme associates with Young, et al. (2003) *Entitlement/Grandiosity* schema: Have I got what I deserve — and I deserve the best! Am I as happy as I could or should be? Can I do better? It also associates with Murray's (1938) *acquisition* or *conservance* drive — the desire to obtain possessions. Fromm (1962) wrote regarding the consumer motive in relationships: 'I am out for a bargain; the object should be desirable from the standpoint of its social value, and at the same time should want me, considering my overt and hidden assets and potentialities. Two persons thus fall in love when they feel they have found the best object available on the market, considering the limitations of their own exchange values' (p. 10).

164 *Exchange Theories of Attraction* are based on the reward-cost dynamic. See, for example, Thibaut and Kelley's (1959) Social-Exchange Theory, and Blau (1964).

165 A person might be drawn to someone with *complementary needs*, either based on attraction to an ego ideal, or on mutual need gratification. In relation to a complementary needs model, see, for example, Winch (1958).

166 See also Li, et al. (2002); and Kenrick, et al. (1993).

167 Buston & Emlen (2003).

168 Prostitution, of course, is the ultimate consumer statement, where the sexual encounter itself is a commodity with a dollar value bought without relationship complications. Using sex as currency can also be found in the drug culture and other settings where people (particularly women) sell their bodies.

169 In this regard, see, for example, Brehm's (1966) *Theory of Reactance*, which predicts that a threat to a couple's freedom of choice — perhaps because of parental displeasure — leads to stronger romantic feelings for that couple.

170 See Meston & Buss' (2007) *revenge* motive.

171 See, for example, Aronson, & Cope (1968).

172 This theme has been explored by many theorists and clinicians. For example, the two aspects are referenced in Murray's (1938) *abasement* (to surrender and accept punishment) and *deference* (to follow a superior and to serve) drives, and his *dominance* or *power* drive (to control and lead others). The power

theme or *will to power* as an underlying drive also plays a central role in Alfred Adler's personality theory, associating with the superiority/inferiority dimension. This theme is echoed in Hill & Preston's (1996) fifth dispositional sexual motive: *enhancing feelings of personal power*, and sixth dispositional sexual motive: *experiencing the power of one's partner*.

173 Note the relationship of ownership and belonging here. The indigenous peoples of Australia traditionally did not think of their land as something that might be bought and 'owned'. Instead, they saw themselves as a people 'belonging to the land' — the land owned them. In that relationship, they became custodians of the land, respecting the land as their source of life and the context of their community. 'Belonging', then, can have emphasis on *the person who belongs to the land* and the associated obligations, rather than on the *land that belongs to the person*, in the sense of it being owned by the person. This, too, can be the emphasis in the sexual relationship. I can emphasise my belonging to the other person, or the other person belonging to me. In the former case, I focus on my obligations to my partner; in the latter, the focus is on my partner's obligations to me. It is in the latter that power issues emerge. When I focus on my partner's obligations to me, I become a 'controlling' partner. This orients me towards potentially abusing my partner when I believe the obligations are not being fulfilled, so that I might be reported on the domestic violence hotline. The worst form of such ownership is found in the practice of sexual slavery.

174 Some argue that rape associates with male domination, or perhaps as a way to control a perceived threat (typically in the woman), but there is also a strong case for arguing that rape represents the association of sexual arousal with arousal linked to aggressive impulses. See Toates (2014), pp. 403-408 for more on this.

175 Winter (1988) and Hofer, et al. (2010).

176 BDSM: Bondage, Sadism, and Masochism. Fromm (1962) refers to *masochism* and *sadism* as being elements of a symbiotic union: 'The masochistic person escapes from the unbearable feeling of isolation and separateness by making himself part and parcel of another person who directs him, guides him, protects him' (p. 20); and: 'The sadistic person wants to escape from his aloneness and his sense of imprisonment by making another person part and parcel of himself' (p. 21). See also Zillman (1984) and Toates (2014), pp. 385-389.

177 See Urada, et al. (2014) with regard to the variety of circumstances and drives relevant to prostitution, including the power motive (pp. 48-49).

178 The *drive to procreation* matches Hill & Preston's (1996) eighth dispositional sexual motive of the same name: *procreation*.

Chapter 6

179 See Tennov (1999), p. 140 for reasons for 'mating relationship', including the practical reasons of economic or procreational purposes, and for companionship and affectional bonding. See also Dion & Dion (1973).

180 See, for example, Birnbaum (2016).

181 Birnbaum (2016) observes: '... women are more likely to associate sex with receiving and expressing love and are therefore more concerned with their romantic relationships during sexual intercourse' (p. 468).

182 See for example Impett, et al. (2014), pp. 271-272; and Birnbaum (2016), p. 469.

183 See Baumeister & Leary (1995). Lehmiller (2014), citing Kiecolt-Glaser & Newton, (2001), notes: 'The need to belong is very powerful, and developing strong social bonds is vital to our physical and psychological well-being. Relationships with family, friends, and various social groups help to fulfil this need; however our sexual and romantic relationships are at least as central... to meeting deep-seated needs and desires for social connection. As some evidence for this, research has found that having a high quality romantic relationship enhances personal health and longevity; in contrast, people who are alone or who lose their partners not only tend to be in worse health, but tend to die sooner' (p. 197). See the work of Shaver & Hazan (1988), who argued for the integration of attachment, care-giving and sex as the expression of adult romantic love, and more recently, Mikulincer & Goodman (2006); and Birnbaum (2016). See also Murray's (1938) *affiliation* drive — the need to make associations and friendships; and Meston & Buss' (2007) *commitment* motive. This is also the drive that comes closest to Fromm's 'deepest need of man': the need to 'overcome separateness, how to achieve union, how to transcend one's own individual life and find at-onement' (Fromm (1962), p. 14). Cooper, et al.'s (2006) *appetitive social motives* would relate to this theme.

184 See, for example, Cooper, et al. (2006).

185 See theories and research relating to the similarity hypothesis of attraction: for example, Newcomb's (1961) *Theory of Attraction*, and the research of Byrne and his colleagues (Byrne & Nelson (1965), and Byrne (1971)). See also Baumeister (2001), pp. 195-196.

186 This relates to the idea of attraction as a function of *consensual validation*: see, for example, Secord & Backman (1965).

187 Mackay (2013) writes: 'For some men, copulation itself is the ultimate expression of the idea of "my place," that intimate enclosure symbolising the sense of acceptance, comfort, tenderness and relief they associate with an idealised home-coming' (p. 58).

188 In this regard, see Meston & Buss' (2007) *mate guarding* motive in sexual relating.

189 See, for example, Young, et al. (2003) *Enmeshment/Undeveloped Self* schema, which is characterised by excessive emotional involvement and closeness with someone else at the expense of full individuation or normal social development, and may accompany a belief that one cannot survive or be happy without the constant support of the other. Feelings of emptiness and floundering, having no direction, or in extreme cases questioning one's existence may result.

190 Basson (2001, 2002, & 2003).

191 Cooper, Shapiro, & Powers (1998).

192 Love for someone helps safeguard the vulnerabilities created in intimacy, and so it is not surprising that clear links have been established between attachment style and love style. See, for example, Birnbaum (2016), p. 466; and Feeney (2016), p. 437.

193 On the variety of meanings of the word 'love', see, for example, Fromm (1962) '...love is primarily *giving*, not receiving. ...giving is 'giving up' something, being deprived of, sacrificing' (p. 22); Marshall (2007); and Tennov (1999) '...how does one distinguish between love and affection, liking, fondness, caring, concern, infatuation, attraction, or desire?' (p. 15). For a more recent and general discussion on the components of love, see Sternberg & Weis (2006).

194 Tennov (1999).

195 This aspect of the *need to love* drive associates with Meston & Buss' (2007) *love* motive, and Murray's (1938) *nurturance* drive: the desire to protect the helpless. Conversely, the *need to be loved* associates with Murray's (1938) *succorance* drive — the drive to seek protection or sympathy. The link of care-giving to attachment and sexual relationships has been researched by Shaver, et al. (1988), and Hazan & Shaver (1994). The *need to love* also associates with Hill & Preston's (1996) second dispositional sexual motive, *showing value for one's partner*, and fourth dispositional sexual motive, *providing nurturance to one's partner*. The *need to feel loved* associates with Hill & Preston's (1996) second dispositional sexual motive: *feeling valued by one's partner*.

196 *Cognitive Dissonance Theory* argues that inconsistencies in thought and behaviour are so uncomfortable that we are normally motivated to align our beliefs and attitudes with our behaviours (see, for example, Aronson (1961)). Where aspects of a relationship cause us distress or discomfort, we can justify such cost on the basis that the person was 'worth it' — we value them accordingly. That is, we tend to love that for which we suffer. This dynamic may explain why people remain in abusive relationships.

197 Unmet childhood needs for love may play a role in having insufficient self-esteem to be able to accept the love of another adult, although that person might be attracted to a mother-figure or father-figure (see *parent-related motives*): one in a strong position and able to meet emotional needs, demanding little in return. Conversely, perhaps in the context of low self-esteem, there may be a desire to relate to a child-figure: a needy person to protect, to rescue even. In order to feel better about one's own capacity, to feel empowered, useful and necessary in another's life, one might want to take pity on someone, to help them become 'somebody' and to feel special. The love-object of such a drive may or may not be a minor, but it is likely to be someone one who represents innocence or neediness: that person is accepting, grateful and easily influenced by the giver. This need is ascendant for those with a history of anxious attachment (see, for example, Davis, et al. (2004)).

198 See, for example, Birnbaum (2016), p. 466.

199 Bem (2001), citing Newcomb (1961), writes: 'Like similarity, familiarity is a major antecedent of liking. In fact, similarity probably promotes liking precisely because it increases familiarity: social norms, situational circumstances, and mutual interests conspire to bring people together who are similar to one another, thereby increasing their mutual familiarity… familiarity turned out to be a stronger facilitator of liking than similarity' (p. 197).

200 Feingold (1988); Murstein (1972); Rubin (1973); and Silverman (1971) (cited in Bem (2001), p. 195). See also Laumann, et al. (1994); and Berscheid, et al. (1971).

201 Reeve (2005), p. 97.

202 Hill, et al. (1976).

203 Meyer & Pepper (1977).

204 Caspi & Herbener (1990).

205 Lehmiller (2014), p. 178; see also Montoya, et al. (2008).

206 There may also be a greater sense of the safety, trust and respect necessary for true intimacy in a lesbian relationship for some women — this would especially be the case for those who have experienced abusive situations with men in the past.

207 Bem (2001), p. 197.

208 This parallels Meston & Buss' (2007) *goal attainment*, including their *resources* and *utilitarian* motives.

209 See, for example, Festinger, et al. (1950), and Athanasiou & Yoshioka (1973).

210 Zajonc (1968).

211 Lehmiller (2014), p. 180.

Chapter 7

212 See in this respect, the 'sexual behaviour sequence model' of Fisher (1986), who conceptualised a continuum between *erotophilia* (being attracted to erotic stimuli) and *erotophobia* (withdrawing from erotic stimuli). However, while a position on a continuum describes the *outcome* of opposing forces in sexual behaviour, it doesn't describe the particular *mix* of activating and inhibiting forces.

213 In a comprehensive study by Brennan, et al. (1998) into adult attachment and love styles, anxiety (about relationship issues) and avoidance (discomfort with closeness and interdependence) emerged as the two primary higher order factors.

214 See Janssen and Bancroft's (2007) dual control model, which describes the interaction of inhibition and activation forces in sexual arousal and behaviour.

215 Self-confidence is listed as one of the higher order factors differentiating the love styles associated with different attachment styles (Feeney & Noller (1990)): both avoidant and anxious-ambivalent attachment styles were characterised by low self-confidence.

216 This drive theme may relate to aspects of the *Dependence/Incompetence* schema of Young, et al. (2003), which reflects the belief that someone is unable to handle their everyday responsibilities in a competent manner, without considerable help from others. It also associates Murray's (1938) *infavoidance* drive (the drive to avoid failure, shame, or to conceal a weakness); and with social difficulties typically found in those on the Autism Spectrum.

217 Murray's (1938) drive to *autonomy* (to resist others and stand strong) is relevant here.

218 Related to this is the desire to avoid responsibility in order to not be held accountable, or to not make a mistake. This may result in passively drifting into a relationship through the initiative of another person (placing the other person in an apparently controlling position), or because of a total decisional paralysis. This associates with a fear of commitment in the sense of avoidance of making *any* decision. Anything negative that emerges in the relationship they have drifted into becomes the responsibility of the other person, and so that they are resented or blamed for subsequent relationship difficulties.

219 This associates with Adler's 'inferiority complex', and Murray's (1938) *infavoidance* drive — the drive to avoid failure, shame, or to conceal a weakness. Young, et al.'s (2003) *Defectiveness/Shame* schema is also relevant to the extent that feelings that one is defective, bad, unwanted, inferior, or invalid in important respects; or that one would be unlovable to others if exposed; resulting in hypersensitivity to criticism, rejection, and blame.

220 Addiction associates with relationship withdrawal and disinterest, as well as accompanying general deception as the addiction is kept from the critical awareness of the other person. Other sources of pleasure preoccupy the person, so that they are distracted from interpersonal relationships and have little energy to invest in relationships. Pornography addiction has a specific impact, generally reducing sexual interest because of desensitising processes, or making sexual demands that alienate the other person.

221 See Shaver & Hazan (1988). Other perceived negative emotional responses from a sexual partner can also lead to withdrawal and inhibition of sexual response: for example, tears in a woman have been found to reduce sexual arousal and testosterone in men: see Gelstein, et al. (2011).

222 Patrick & Lee (2010) identify three major motivations to inhibit sexual behaviour: *health reasons, morals,* and *not being ready for sex.* Both *health reasons* and *not being ready for sex* are included here under *the need for self-protection.* The third, *morals,* appears as the negative aspect of *the need for social acceptance,* but also relates in this model to the adopted socio-cultural sexual script.

223 Murray's (1938) *counteraction* drive is relevant here: the drive to defend honour.

224 This relates to a number of schemas of Young, et al. (2003), including *Abandonment/Instability* schema; the *Mistrust/Abuse* schema; *Emotional Deprivation* schema; and the *Social Isolation/Alienation* schema.

225 With regard to fear of intimacy and commitment in avoidant and anxious-ambivalent attachment styles, see Levy & Davis (1988), Feeney & Noller (1990), and Stefanou & McCabe (2012).

226 Kelly (2011).

227 Stevenson, et al. (2011). de Jong, et al. (2013) describes disgust as 'a defensive emotion that protects the organism from contamination' (p. 247).

228 This drive might relate to Young, et al.'s (2003) *Unrelenting Standards/Hypercriticalness and Punitiveness* schemas, which includes hyper-criticalness toward others, and unrealistically high moral, ethical, cultural, or religious precepts. This drive also associates with Murray's (1938) *rejection* drive — the drive to exclude another.

229 de Jong, et al. (2013) observe that 'the mouth and vagina [are] the body parts that show strongest disgust sensitivity' (p. 247). They observe that given these play such a central role in sexual activity, it isn't surprising that sex can create a disgust reaction where the level of sexual arousal fails to counteract and overcome the disgust-induced avoidance.

Chapter 8

230 Kuehne (2009) notes: 'we [as a society] are able to function in relative peace and harmony because we share a common answer that helps us each regulate our life' (p. 45). Also, Mitterauer & Sieder (1982), in their review of the history of marriage, reproduction and sexuality in the European family noted: 'Fluctuations in sexual desire and differences in sexual behaviour among human beings should rather be seen in a social context, as responses to social rather than biological stimuli. Yet the continuous presence of sexual impulses has to be managed and controlled. Since human sexuality is largely socially determined, the adaptation of people to the social system prevalent at any given time is achieved to a large extent through the disciplining of their sexuality' (p. 120).

231 See Reeve (2005), p. 94, and the material by Simon & Gagnon (1986).

232 Coontz (2006) observes: '…the connection between what people believe in the abstract and what they do in real life is often tenuous at best' (p. 287). There may also be gender differences in the extent to which sexual desire and sexual behaviour is governed by internalised socio-cultural scripts. Vohs & Baumeister (2004) conclude 'whereas the male sex drive appears to conform to the pattern of an innate set of desires that are relatively immune to sociocultural influence, the female sex drive is much more malleable' (p.197).

233 Toates (2014) wrote: 'Sexual desire arises within an historical, cultural, and religious context, which powerfully influences how it is interpreted' (p. 68). See also his further observations regarding the various religious and cultural traditions in understanding and role of sexual desire.

234 Pfaus et al. (2014) noted: 'it is assumed that cultures superimpose a moral value of "right" and "wrong" on the hierarchies so that some behaviours that feel good are right and can be experienced without guilt, whereas others are wrong and carry the weight of guilt or rule of law against them. This type of inhibition represents an approach-avoidance conflict in which the expectation of reward drives the desire, but the inhibition imposed by the real or perceived aversive consequences of engaging in sexual activity blunts the initiation of behaviour' (p. 179).

235 See the work of Tiefer (2001). Katz-Wise & Hyde (2014) observed in regard to women's sexual problems, that the 'meaning and motivation for sexual activity are largely derived from cultural sexual scripts' (pp. 49-50). Marshall (2010) writes: 'According to sexual script theory, culturally derived rules and norms guide courtship and sexual behaviour (Green & Faulkner, 2005; Simon & Gagnon, 1986). These scripts, familiar to individuals socialised within the cultural setting from which they derive — most North Americans, for example, are aware of narratives for first dates or one-night stands — operate at cultural, interpersonal, and intrapsychic levels (Simon & Gagnon, 1986). Cultural-level

scripts, learned from schools, religious institutions, sex educators, and the mass media, address shared expectations about the who, what, when, where, and how of sexual behaviour (Gagnon, 1990; Greene & Faulkner, 2005). In the ambiguous world of dating, adherence to these scripts can help to reduce uncertainty, anxiety, and awkwardness (Laner & Ventrone, 1998)' (p. 289).

236 See, for example, Drehle (2013).

237 Although this has not been without its challengers: see, for example, Wilson (1981).

238 For a review of the many scripts found in different societies at different times, see, for example, Coontz (2006) and de Munck (1998). Lehmiller (2014) notes 'Virtually all societies around the world regulate sexuality in one form or another' (p. 3). See also Delamater (1987) and Delamater & Hyde (1998).

239 The presence of competing socio-cultural sexual scripts and subscripts within a single community means that where once a script set the common standard for behaviour, it is now possible for someone to choose which sexual script or subscript best suits their desired sexual lifestyle: the sexual lifestyle determines the adopted socio-cultural script, rather than the script determining the lifestyle.

240 Many tenants of the Mosaic laws are also reflected in Islamic teaching. The ancient Mosaic laws proscribed certain sexual behaviours because they were seen to be against divine and natural order, with severe consequences when these acts are committed: these teachings concern bestiality, adultery, having sex with a woman while she was menstruating, sex between men, prostitution, and incest.

241 See also the discussion by Kuehne (2009) regarding the traditional emphasis on the obligations of the couple in a sexual relationship to the family and society.

242 We read in the Quran, for example: 'Men are in charge of women by [right of] what Allah has given one over the other and what they spend [for maintenance] from their wealth. So righteous women are devoutly obedient, guarding in [the husband's] absence what Allah would have them guard' (Quran 4:34).

243 Coontz (2006) notes exceptions in some cultures.

244 Fromm (1962) wrote in this respect: 'In the Victorian age, as in many traditional cultures, love was mostly not a spontaneous personal experience which then might lead to marriage. On the contrary, marriage was contracted by convention — either by the respective families, or by a marriage broker, or without the help of such intermediaries; it was concluded on the basis of social considerations, and love was supposed to develop once the marriage was concluded' (pp. 9-10). Surprisingly, psychological research aligns with this: 'for women, desire often follows from sexual stimulation rather than preceding it, particularly in long term relationships' (Katz-Wise & Hyde (2014), p. 50).

245 And so Mangalwadi, for example, notes that in the Roman classical culture 'Adultery was a crime with serious consequences because it was an *economic* offense, taking another man's property (wife) — not because it was a matter of sexual impurity, a disruption of the holy union of husband and wife or a violation of sacred vows' (Mangalwadi (2011), p. 285).

246 See, for example, the Levitical codes in the Old Testament.

247 Note Coontz' observation about homosexual marriage in Roman society: 'The ancient Romans had no problem with homosexuality, and did not think that heterosexual marriage was sacred. The reason they found male-male marriage repugnant was that no real man would ever agree to play the subordinate role demanded of a Roman wife.' (Coontz (2006), p. 11) Of course, unless it occurred within a master/slave relationship where one was the property of the other, the economic implications of such a union created a problem.

248 A covenant in traditional times was a form of agreement or contract involving vows made before witnesses that articulated promises and obligations that both parties were honour-bound to keep, according to the terms of the covenant. It had legal status and the trust and shared expectations it was based on was foundational to social order.

249 Hernandez, Mahoney, & Pargament (2014) note: 'Christianity maintains that sexual intercourse within heterosexual marriage is intended for procreation and bonding. …premarital and extramarital sexuality is viewed nearly universally as sinful and prohibited' (p. 427). Consistent with this view, they further note (citing Fontenot (2013)) that, until recently, 'religious institutions also have understood homosexuality to be a desecration of the sacred' (p. 427).

250 The notions of belonging and exclusiveness as inherent in the sexual relationship are foundational to the traditional sexual scripts and key to the significance of loss of virginity. In this context, Freud wrote in *The Virginity Taboo* in 1918: 'The requirement that the girl should not bring into marriage to one husband a memory of sexual intercourse with another is of course nothing but the consistent continuation of the exclusive property right to a woman which constitutes the essence of monogamy, and the extension of this monopoly to include the past. …The person who is first able to satisfy the virgin's longing for love, arduously contained over long periods of time, and who has thus overcome the resistances erected in her by the influences of milieu and her education, will be drawn by her into a lasting relationship that will no longer be possible with anyone else. On the basis of this experience the woman enters a state of dependence which guarantees the untroubled permanence of her possession and makes her capable of resisting new impressions and the temptations of stranger' (Freud (2006), p. 262). Freud further explores how a relationship remains stable even when love fades, because there is no memory of sexual relationship being possible with another person.

251 See for example, the gospel of St Matthew 19:4-6: '…at the beginning the creator "made them male and female," and said "For this reason a man will… be united to his wife, and the two will become one flesh." So they are no longer two, but one. Therefore what God has joined together, let man not separate.' This idea of belonging and becoming 'one' is a critical notion of the traditional scripts not reflected in the various subscripts of the *secular Western* script.

252 The linking of sexuality and spirituality is also found in other religious traditions such as Taoism, Hinduism, and Buddhism. Regarding the Christian tradition, Hernandez, Mahoney, & Pargament (2014), citing Gardner (2002), observe that 'marital sex represents God's love and presence, unites the couple to God, and is holy and sacred' (p. 427).

253 The issue of the inherent seriousness of marriage and the associated issue of 'honour' is also relevant in other traditional scripts, but not so much in the *secular Western* script, where sexual behaviour is regarded much more casually, with sexual behaviour often being dismissed as inconsequential and commonly subjected to humour.

254 See, for example, the letters of the apostles Peter and Paul, in 1 Peter 3:1-7 and Ephesians 5: 22-33.

255 Brown (1988).

256 Of Tudor England of the 1500s, Briggs writes: '…order was considered essential to the stability and security of the state. The belief that the law of nature itself lay behind the one law of the realm lent sanctity to the whole system… The laws of society therefore required that 'every part do obey one head or governor' and that 'order, moderation and reason' should 'bridle the affections'… They were reinforced by paternal authority within the family and the preaching of the church. Each household, like society as a whole, had its 'head' who, in theory at least, expected obedience in his small realm. Wives, by law as well as by custom, were held to be subordinate to their husbands… Order, therefore, lay at the centre of all things' (Briggs (1983), p. 106).

257 Having said this, Christian New Testament teaching invites a husband and wife to submit to *each other* — to voluntarily give up perceived rights and desires for the benefit of the other (see Ephesians 5:21).

Chapter 9

258 See Peterson's (2018) commentary on post-modernism, Marxism, and the reaction to traditional patriarchal culture (p. 302).

259 Many writers in the field of sexuality (such as Tolman & Diamond (2014)) make reference to the traditional script as 'the dominant culture', implying the masculine 'dominant' nature of the culture. The reality, however, is that the *secular Western* script has largely become the 'dominant culture' in the Western

world, in the sense of its widespread embrace, especially in its representation in the media, and the changes in legislation that have resulted.

260 A comparison of the literature on the psychology of sexuality in the 1970s with that of the 2010s is revealing, in the changes of perspective that can be seen to have taken place over this time. For example, the heteronormative perspectives of that time have largely changed.

261 This raises the question of what scientific evidence might be relevant to the rules of relationships, and to morality more generally. From the perspective of the 'science' of psychology, relational research tends to focus on the promotion of the health and wellbeing of the individual rather than that of the relationship itself or of the community at large. Alternatively, research (generally based on surveys) gives information about *what happens to be common*, rather than how things *ought to be*. The evidence about *what happens to be common* then becomes the basis of social theory and policy. Furthermore, what is found to be common becomes 'normal', which in turn frequently forms the basis for what *should be*. This 'science' is given authority in matters of social morality. The philosopher David Hume explored the problem of converting *what is* into *what ought to be*, discussed at length in Hume (1978), pp. 469-470. But in more recent developments in gender theory, even 'common' or 'normal' is no longer seen as a basis for what should be. In fact, it is argued that there should no longer *be* any 'should be'.

262 The focus became increasingly self-focused, although recognition by others was still sought. Various writers have documented these social changes, with some referring to it as the 'celebration of narcissism': see, for example Andrews (2012) and Manne (2014).

263 Peterson (2004) presents romantic love as an ideology: 'One of the most basic prerequisites for falling in love is a belief that the phenomenon of couple love, or romantic attraction, actually exists as a potential life experience. Some men and women are such strong believers in romantic love that they would feel cheated or abnormal unless they managed to fall "head-over-heels" in love at least once in their lives...' (p. 440). See also Cunningham & Antill (1981, 1994) and Andrews (2012).

264 This was not without its challenges. For example, men were more likely than women to cite sex as their primary motivation in FWB, but women were more likely to seek an 'emotional connection'. Men liked the FWB to stay as it was; women often saw it as a step to a more committed relationship; and generally, those in FWB were less satisfied and had lower levels of sexual communication than those in committed relationships (Lehmiller (2014), p. 203).

265 Lehmiller (2014), citing Cohn, et al. (2011) and Blackwell & Lichter (2000), observes: '...Worldwide, the marriage rate has declined in recent years, whereas the number of couples who cohabit or seek to define their relationships in other

ways has increased … couples who cohabit tend to have more equality in their relationships and are less likely to subscribe to traditional gender role beliefs …Cohabitation makes it easier to end the relationship, but offers fewer legal rights and protections' (p. 215). He also notes, citing Jose, et al. (2010): '…couples who cohabit before marriage report lower marital quality …[but] a higher likelihood of divorce only occurs among individuals who have had prior experience moving in and out with multiple partners' (p. 216).

266 See Kuehne (2009), p. 51.

267 In this regard, Coontz (2006) writes: 'Marriage has become more joyful, more loving, and more satisfying for many couples than ever before in history. At the same time, it has become optional and brittle' (p. 306). And: '[The revolution in marriage] has liberated some people from restrictive, inherited roles in society. But it has stripped others of the traditional support systems and rules of behaviour without establishing new ones' (p. 308). And: '[Marriage] remains the highest expression of commitment in our culture and comes packaged with exacting expectations about responsibility, fidelity and intimacy. Married couples may no longer have a clear set of rules about which partner should do what in their marriage. But they do have a clear set of rules about what each partner should *not* do. …Arrangements other than marriage are still treated as makeshift or temporary, no matter how long they last. There is no consensus on what rules apply to these relationships' (p. 309).

268 See the psychological literature relating the capacity for delayed gratification (that is, self-discipline) to emotional maturity and the valuing of the objects of delayed gratification (for example, Peck (1978), Coleman (1995), Baumeister & Tierney (2011), and Peterson's (2018) chapter 7 *Pursue what is meaningful (not what is expedient)*). Also see the discussion regarding the *virtual sex* subscript.

269 See, for example, Andrews (2012) p. 118.

270 Having said this, one could argue that the individual rights sub references scienticism and evolutionary psychology. In regard to scientism and the individual, Byrnes, et al. (2009) note: 'Some scholars see the rise of modern scientific method in the 18th century enlightenment as grounded in the affirmation of freedom of thought and inquiry that each individual was able to exercise on the basis of rational thought and analysis, free from externally imposed "authoritative" views' (p. 3). The 'values-free' approach to sexual behaviour lends itself well to the scientific community, which seeks to 'objectively' study and interpret behaviour (see also Pettit & Hegarty (2014)).

271 This theme is evident in events that promote the sexual diversity celebrated in the human rights movement, such as in the *Sydney Gay and Lesbian Mardi Gras* festival, where traditional social institutions and values — representing the 'dominant culture' — are routinely pilloried.

272 But herein was a difficulty: just how 'private' are our lives when it comes to relationships and sexual behaviour? For example, ill-treatment by a partner in private will eventually manifest publically, perhaps leading to separation of the two parties involved, affecting many people — not least of all any children involved. Issues of domestic violence and separation — 'private' events — are also issues with major mental health repercussions both for the adults involved and for their children, becoming events of public concern. The sexual exploitation of a child has long-term mental health implications and social and relational ramifications. Although the damage caused to a child might be difficult to assess at the time, the mental and relational health issues surface later. What happens privately can influence things publically because it shapes the individual's thinking, feelings and behaviour, which in turn affects how they relate to others in the public domain. And although legislation concerns community governance, not private lives, it is the public face of private thoughts and acts that becomes its focus.

273 Unfortunately, to the degree that such freedom represented a freedom from past traditions or beliefs, and from authoritative institutions, it was potentially at the cost of certainty, stability, and socially accepted parameters for decision-making, which in turn created personal vulnerabilities and associated mental health problems for some.

274 In relation to some of the issues emerging from this idea, see Byrnes, et al. (2009), pp. 9-13. Paradoxically, although people look to laws to *safeguard* individual freedoms, laws normally *restrict* individual freedoms, ostensibly for the benefit, order and safety of the wider community. Byrnes, et al. (2009) observe that one of the fathers of the *French Declaration of the Rights of Man and the Citizen* of 1789, Jean-Jacques Rousseau, understood this dilemma: 'Rousseau's book *The Social Contract*, published in 1762, argued that the basis of entering the social contract involved giving up natural liberty for civil liberty' (p. 5). 'Rights' is a legal notion; not a biological or scientific one. Traditionally, rights are defined by legislation, rather than legislation being defined by (natural) 'human rights'. Rights come into being when the relevant law is enacted — that is, where there is community agreement to, and recognition of, that law. Generally laws are developed to create good order, safety and wellbeing for the wider community. This allows each person to be respected, to retain the integrity of their being, and to not live in fear — not so much because they have a natural *right* to this, but because by social agreement this is a good and productive thing to agree to. Yet a law typically restricts 'natural' individual freedoms, and necessarily discriminates against those whose actions happen to be restricted under that law. And so anti-discrimination laws create a conundrum, given that a law in and of itself discriminates. Nevertheless, well-formulated laws relating to sexual behaviour and restricting certain individual freedoms   on such issues as the age of consent, incest, and governing the

institution of marriage — appropriately become the basis upon which human rights and obligations are established.

275 This becomes more extreme as advances in technology moves from the range of sex toys (or 'aids') currently available to the creation of robots that can interact as sexual partners (see, for example, Ostrow (2017)).

276 Pratt (2015) observes: 'Not only are we struggling to comprehend the extent and type of pornography our youth are being exposed to, but we also have to grapple with the impact this is having on their sexual practices and relational templates. The pornography industry appears to have brought about changes to both body image and sexual practices among young people. Here's some examples: the complete lack of pubic hair on virtually everyone under 30 — thank the porn industry; the research indicating that large cohorts of teenage girls do not regard oral sex as sex, but rather something that is provided to young men as a way of not having sex — thank the porn industry; the growing rates of reported anal sex amongst adult and teenaged heterosexual couples, to the point that for the first time ever, rates of practising anal sex were polled among Victorian school students in Years 10-12 in a recent survey of sexual practices (the rates were recorded as nine per cent of the sample of just over 2,000 youth)' (p. 12).

277 McLean (2014) quotes Dr David Greenfield from the *Center for Internet Behaviour USA*: 'The internet appears to be capable of altering mood, motivation, concentration, and producing a dissociating and disinhibiting experience for users; for some individuals, patterns of use can transform into abuse, taking on a compulsive quality...' (p. 97).

278 Language plays a subtle but powerful role in the construction of meanings. In the scientific community, terms can be objective and impersonal, deemphasising the personal nature of sexual events. Although the form of language used colours all narratives, a depersonalising theme becomes a narrative in its own right, reinforcing the idea that sexual behaviour simply represents the expression of animal instincts, and need carry no other meaning. But this is not limited to the scientific community. Terms used for sexual interest or desire and for sexual intercourse can carry meanings that are exploitive, demeaning or belittling and even abusive of the sexual relationship, or disrespectful of the sexual partner. When terms for human sexual behaviour are used that are commonly used to describe the sexual activity of animals, for example, the sexual relationship becomes depersonalised: in depersonalising the sexual act, the actors also become depersonalised, which can result in alienation. Such depersonalising language has found its way into songs, books, movies, and comedy. Most of all, it is a common feature of pornography, which has become highly accessible through the internet. If the sexual act is the apex of the expression of human intimacy, love, belonging and connection, then its depersonalisation destroys all these meanings.

Chapter 10

279 These individual narratives have also been referred to as *working models*. Feeney, (2016) (citing Collins, et al. 2014, and Mikulincer & Shaver 2015), suggested that 'working models include four components: memories of attachment-related experiences; beliefs, attitudes, and expectations of self and others in relation to attachment; attachment-related goals and needs; and strategies and plans for achieving these goals... working models shape our cognitive, emotional, and behavioural responses to others' (p. 441). Here of course, we include not only attachment history, but also a person's sexual history. Individual sexual narratives articulate part of a person's *mind map* (or mental map) as described in Schneider (2013).

280 Although strictly speaking we are dealing with *infant-caregiver* attachment, because parents are generally an infant's caregivers (and for ease of writing) I will refer to *infant-parent* attachment.

281 Hazan & Shaver (1987) and Hazan & Zeifman (1994).

282 See also Byers & Rehman (2014), p. 321, Carter (2010), and Siegel (2012).

283 Peterson (2004), p.151.

284 Schaffer & Emerson (1964).

285 Cozolino (2006).

286 Schaffer & Emerson (1964).

287 This was earlier referenced in the negative sense from a sexual relational point of view in the fear of entrapment drive.

288 See, for example, Siegel (2012).

289 Adults seeking sexual behaviour with children comprise a heterogeneous group with varying drive profiles and outlooks. In developing a motivational continuum, from *situational* to *preferential* circumstances, Lanning (2010) suggests various motives in child sexual offenders. At the situational end, there are those with no particular interest in children as such, whose actions are impulsive and opportunistic. Indiscriminate sexual desire or non-sexual motives such as anger or power may play a role. Some have poor social skills, general poor coping, poor self-esteem, or lack the confidence to initiate a sexual relationship with an appropriate person. Along similar lines are those with inadequate or withdrawn personalities who are drawn to children (and sometimes also the elderly) because they are non-threatening. Then there are those that simply don't care — antisocial or psychopathic people who may manipulate, force or lure vulnerable children should the opportunity arise, simply because they are able. Their activity is *indiscriminate* in the sense that they might equally approach vulnerable adults, and *opportunistic* in the sense that it is non-relational, impulsive, and either a one-off event or short-lived.

But there are also those that prefer children sexually. Most commonly, they seduce children into an ongoing sexual relationship, seeking both emotional and sexual intimacy. They have good relational skills and empathy, and may identify with a child's vulnerabilities — often their sense of loneliness (non-belonging) or emotional neglect. The offender views their own behaviour as loving and acceptable, and believes the child is making their own choices, and benefits from the relationship (see, for example, Wilson (1981)). In this instance there is an active grooming that seduces the child, first into an affectionate and close relationship, and then into a sexual one. Ultimately, the child's emotional needs are exploited, and their natural interpersonal boundaries are compromised because they feel safe, understood, and loved. This can take place over a lengthy period so that bonding and interpersonal belonging results. While the child may not always be traumatised and upset at the time, they later struggle with guilt and shame.

The sadistic pattern in child preference is relatively rare. This involves sexual arousal conditioned to seeing a vulnerable child suffering or humiliated: it suggests underlying issues with anger and power. Finally, Lanning describes the 'diverse' profile, which describes offenders that are essentially indiscriminate in their sexual interests, seeking a variety of sexual experiences which are not limited to children, but nor are their responses simply reactive to circumstance. It is an aspect of their sexual interest, rather than having a more generally sociopathic or psychopathic base.

The most common danger occurs within the family system. The ready sexualisation of intimacy and affection behaviours can see relationships between certain family members transform over time from 'innocent' love and affection into sexualised behaviours, including sexual innuendo, covert or overt observing, exposure, invasive touch and caress, and genital involvement either of the offender or the victim or both. These behaviours may be restricted to family members: that is, those that are already in trusting relationships and with whom the offender has ready contact. A person's interpersonal boundaries tend to be more relaxed in the family, as familiarity, trust, closeness and belonging are already established: these factors makes the transition into sexualised behaviours much easier. Typically, the offender is male, but female members can also relate in inappropriate sexual ways. These situations are often situational rather than preferential. An important question is not just what has activated sexual arousal or desire towards a child, but why have inhibiting drives not been activated?

Socio-cultural scripts can contribute positively and protectively to such inhibitory drives. But there is disturbingly an alternative script (echoing the *individual freedoms* subscript) that some child sexual offenders use that compromises such inhibitory drives (e.g. Wilson (1981)), suggesting that children and adolescents should be allowed to engage in sexual relations with whom they want, that men who have consenting sex with boys might be considered 'benevolent father figures' rather than sex offenders, that boys might play a role in seducing men as much as men might boys, and that we may have misunderstood the sexual and emotional 'needs' of young males. (In this respect, a distinction may also be made between homosexual child abuse and heterosexual child abuse.)

290 This is not legal guilt — Alicia was a minor and victim of abuse — but the psychological guilt feelings that result from association with or complicity in immoral actions, and the failure and sense of self-betrayal for not maintaining personal boundaries, even when powerless to do otherwise.

291 Freud's theory of sexual development posited that 'sexual pleasure' was experienced in childhood in different ways (that is, focused on different body parts) at different times of development. However, his theory raises the question: what makes pleasure 'sexual'?

292 See Lamb & Plocha (2014), p. 416.

293 Ibid, pp. 422-424.

294 Foucault suggests it is 'repressive' when we think we need to 'protect childhood innocence', and declares that we take away sexual pleasure without guilt from children when we define what is traumatic and harmful for children in sexual matters. Foucault's philosophy is periodically promoted by research psychologists dealing with issues of sexuality (see, for example, Lamb & Plocha (2014)). I believe his approach is badly flawed for many reasons (see Andrews (2012) on Foucault). In this case, the issue is how we understand childhood sexuality. Childhood innocence represents a beauty of its own that may associate with happy childhood memories, but which may also become confused with inappropriate sexual overlays. Childhood innocence associates with the promise of loveliness, hope, a future still to unfold, something as yet untouched, unmarked, and free of the complexities of adult sexual relating.

295 Nevertheless, initial sexual relationship experiences at *whatever* age — whether far too early or long after the child has reached sexual and relational maturity — will affect drives and decisions through association, conditioning, and a changed neural orientation (that is, the brain shapes itself around its decisions and experience). First experiences and decisions in relation to sexual behaviour may be of lasting consequence: hopefully, positively; but not always.

296 This has long been known. In 1931, for example, Freud (2006) notes: 'As we have long known with the effects of seduction, other elements — the time of the birth of brothers and sisters, the time of discovery of sexual difference, the direct observation of sexual intercourse, the encouraging or prohibiting attitude of parents, and so on — can provoke an acceleration and maturing of child sexual development' (p. 325).

297 Peterson (2004), p. 343, citing Steinberg (1988).

298 Comings, et al. (2002).

299 Lamb & Plocha (2014), p. 426.

300 Much could be said about the role of self-discipline, learned during the early years of childhood, and later capacity for successful relationships — sexual and otherwise. This would take us down another track, but see, for example, Peck's (1983) chapter on discipline, and Peterson's (2018) Rule 5: *Do not let your children do anything that makes you dislike them.*

301 Peterson (2004) pp. 266-268.

302 Bem (2000) argues that the 'exotic species' also comes to be associated with physiological arousal because of the differences, and that memory of arousal becomes the basis for later sexual 'erotic' attraction to the 'exotic species'.

303 See, for example, Meyer-Bahlberg (1980), referenced in Bailey & Zucker (1995). Although generally sexual orientation is established during the adolescent years, change in sexual orientation can take place in later adult life (Rosario & Scrimshaw (2014), p.561), presumably due to changes in drive profile.

304 See, for example, Fagot (1985) referenced in Bailey & Zucker (1995).

305 See Green (1987). Importantly, effeminate tendencies during primary school or later do not necessarily result in homosexual interest or behaviour. Green's study found that for one-third of the boys with feminine tendencies, no homosexual patterns resulted.

306 See Bem (2002).

307 See, for example, Bell, Weinberg, & Hammersmith (1981) and Newman & Muzzonigro (1993). As we have seen, this may in part be the result of the hormonal activity in the second trimester of prenatal development, where insufficient testosterone results in the feminisation of the brain (see Rosario & Schrimshaw (2014), pp. 568-569).

308 Isay (2009), p. 18. Others have made similar observations, such as Green (1987) and Storms (1983), cited by Bayley & Zucker (1995).

309 See the work of social learning theorists (Peterson (2004), pp. 272-273). This social learning includes learning about relationship skills: patterns of communication and conflict resolution. In this respect, the stability of the parental relationship becomes an important source of learning and expectation with regard to the child's own future sexual relationships.

Chapter 11

310 Birnbaum (2016), Mikulincer & Shaver (2007), Tracy, et al. (2003) and O'Sullivan & Thompson (2014) observe that 'adolescents report intimacy is the primary motive for engaging in a variety of sexual behaviours' (p. 458).

311 Birnbuam (2010) and Mikulincer & Shaver (2007).

312 Baumeister (2001), p. 155.

313 Allen & Tan (2016) note: 'During adolescence, rapidly developing competencies decrease the need for dependence on parental attachment figures, and the strong need to explore and master new environments promotes healthy growth in the exploratory system' (p. 400). That is, the *drive to curiosity and discovery* is generally ascendant at this time.

314 As she matures, she also begins to consider what the male can offer her as a provider and the door to a new life — perhaps a stable and protected future in which to raise a family, or an adventurous and interesting future providing personal stimulation, or perhaps a socially privileged life that allows her competitive side to know success, depending on her SDP of the time.

315 Individual differences in the preparedness for entering a stable romantic relationship relate in part to the adolescent's parental attachment history (see Furman (2001) and Dykas, et al. (2006)).

316 The notion that the drive profile fluctuates, especially during adolescence, explains, for example, why same-sex orientation is frequently unstable during this time. Studies suggest that some two-thirds of those describing themselves as same-sex attracted during adolescence are opposite-sex attracted by their twenties (See Savin & Williams (2007), and Ott & Corliss (2010)). This indicates fluidity in sexual orientation because of changing natural circumstances and drive profile.

317 Erikson argues for the need for a certain readiness in social/emotional maturity before a sexual relationship can function effectively. Peterson (2004) (citing Erikson (1968)), observes that Erikson defined intimacy as 'the personality dimension that develops out of a successful resolution of the central developmental crisis of early adulthood. For Erikson, intimacy is "Mutual devotion [which] overcomes the antagonisms inherent in divided sexual and functional polarisation [and] the guardian of that elusive and yet all-persuasive power... which binds into a 'way of life' the affiliations and competition and cooperation, production and procreation" [Erikson, p. 137] For Erikson, genuine intimacy implies something more than the exclusivity of 'steady' dating or sexual monogamy, and more than the togetherness of sharing a home, a bed or even one's most private thoughts and feelings. As he defined it, intimacy entails a major reorganisation of each partner's entire psychological make-up through "a counterpointing as well as a fusing of identities." This means that a stable, achieved identity is one of the pre-requisites for mature, intimate love.' (Peterson (2004), p. 447)

318 Wallmyr & Welin (2006), cited in O'Sullivan, & Thompson (2014), p. 448.

319 The question as to the age considered appropriate for engaging in sexual activity or entering a sexual relationship varies from culture to culture. Furthermore, in many countries an arbitrary age is set defining when sexual activity is legal: although the intent is clearly to protect against the negative consequences of sexual relationships entered into in immaturity, the basis for the 'age of consent' is unclear. What some regard as protective, however, others regard as repressive.

320 Lerner (1989) notes: 'At the simplest level, "being a self" means we can be pretty much who we are in relationships rather than what others wish, need, and expect us to be. It also means that we can allow others to be the same. It means we do not participate in relationships at the expense of the "I" (as women are encouraged to do) and we do not bolster the "I" at the expense of the other (as men are encouraged to do). As simple as this may sound, its translation into action is enormously complex' (pp. 21-22).

321 Bowlby (1975) noted: 'confidence in the availability of attachment figures, or lack of it, is built up slowly during the years of immaturity — infancy, child-hood, and adolescence — and that whatever expectations are developed during those years tend to persist relatively unchanged throughout the rest of life' (p. 235). Fear and anxiety tend to inhibit relational drives, but not necessarily sexual desire or arousal. This would predict a greater likelihood of sexual activity outside a relational context by those suffering insecure attachment, reinforcing existing patterns of insecure attachment. While Bowlby does not comment on the role of a first sexual experience in subsequent attachment processes, new research provides increasing evidence for the central role of attachment styles in both early and subsequent sexual experiences.

322 We notice that with *belonging* also comes the presence of *boundaries*. That is, a discrimination between the one to whom I belong, and those to whom *I do not belong*. A poor history of interpersonal boundaries can indirectly result in a confused sense of belonging.

323 For example, Bretherton & Waters (1985), and the many recent studies cited in, for example, Cassidy & Shaver (2016).

324 See, for example, Hazan & Shaver (1987). Peterson (2004) observes that 'securely attached infants, who grow up to become securely attached children, adolescents and adults, are likely to enjoy different experiences with peers, romantic partners, spouses and colleagues at work than those whose attachment styles remain insecure' (p. 159).

325 Hazan & Shaver (1987, 1990, 1994) and Hazan & Zeifman (1994).

326 Feeney & Noller (1996). See also Feeney & Noller (1990, 1992).

327 Peterson (2004), p. 394.

328 Tracy, et al. (2003), Davis, et al. (2003, 2004), Gentzler & Kerns (2004), and Stefanou & McCabe (2012).

329 Szielasko, et al. (2013), Paulk & Zayac (2013), and Birnbaum (2016).

330 Birnbaum (2007) and Birnbaum, et al. (2006).

331 Davis, et al. (2004) and Birnbaum (2007).

332 Tracy, et al. (2003), Cooper, et al. (2006), and Schachner & Shaver (2004).

333 Cooper, et al. (2006) and Gentzler & Kerns (2004).

334 Gentzler & Kerns (2004), Bogaert & Sadava (2002), Davis (2006), and Szymaski & Stewart-Richardson (2014).

335 For example, Birnbaum (2007) and Cohen & Belski (2008).

336 See also Mikulincer & Shaver (2007).

337 Mikulincer & Shaver (2007) and Birnbaum (2010).

338 See Impett, et al. (2014), pp. 279-280.

339 Davis, et al. (2003, 2004) and Impett, Gordon, Strachman (2008), cited in Impett, et al. (2014), p. 279.

340 Schachner & Shaver (2004) cited in Impett, et al. (2014).

341 From Stephanou & McCabe (2014): 'Mikulincer and Shaver introduced a model specifying the activation and operation of the adult attachment system. When attachment figures are perceived as available and responsive, a sense of felt security is developed which encourages the formation of close bonds with others. However, if attachment figures are perceived as unavailable and unresponsive, secondary attachment strategies are activated to cope with the sense of insecurity... It has been proposed that attachment and sexual behavior are two instinctual systems that are central to human behavior. Empirical research indicates that these two systems have a reciprocal relationship, as attachment styles shape the way sexual interactions are experienced... Sexual hyperactivation involves effortful attempts to encourage a partner to have sex, placing significant value on the importance of sex within a relationship, and adopting a hypervigilant stance toward perceived sexual rejection. In contrast, sexual deactivation involves inhibition of sexual desire, avoidant attitudes toward sex, distancing from a partner who is interested in sex, and inhibition of sexual arousal and orgasmic joy. Therefore, the attachment and sexual behaviour systems can impact sexual function and dysfunction within romantic relationships' (p. 2500).

342 Peterson (2004) reports that '...most adolescents in Australia, New Zealand, Europe and North America today become sexually active while still in their teens (Bingham & Crockett, 1996; Noller, Feeney & Peterson, 2001) though a minority remain virgins until the age of 20, 25, or even later' (p. 349).

343 Jessor (1992), cited in Peterson (2004), p. 349.

344 Peterson (2004), p. 349.

345 See, for example, Billy & Udry (2001).

346 This is especially so for males: see Baumeister (2001), p. 136.

347 Collins & Harper (1985), cited in Peterson (2004), p. 350.

348 'Many agreed with the statement "If you don't take risks you don't have any fun"' (Peterson (2004), p. 348, citing Goldman (1990)).

349 Peterson notes that teenagers had a tendency to experiment with multiple partners without using a condom (Peterson (2004), p. 347, citing Chapman. & Hodgson (1988)) and also notes 'teenagers' sexual risk-taking may be enhanced by feelings of invulnerability' (Peterson (2014), p. 348, citing Goldman (1990)).

350 This will be open to dispute: see Impett, et al. (2014), p. 290. There certainly are negative experiences — but also positive ones. Gender makes a difference here, with men consistently reporting more satisfying first sexual experiences than women (reflecting a SDP often not linked as strongly with relational themes as it does for women — see elsewhere), and women more commonly reporting feelings of guilt, shame, and regret about engaging in sexual activity (Crockett, et al. 1996; and Higgins, et al. 2010). Not surprisingly, adolescents found their first sexual experiences more satisfying when they occur in the context of healthy 'steady' relationships (Donald, et al. 1995; and Weinberg, et al. 1995), although this again is more so for women. Importantly, Impett, et al. (2014) note: 'Initial sexual experiences lay an important foundation for sexual and relational development...' (p. 290).

351 Baumeister (2001), pp. 135-136.

352 Emmanuele (2008) in O'Sullivan, & Thompson (2014), p. 461.

353 Feeney (2016) researched *limerence*, and identified four factors associated with this form of 'anxious love': 'obsessive preoccupation', 'self-conscious pre-occupation with partners', 'emotional dependence', and 'idealisation'. She differentiated between this and anxious-ambivalent attachment, and found that four higher order factors helped to distinguish the various types of attachment in sexual relationships: 'neurotic love', 'circumspect love', 'self-confidence', and 'avoidance of intimacy' (p. 437).

354 Or to intentionally *inhibit* sexual desire or behaviour, where such desire or behaviour is problematic: see Toates (2014), pp.202-205.

355 Tennov (1999) observes that 'affectional bonding' is not the same as limerence. She writes that affectional bonding is about 'compatibility of interests, mutual preferences in leisure activities, ability to work together, pleasurable sexual experiences, and contentment' as compared to the limerent experience of 'con-

tinuous and unwanted intrusive thinking, an intense need for exclusivity, the goal of reciprocity, and ecstasy' (p. 130).

356 The unstable physiology of passion makes its decline almost inevitable, according to Walster & Walster (1978), cited in Peterson (2004): '...the human body cannot maintain such aberrant physiological states indefinitely... the body eventually gravitates back to a stable equilibrium... A decline in love's bodily upheavals need not always terminate the couple's involvement with each other, but often this does happen, particularly among young or inexperienced lovers who are uncertain enough about what love is to require physiological confirmation' (pp. 442-443).

357 This observation also underscores the need for any effective narrative to account for such changes, and to allow interpretation of a relationship as being successful even when there is a change in physiological processes.

358 Traupmann and Hatfield's (1981) two-stage model of love sees 'romantic passionate' love giving way to 'companionate' love. Driscoll, et al. (1972) observed that the companionate love of married couples focused more on qualities of companionship, trust, and mutual respect rather than intense physical emotions and sexual arousal (which, by their very nature, are short-lived) when compared to dating couples. Hatfield (1988) talked of *equity* in the companionate relationship — the subjective sense of balance between two lovers' contributions to the relationship and what each gain or lose from being involved in it. The one with greater investment expects greater returns — their research showed such equity to be common in all successful long-term relationships, and that poor equity played a role in extramarital affairs, with either the under-benefitted partner or the over-benefitted partner initiating the affair (Peterson (2004), pp. 444-446).

Chapter 12

359 There is a considerable body of research that links romantic attachment security with the quality of couple relationships. For a recent summary review of the research regarding the factors predicting good romantic relationship quality, see Feeney (2016), pp. 444-453. See also Uchino, et al. (1996), Diener & Seligman (2002), Diamond & Huebner (2012), and Impett, et al. (2014).

360 For example, 'insecurity in measures of both current attachment styles and qualities of current attachment relationships have also been linked to mental health difficulties [in adolescents]' (Allen & Tan (2016), p. 408). See also Stephenson, et al. (2011), for the relationship between sexual and relationship satisfaction.

361 Byers & Rehman (2014), p. 321, citing Lawrence & Byers (1995), MacNeil & Byers (2005, 2009), and Purnine & Carey (1997).

362 Byers & Rehman (2014), p. 321.

363 Reeve (2005). See also Kiecolt-Glaser & Newton (2001) and Musick & Bumpass (2012).

364 Reeve (2005), pp. 121-122 (summarising Cohen, et al. (1986), Lepore (1992), Ryan, et al. (1994), Sarason, et al. (1991), and Windle (1992). See also Carstensen, et al. (1995).

365 Reeve (2005), p. 123, citing Ryan & Lynch (1989), Pierce, Sarason & Sarason (1991), and Windle (1992). See also Baumeister & Leary (1995) and Williams & Solano (1983).

366 Reeve (2005), p. 123, citing Williams & Solano (1983). Also from George, et al. (2014), p. 661: There appear to be gender differences, possibly reflecting the greater integration of emotional connectedness and sexual activity in women, in that depressive symptoms seem to be associated with lower feelings of connectedness to their partner during sex among women, but with greater feelings of connectedness among men (Kashdan, et al. (2011)).

367 Amato (2000), cited in Stefanou & McCabe (2012), p. 2499.

368 Amato & Previti (2003), and Cano & O'Leary (2000), in Impett, et al. (2014), p. 298.

369 Perilloux & Buss (2008), in Lehmiller (2014), p. 224.

370 The most common cause of death between the age of fifteen and the mid-twenties is suicide. It is also the time that falling in love is common. How many people suicide because of failed love, and why do they do so? Tennov (1999), p. 149, reports that a large proportion of college report being depressed 'about a love affair'. It is not surprising that where so much is invested in a relationship, its cessation means everything is lost. And if meaning is about connection, and connection is lost, meaning is lost. And so suicide as a statement that I have no life or future or meaning anymore is hardly surprising.

371 For the possible psychological problems that arise in poor marriages, see Coontz (2006), p. 310. See also Impett, et al. (2014), p. 298.

372 For example, Putnam (2003).

373 Browne & Finkelhor (1986).

374 Bailey, et al. (2007) and Madigan, et al. (2012).

375 Beitchman, et al. (1992).

376 Mullen, et al. (1993).

377 Paolucci, et al. (2001).

378 Coker, et al. (2002).

379 Plichta & Falik (2001) and Temple, et al. (2007), cited in Impett, et al. (2014), p. 297.

380 See, for example, Bailey (1999) and Fergusson, et al. (1999).

381 Kerr, et al. (2003).

382 Oswalt & Wyatt (2011).

383 Burgess, et al. (2008). The research of de Bolger, et al. (2014) also found, for example, that a majority of 'trans men' reported 'a diagnosis of depression or anxiety within the last 12 months and attributed suicidal ideation and self-harm and attempted suicide to personal issues with gender identity' (p. 395).

384 Rosser, et al. (2008).

385 Mathy (2003), cited by Bockting (2014), pp. 744-745.

386 Zeifman & Hazan (2016), p. 429, citing Hall & Fincham (2006).

387 Paul, McManus, and Hays (2000); Justin Garcia, et al. (2012).

388 George, et al. (2014), p. 661 note that there is extensive empirical evidence of the comorbidity between sexual dysfunctions and mood disorders — particularly depression (see reviews by Hartmann (2007) and Michael & O'Keane (2000)) and anxiety (see reviews by Norton & Jehu (1984) and Seto (1992)).

389 Ibid (p. 662), citing Nobre & Pinto-Gouveia (2006, 2008).

390 Ibid (p. 661), citing Michael & O'Keane (2000).

391 Ibid (p. 663); see also Meade, et al. (2011).

392 Ibid (p. 661), citing Schnatz, et al. (2010) and Dell'osso, et al. (2009); see also Brotto & Smith (2014), p. 229.

393 Ibid (p. 661); see also Laurent & Simons (2009).

394 Ibid (p. 663).

395 Ibid (p. 663); see also Dunn, et al. (1999).

396 Ibid (p. 663). Of course, this would depend on what 'sexually active' means — especially whether or not it involved multiple partners.

397 I note that much sexual research tends to be of the survey kind, which tells us about current social patterns rather than the underlying dynamics of, and reasons for, sexual behaviour. A regular conclusion is that when a social pattern is common, it is 'normal'; and because it is 'normal', it must somehow be functional and healthy — or at least, not dysfunctional and unhealthy. I suggest that this represents a community's current lived values, rather than 'psychological science' as such. (See King (1945) on the meaning of 'normal'.)

398 There has been much debate over the years with philosophers, social scientists and theologians all making extensive contribution as to what the 'shoulds' (or norms) should be in the practice of sexual relationships. The important thing to note is that the ongoing debate centres largely on the issue of human freedom and on the goal of the sexual relationship: specifically, whether the ultimate goal of the sexual relationship is one of individual pleasure and fulfilment; or one of 'belonging' to one's sexual partner, with a view to interpersonal wellbeing and social order. My own position, and the reasons for it, I have made clear. This debate has direct bearing not only on the patterns of sexual behaviour that are studied, but also on the focus of psychological theory and research.

399 See, for example, Isay's argument in relation to homosexual impulses (Isay (2009), p. 8).

400 I note that the empty chair technique used in traditional Gestalt Therapy is one of several that externalised the internal dialogue that can be used to represent conflicting drives. Externalising such dialogue can help towards the process of resolution.

401 This could also be said of those suffering Gender Dysphoria (GD). The resolution of the dysphoria (that is, the emotional distress) as such is not the point: rather, the perception of being a gender different from that of the physical body (that is, physical reality) is the problem. Cretella (2016) observes: 'Psychology has increasingly rejected the concept of norms for mental health, focusing instead on emotional distress. The American Psychiatric Association (APA), for example, explains in [the DSM-V] that GD is listed therein not due to the discrepancy between the individual's thoughts and physical reality, but due to the presence of emotional distress that hampers his social functioning' (p. 51).

402 As is argued by Isay (2009) in his work with gay patients.

403 For a relationship to last, self-regulation (self-control) surely plays a role. This, in part, means managing the SDP and BDP. Lehmiller (2014) discusses this (pp. 249-250), although he relates it more to the likelihood of engaging in sexual practice, and observes that our 'ability to exert self-control is finite', quoting Baumeister, et al. (2007). Self-control is also a trait in the sense that some are naturally more able to assert self-discipline than others. Those with poor self-control engage in riskier behaviours (Raffaelli & Crockett (2003)), or are more tempted to cheat on their partner (Pronk, et al. (2011)). Gailliot & Baumeister (2007) reported that those whose self-regulatory abilities were temporarily weakened engaged in more extensive sexual activities with their partner, and also a greater likelihood of cheating on their partner.

404 Indeed, the brain may fail in one of its primary functions — to make sense of events in such a way that there is alignment between internal and external reality (including the prevailing social reality). Instead, external or social reality is not properly internalised. Whether or not poor alignment creates personal

distress, faulty and misaligned perceptions become a legitimate focus for thera-peutic intervention. This contrasts with the idea that intervention is simply about alleviating personal distress.

405 Feeney (2016) notes that 'Working models affect cognitive processes by direct-ing us to pay attention to certain aspects of social stimuli (particularly goal-related stimuli), by creating biases in memory encoding and retrieval, and by affecting explanation processes' (p. 441).

406 See, for example, Feeney's (2016) discussion on the stability, change, and the conceptualization of attachment (p. 443). See also Seligman's (1994) views on 'difficulty to change' arguments.

407 See for example, Cohen-Kettenis, et al. (2008), Shechner (2010), and Cretella (2016).

408 See thoughts of Cass (1979) on accepting responsibility for one's sexual self-image (p. 228).

409 In fact, the same drive profile that lead one into relationship can predispose towards unfaithfulness: drives such as curiosity ('what would it be like to have sex with him/her?'), not wanting to miss out ('I'm getting older — what if I never get the chance again: will I regret it?'), and the reignition of limerence ('I just want to have that heady feeling of being in love again') could encourage a person to go from one relationship to the next.

410 Social disapproval (for reasons of race, ethnicity, religion, social class, age, gender, sexuality, or relationship status) by family, friends, society at large, links to less commitment (Lehmiller & Agnew (2006)) and greater chance of breaking up (Lehmiller & Agnew (2007)), and worse physical and psychological health outcomes (Lehmiller (2014)) — 'lacking relationship acceptance and approval may be destructive to both the health of the partners and their romance.' (p.221) (This reflects the fact that belonging is not only to one another, but also to the wider social group, and for the social group to *recognise our belonging together* (hence the wedding ring) — we want to belong all round.)

411 Not making a decision — that is, drifting into a relationship — means a clear decision for the relationship has still to be made, and no doubt it *will* be made (by leaving the relationship) when things get tough. Lehmiller observes that cohabitation tends to have a 'shorter shelf-life' than marriage (Lehmiller (2014), p. 220).

412 *Insecurity and jealousy* — because of attachment style (Hazan & Shaver (1987), which partially develop out of our early experiences with primary caregivers, but new experiences and relationships also play a role in this (Simpson, et al. (2003)). Securely attached people find it easy to get close (intimate), are trusting (that the partner is reliable), and don't worry about abandonment; anxiously attached people are more likely to be jealous because they worry their partner

may not want to be close and that they won't love them, and might leave. Avoidantly attached people don't want too much intimacy, or to be dependent; they see love and the relationship as temporary, and that their partner could leave at any point. Anxious and avoidant attachment styles tend to lead to relationship breakup (Deummler & Kobak (2001)). When it comes to gender differences, men are more jealous about their partner becoming *physically* involved with someone else, while women become jealous that their partner might become *emotionally* involved with someone else (Buss, et al. (1992); see also Lehmiller (2014), p. 221).

413 Infidelity is the most frequently cited reason for divorce — Amato & Previti (2003). The definition of infidelity or cheating varies hugely: it can include the use of pornography, visiting prostitutes, one-night stands, and flirting. Men admit to cheating more than women. Cheating has a devastating effect on a relationship as it transgresses the expectations of what *belonging* means to a person: it is the ultimate betrayal of trust. Note also the prevalence of 'mate-guarding behaviour' and becoming jealous when a partner's eyes wander, which attests to the common expectation of relationship belonging. (Lehmiller (2014), p. 223).

414 An insecure person may want the other person to fit into their world and expectations. There's no room for another opinion: you can come into my home, but you can't bring in anything that belongs to you. You actually don't belong; it's my home, my space, which you can enter only when you leave all else behind. It is not shared space: it is *my* space. You can only have what I give you — you are altogether disempowered. There is no negotiating. It is important for such a person to be right: they have a fragile view of reality. If they are wrong about something, they could be wrong about other things too, and this loss of certainty destabilises them. But it also prevents the relationship negotiation necessary for long-term shared space.

415 To the extent that our belonging to someone else orients our sense of self, any violation, fracturing, or confusion in that sense of belonging can have immediate ramifications for our sense of self, and, by extension, our mental health, in the short term or the long term. The question must be asked: does the repeated fracturing of sexual relationships and the attendant sense of belonging have implications for mental health? Furthermore, as we have seen, this sense of belonging tends to have a territorial aspect in males. If this innate impulse to territoriality is denied, is masculinity then compromised, and does this contribute to identity confusion and mental health issues for men?

Chapter 13

416 Pratt (2015) notes: 'Research has shown some worrying trends, particularly related to earlier onset exposure (Kraus & Russell, 2008; Mitchell, et al., 2014),

with one study indicating the average age of first-time exposure to pornography was 12.2 years old. Sabina and colleagues (2008) found that 93 per cent of males and 62 per cent of females in their sample reported exposure to pornography prior to age 18, the majority between the ages of 14 and 17. It also appears that youth are the main consumers of pornography, with research indicating that young males aged 12-17 years were the most frequent consumers of online pornography (Haggstrom-Nordin, Hanson & Tyden, 2005)' (p. 12).

417 Smith (2015) notes that research suggests there is a range of reported pornography-viewing behaviour, from 'healthy, positive and educative' to 'exploitative, detrimental and addictive'. However, one of the difficulties with such research is that conclusions are drawn from the reported experiences of consumers of pornography. This is a bit like doing research on the effects of smoking by asking smokers about their experience. Few will admit to it being a problem or recognise longer-term effects.

418 Fantasy needs to be distinguished from intrusive images. The former involves a choice to engage in thoughts and mental images that are constructed intentionally, which may lead to sexual arousal, which, in turn, become conditioned to those images. As such they may reflect pre-existing sexual desire or interest, and they certainly reinforce sexual desire in relation to the images. The latter are involuntary, and generally result from intense and sometimes traumatic emotional experiences.

419 Smith (2015) notes: 'For relationships, another potential negative is that sexual behaviour in pornography is depicted as disconnected from the domain of a loving relationship, leading to unrealistic expectations and beliefs about sexual encounters and sexual intimacy. Differences between partners in terms of expectation and meaning about the use of pornography and cyber sex sites, in the absence of effective communication regarding sexual needs, increases the risk of relationship dissatisfaction. One partner's use of pornography may be viewed as evidence of rejection and personal inadequacy, the conclusion being that their partner does not find them sufficiently attractive or valuable' (p. 9).

420 Gemmel (2015), p. 8.

421 Komarovsky (1976), p. 146.

References

Agocha, V.B., Asencio, M., & Decena, C.U. (2014). Sexuality and Culture. In D.L. Tolman & L.M. Diamond (Eds.), *APA Handbook of Sexuality and Psychology Vol 2*. (pp. 183–228). Washington: American Psychological Association.

Ainsworth, M.D.S. (1973). The development of infant-mother attachment. In B.M. Caldwell & H.N. Ricciuti (Eds.), *Review of Child Development Research Vol 3: Child development and social policy*. Chicago: University of Chicago Press.

Allen, J.P., & Tan, J.S. (2016). The multiple facets of attachment in adolescence. In Cassidy, J., & Shaver, P.R. *Handbook of Attachment: Theory, research, and clinical applications Third edition*. (pp. 399–415). New York: The Guilford Press.

Amato, P.R. (2000). The consequences of divorce for adults and children. *Journal of Marriage and Family, 62*, 1269–1287.

Amato, P.R., & Previti, D. (2003). People's reasons for divorcing: Gender, social class, the life course, and adjustment. *Journal of Family Issues, 24*, 602–626. doi:10.1177/0192513X03024005002.

Amodeo, J., & Amodeo, K. (1986). *Being Intimate: A guide to successful relationships*. London and New York: Arkana.

Anderson, P.A., Eloy, S.V., Guerrero, L.K., & Spitzberg, B.H. (1995). Romantic jealousy and relational satisfaction: A look at the impact of jealousy experience and expression. *Communication Reports, 8*, 77–85. doi:10.1080/08934219509367613.

Andrews, K. (2012). *Maybe I do: Modern marriage and the pursuit of happiness*. Ballan: Connor Court Publishing.

Aron, A.P., Mashek, D.J., & Aron, E.N. (2004) Closeness as including other in the self. In D.J. Mashek & A. Aron (Eds.), *Handbook of Closeness and Intimacy* (pp. 27–41). Mahwah, New Jersey: Lawrence Erlbaum Associates.

Aronson, E. (1961). The effect of effort on the attractiveness of rewarded and unrewarded stimuli. *Journal of Abnormal and Social Psychology, 63*, 375–380.

Aronson, E., & Cope, V. (1968). My enemy's enemy is my friend. *Journal of Personality and Social Psychology, 8*, 8–12.

Athanasiou, R., & Yoshioka, A. (1973). The spatial character of friendship formation. *Environment and Behaviour, 5*, 43–65.

Bailey, H.N., Moran, G., & Pederson, D.R. (2007). Childhood maltreatment, complex trauma symptoms, and unresolved attachment in an at-risk sample of adolescent mothers. *Attachment and Human Development, 9 (2)*, 139–161.

Bailey, J. M. (1999). Homosexuality and mental illness. *Archives of General Psychiatry, 56 (10)*, 883–884. doi:10.1001/archpsyc.56.10.883.

Bailey, J.M., & Pillard, R.C. (1991). A genetic study of male homosexual orientation. *Archives of General Psychology, 48*, 1089–1097.

Bailey, J.M., Pillard, R.C., Neale, M.C.I., & Agyei, Y. (1993). Heritable factors influence sexual orientation in women. *Archives of General Psychiatry, 50*, 217–223.

Bailey, M.J., & Triea, K. (2007). What many transsexual activists don't want you to know and why you should know it anyway. *Perspectives in Biology and Medicine, 50*, 521–534. doi:10.1353/pbm.2007.0041.

Bailey, J.M., & Zucker, K.J. (1995). Childhood sex-typed behaviour and sexual orientation: A conceptual analysis and quantitative review. *Developmental Psychology, 31 (1)*, 43-55. doi:10.1037/0012-1649.31.1.43.

Basson, R. (2001). Human sex-response cycles. *Journal of Sex and Marital Therapy, 27*, 33–43.

Basson, R. (2002). Women's sexual desire – disordered or misunderstood? *Journal of Sex and Marital Therapy, 28*, 17–28.

Basson, R. (2003). Commentary on "In the mood for sex – the value of androgens." *Journal of Sex and Marital Therapy, 29*, 177–179.

Baumeister, R.F. (Ed.) (2001). *Social Psychology and Human Sexuality: Key Readings in Social Psychology*. Philadelphia, PA: Psychology Press.

Baumeister, R.F., & Leary, M.R. (1995). The need to belong: desire for interpersonal attachments as a fundamental human motivation. *Psychological Bulletin 117*, 497–529. doi:10:1037/0033-2909.117.3.497.

Baumeister, R.F., & Tierney, J. (2011). *Willpower: Rediscovering the greatest human strength*. New York: Penguin Press.

Baumeister, R.F., Vohs, K.D., & Tice, D.M. (2007). The strength model of self-control. *Current Directions in Psychological Science, 16*, 351-355. doi:10:1111/j1467–8721.2007.00534.x.

Beitchman, J.H., Zucker, K.J., Hood, J.E., DaCosta, G.A., & Akman, D. (1992). A review of the long-term effects of child sexual abuse. *Child Abuse & Neglect, 16 (1)*, 101–118. doi.org/10.1016/0145-2134(92)90011.

Bell, A., & Weinberg, M. (1978). *Homosexualities: A study of diversity among men and women*. New York: Simon & Schuster.

Bell, A.P., Weinberg, M.S., & Hammersmith, S.K. (1981). *Sexual preference: Its development in men and women.* Bloomington. Indiana University Press.

Bell, A.P. (1982). Sexual preference: A postscript. *Siecus Report, 11, 2.*

Bem, D.J. (1996). Exotic becomes erotic: A developmental theory of sexual orientation. *Psychological Review, 103*: 320–335; also in Baumeister, R.F. (Ed.) (2001) *Social Psychology and Human Sexuality: Key readings in Social Psychology.* Philadelphia, PA: Psychology Press, pp.191–212.

Bem, D.J. (1998). Is EBE Theory Supported by the Evidence? A Reply to Peplau et al (1998). *Psychological Review, 105*, 395–398.

Bem, D.J., Herdt, G., & McClintock, M. (2000). Exotic becomes erotic: interpreting the biological correlates of sexual orientation. *Archives of Sexual Behaviour, 29* (6), 531–548. doi:10.1023/A:1002050303320. PMID 11100261. PDF.

Bem, S.L. (1985). Androgyny and gender schema theory: A conceptual and empirical integration. In Sondregger, T.B. (Ed), *Nebraska Symposium on Motivation, 1984: Psychology and Gender (Vol 32).* Lincoln: University of Nebraska Press

Berenbaum, S.A., & Snyder, E. (1995). Early hormonal influences on childhood sex-typed activity and playmate preferences: implications for the development of sexual orientation. *Developmental Psychology, 31*, 31–42.

Berg, S.J., & Wynne-Edwards, K.E. (2001). Changes in testosterone, cortisol, and estradiol levels in men becoming fathers. *Mayo Clinic Proceedings, 76*, (1), 582–592. doi:10.4065/76.6.582.

Berger, P., & Luckmann, T. (1967). *The Social Construction of Reality: A treatise in the sociology of knowledge.* Garden City, NY: Doubleday.

Berry, D.S., & Hansen, J. (1996). Positive affect, negative affect, and social interaction. *Journal of Personality and Social Psychology, 71*, 796–809. doi:10.1037/0022-3514.71.4.796.h.

Berscheid, E., Dion, K., Walster, E., & Walster, G.W. (1971). Physical attractiveness and dating choice: a test of the matching hypothesis. *Journal of Experimental Social Psychology, 7*, 173–189. doi:10.1016/0022-1031(71)90065-5.

Bingham, C.R., & Crockett, L.J. (1996) . Longitudinal adjustment patterns of boys and girls experiencing early, middle, and later sexual intercourse. *Developmental Psychology, 32*, 647–658.

Billy, J.O.G., & Udry, J.R. (2001). Patterns of adolescent friendship and effects on sexual behaviour. In Baumeister, R. F., *Social Psychology and Human Sexuality: Key readings in Social Psychology* Philadelphia, PA: Psychology Press.

Birnbaum, G.E. (2007). Attachment orientations, sexual functioning, and relationship satisfaction in a community sample of women. *Journal of Social and Personal Relationships, 24*, 21–35.

Birnbaum, G.E., Reis, H.T., Mikulincer, M., Gillath, O., & Orpaz, A. (2006). When sex is more than just sex: Attachment orientations, sexual experience, and relationship quality. *Journal of Personality and Social Psychology, 91*, 929–943.

Birnbaum, G.E. (2010). Bound to interact: The divergent gaols and complex interplay of attachment and sex within romantic relationships. *Journal of Social and Personal Relationships, 27*, 245–252.

Birnbaum, G.E. (2016). Attachment and sexual mating: the joint operation of separate motivational systems. In Cassidy, J., & Shaver, P.R. *Handbook of Attachment: Theory, research, and clinical applications Third edition* (pp.464–483). New York: The Guilford Press.

Blackwell, D.L., & Lichter, D.T. (2000). Mate selection among married and cohabiting couples. *Journal of Family Issues, 21*, 275–302. doi:10.1080/00224490409552235.

Blau, P.M. (1964). *Exchange and Power in Social Life*. New York: John Wiley & Sons.

Bockting, W.O. (2014).Transgender identity development. In D.L. Tolman & L.M. Diamond (Eds.), *APA Handbook of Sexuality and Psychology, Vol 1*. (pp. 739–758). Washington: American Psychological Association.

Bogaert, A.F., & Sadava, S. (2002). Adult attachment and sexual behaviour. *Personal Relationship, 9*, 191–204.

Booth, A., Johnson, D.R., & Granger, D.A. (1999.) Testosterone and men's health. *Journal of Behavioral Medicine, 22* (1), 1–19. doi:10.1023/A:1018705001117.

Bowlby, J. (1975). *Attachment and Loss – Vol 2, Separation: Anxiety and Anger*. Harmondsworth: Penguin Books.

Breedlove, S.M. (1994). Sexual differentiation of the human nervous system. *Annual Review of Psychology, 45*, 389–418.

Brehm, J.W. (1966). *A Theory of Psychological Reactance*. New York: Academic Press.

Brennan, K.A., Clark, C.L., & Shaver, P.R. (1998). Self-report measurement of adult attachment: An integrative interview. In J.A. Simpson & W.S. Rholes (Eds.), *Attachment Theory and Close Relationships* (pp.46–76). New York: Guildford Press.

Bretherton, I., & Waters, E. (1985). Growing points of attachment theory and research. *Monographs of the Society for Research in Child Development, 50* (209), 1–211.

Briggs, A. (1983). *A Social History of England*. London: Weidenfeld and Nicolson.

Brislin, R.W., & Lewis, S.A. (1968). Dating and physical attractiveness: replication. *Psychological Reports, 22*, 976.

Brotto, L.A., & Smith, K.B. (2014). Sexual desire and pleasure. In D.L. Tolman & L.M. Diamond (Eds.), *APA Handbook of Sexuality and Psychology, Vol 1.* (pp. 205–244). Washington: American Psychological Association.

Brown, P. (1988). *The Body and Society: Men, women, and sexual renunciation in early Christianity.* New York: Columbia University Press.

Browne, A., & Finkelhor, D. (1986). Impact of child sexual abuse: A review of the research. *Psychological Bulletin, 99* (1), 66–77. doi:10.1037/0033-2909.99.1.66.

Buck, R. (1988). *Human Motivation and Emotion.* New York: John Wiley & Sons.

Burchell, J.L., & Ward, J. (2011). Sex drive, attachment style, relationship status and previous infidelity as predictors of sex differences in romantic jealousy. *Personality and Individual Differences, 51,* 657–661. doi:10.1016/j.paid.2011.06.002.

Burgess, D., Lee, R., Tran, A., & van Ryn, M. (2008). Effects of perceived discrimination on mental health and mental health services utilization among gay, lesbian, bisexual, and transgender persons. *Journal of LGBT Health Research, 3* (4), 1–14. doi:10.1080/ 15574090802226626.

Buss, D.M. (1994). *The Evolution of Desire.* New York: Basic Books.

Buss, D.M., Larsen, R.J., Westen, D., & Semmelroth, J. (2001). Sex differences in jealousy: Evolution, physiology, and psychology. In Baumeister, R.F. (Ed.), *Social Psychology and Human Sexuality: Key readings in Social Psychology* (pp. 278–291). Philadelphia, PA: Psychology Press.

Buston, P.M., & Emlen, S.T. (2003). Cognitive processes underlying human mate choice: the relationship between self-perception and mate preference in Western society. *Proceedings of the National Academy of Sciences, 100,* 8805–8810.

Byers, S.E., & Rehman, U.S. (2014). Sexual wellbeing. In D.L. & Diamond, L.M. (Eds.), *APA Handbook of Sexuality and Psychology Vol 1.* (pp. 317–338). Washington: American Psychological Association.

Byrne, D. (1971). *The Attraction Paradigm.* New York: Academic Press.

Byrne, D., & Nelson, D.A. (1965). Attraction as a linear function of proportion of positive reinforcements. *Journal of Personality and Social Psychology, 1,* 659–663.

Byrnes, A., Charlesworth, H., & McKinnon, G. (2009). *Bills of Rights in Australia: History, Politics, and Law.* Sydney: UNSW Press.

Cano, A., & O'Leary, K. (2000). Infidelity and separation predict major depressive episodes and symptoms of nonspecific depression and anxiety. *Journal of Consulting and Clinical Psychology, 68,* 774–781. doi:10.1037/0022-006X.68.5.774

Carnes, P. (1992). *Don't Call it Love: Recovery from sexual addiction.* New York: Bantam Books.

Carnes, P. (2001). *Out of the Shadows: Understanding sexual addiction (3rd ed.).* Minnesota: Hazelden Publishing.

Carrington, J. (2012). Using Hormones to Heal Traumatic Brain Injuries. *Life Extension Magazine, Jan:* www.lifeextension.com.

Carstensen, L.L., Gottman, J.M., & Levenson, R.W. (1995). Emotion behaviour in long-term marriage. *Psychology and Aging, 10,* 140–149.

Carter, R. (2010). *Mapping the Mind.* London: Orion Publishing Group.

Caspi, A., & Herbener, E.S. (1990). Continuity and change: Assortative marriage and the consistency of personality in adulthood. *Journal of Personality and Social Psychology, 58,* 250–258.

Cass, V. (1979). Homosexual identity formation: A theoretical model. *Journal of Homosexuality, 4* (3), 219–235.

Cassidy, J., & Shaver, P.R. (2016). *Handbook of Attachment: Theory, research, and clinical application. Third edition.* New York: The Guilford Press.

Chapman, S., & Hodgson, J. (1988). Showers in raincoats: Attitudinal barriers to condom use in high-risk heterosexuals. *Community Health Studies 12,* 97–105.

Chivers, M.L., Suschinsky, K.D., Timmers, A.D., & Bossio, J.A. (2014). Experimental, neuroimaging, and psychophysiological methods in sexuality research. In D.L. Tolman & L.M. Diamond (Eds.), *APA Handbook of Sexuality and Psychology, Vol 1.* (pp. 99–120).Washington: American Psychological Association.

Cohen, D., & Belski, J. (2008). Avoidant romantic attachment and female orgasm: Testing an emotion-regulation hypothesis. *Attachment and Human Development, 10,* 1–11.

Cohen, S. (2004). Social relationships and health. *American Psychologist.* (Special issue: Awards issue), *59,* 676–684.

Cohen, S., Sherrod, D.R., & Clark, M.S. (1986). Social skills and the stress-protective role of social support. *Journal of Personality and Social Psychology, 50,* 963–973.

Cohen-Kettenis P.T., Delemarre-van de Waal H.A., & Gooren L.J. (2008). The treatment of adolescent transsexuals: changing insights. *Journal of Sexual Medicine, 5,*1892–1897.

Cohn, D., Passel, J., Wang., & Livingston, G. (2011). Barely half of U.S. adults are married – a record low. *Pew Research Center.* Retrieved from http://www.pew-socialtrends.org/2011/12/14/barely-half-of-u-s-adults-are-married-a-record-low/

Coker, A.L., Davis, K.E., Arias, I., Desai, S., Sanderson, M., Brandt, H.M., & Smith, P.H. (2002). Physical and mental health effects of intimate partner violence for men and women. *American Journal of Preventive Medicine, 23* (4), 260–268. doi:10.1016/S0749-3979(02)00514-7.

Collins, J.K., & Harper, J.F. (1985). Sexual behaviour and peer pressure in adolescent girls. *Australian Journal of Sex, Marriage and Family, 6,* 137–142.

Collins, N.L., Guichard, A.C., Ford, M.B., & Feeney, B.C. (2004). Working models of attachment: New developments and emerging themes. In W.S. Rholes & J.A. Simpson (Eds.), *Adult Attachment: Theory, research, and clinical implications* (pp.196–239). New York: Guildford Press.

Comings, D., Muhleman, D., Johnson, J., & MacMurray, J. (2002). Parent-daughter transmission of the androgen receptor (AR) gene as an explanation of the effect of father absence on age of menarche. *Child Development, 73,* 1036–1042.

Coontz, S. (2006). *Marriage, a History: How Love Conquered Marriage.* New York: Penguin Books.

Cooper, M.L., Pioli, M., Levitt, A., Micheas, L., & Collins, N.L. (2006). Attachment styles, sex motives, and sexual behaviour: Evidence for gender specific expressions of attachment dynamics. In M. Mikulincer & G.S. Goodman (Eds.), *Dynamics of Love: Attachment, caregiving, and sex* (pp. 243–274). New York: Guilford Press.

Cooper, M.L., Shapiro, C.M., & Powers, A.M. (1998). Motivations for sex and risky sexual behaviour among adolescents and young adults: A functional perspective. *Journal of Personality and Social Psychology, 75,* 1528–1558.

Costa, P.T., Terracciano, A., & McCrae, R.R. (2001). Gender differences in personality traits across cultures: Robust and surprising findings. *Journal of Personality and Social Psychology, 81,* 322–331. doi:10.1037//0022-3514.81.2.322.

Cozolino, L. (2006). *The Neuroscience of Human Relationships.* New York: W.W. Norton and Company.

Cretella, M.A. (2016). Gender dysphoria in children and suppression of debate. *Journal of American Physicians and Surgeons, 21* (2), 50–55.

Crockett, L.J., Bingham, C.R., Chopak, J.S., & Vicary, J.R. (1996). Timing of first sexual intercourse: the role of social control, social learning, and problem behaviour. *Journal of Youth and Adolescence, 25,* 89–111. doi:10.1007/BF01537382.

Cunningham, M.R. (1986). Measuring the physical in physical attractiveness: Quasi-experiments on the socio-biology of female facial beauty. *Journal of Personality and Social Psychology 50,* 925–935.

Cunningham, J.D., & Antill, J.K. (1981). Love in developing relationships. In S. Duck & R. Gilmour (Eds.), *Personal relationships 2: Developing personal relationships*. New York: Academic Press.

Cunningham, J.D., & Antill, J.K. (1994). Cohabitation and Marriage: Retrospective and predictive comparisons. *Journal of Social and Personal Relationships, 11*, 77–93.

Dabbs, J.M. (1993). Testosterone and men's marriages. *Social Forces, 72*, (2), 463–477. doi:10.1093/sf/ 72.2.463.

Davis, D. (2006). Attachment-related pathways to sexual coercion. In M. Mikulincer & G. Goodman (Eds.), *Dynamics of Romantic love: Attachment, caregiving, and sex* (pp. 293–336). New York: Guildford Press.

Davis, D., Shaver, P.R., & Vernon, M.L. (2003). Physical, emotional, and behavioural reactions to breaking up. *Personality and Social Psychology Bulletin, 29*, 871–884.

Davis, D., Shaver, P.R., & Vernon, M.L. (2004). Attachment style and subjective motivations for sex. *Personality and Social Psychology Bulletin, 30*, 1076–1090.

de Bolger, A. del pozo, Jones, T., Dunstan, D., & Lykins, A. Australian trans men: development, sexuality, and mental health. *Australian Psychologist, 49* (6), 395–402.

Delamater, J. (1987). A sociological perspective. In J.H. Geer & W.T. O'Donohue (Eds.), *Theories of Human Sexuality* (pp. 237–256). New York: Plenum.

Delamater, J.D., & Hyde, J.S. (1998). Existentialism vs. social constructionism in the study of human sexuality. *Journal of Sex Research, 35*, 10–8. doi:10.1080/00224499809551913.

Dell'osso, L., Carmassi, C., Carlinni, M., Rucci, P., Torri, P., Cesari, D., Landi, P., Ciapparelli, A., & Maggi, M. (2009). Sexual dysfunctions and suicidality in patients with bipolar disorder and unipolar depression. *Journal of Sexual Medicine, 6*, 3036–3070. doi:10.1111/j.1743-6109.2009.01455.x.

de Munck, V.C. (1998). *Romantic Love and Sexual Behaviour: Perspectives from the social sciences*. Santa Barbara: Greenwood Publishing Group.

Dennerstein, L., Lehert, P., Burger, H., & Dudley, E. (1999). Factors affecting sexual functioning of women in the mid-life years. *Climacteric, 2*, 254–262. doi:10.3109/ 13697139909038085.

De Steno, D., Bartlett, M.Y., Braverman, J., & Salovey, P. (2002). Sex differences in jealousy: Evolutionary mechanism or artifact of measurement? *Journal of Personality and Social Psychology, 83*, 1103–1116. doi:101037/0022-3514.83.5.1103.

de Jong, J.P., van Overveld, M., & Borg, C. (2013). Giving in to arousal or staying stuck in disgust? Disgust-based mechanisms in sex and sexual dysfunction. *Journal of Sexual Research, 50* (3–4), 247–262. doi:10.1080/00224499.2012.746280.

Diamond, L.M., & Dickenson, J. (2012) The neuroimaging of love and desire: review and future directions. *Clinical Neuropsychiatry, 9*, 39–46.

Diamond, L.M., & Huebner, D.M. (2012). Is good sex good for you? Rethinking sexuality and health. *Social and Personality Psychology Compass, 6*, 54–69. doi:10:1111/j.1751-9004.2011.00408.x.

Diamond, L. M., & Wallen, K. (2011). Sexual minority women's sexual motivation around the time of ovulation. *Archives of Sexual Behaviour, 40*, 237–246.

Diener, E., & Seligman, M.E.P. (2002). Very happy people. *Psychological Science,13*, 81–84. doi:10.1111/1467-9280.00415.

Dion, K.L., & Dion, K.K. (1973). Correlates of romantic love. *The Journal of Consulting and Clinical Psychology 41*, 51–56.

Doerr, P., Pirke, K.M., Kockott, G., & Dittmor, F. (1976). Further studies on sex hormones in male homosexuals. *Archives of General Psychiatry, 33*, 611–614.

Donald, M., Lucke, J., Dunne, M., & Raphael, B. (1995). Gender differences associated with young people's emotional reactions to sexual intercourse. *Journal of Youth and Adolescence, 24*, 453-464. doi:10.1007/BF01537191.

Dörner, G. (1988). Neuroendocrine response to brain estrogen and brain differentiation. *Archives of Sexual Behaviour, 17* (1), 57–75.

Dörner, G., Rohde, W., Stahl, F., Krell, L., & Masius, W.G. (1975). A neuroendocrine predisposition for homosexuality in men. *Archives of Sexual Behaviour 4* (1), 1–8.

Driscoll, R., Davis, K.E., & Lipetz, M.A. (1972). Parental interference and romantic love. *Journal of Personality and Social Psychology, 24*, 10.

Duemmler, S.L., & Kobak, R. (2001). The development of commitment and attachment in dating relationships: Attachment security as relationship construct. *Journal of Adolescence, 24*, 401–415. doi:10.1006/jado.2001.0406.

Dunn, K.M., Croft, P.R., & Hackett, G.I. (1999). Association of sexual problems with social, psychological, and physical problems in men and women: A cross sectional population survey. *Journal of Epidemiology and Community Health, 53*, 99–102. doi:10.1136/jech.53.3.144.

Dutton, D.G., & Aron, A.P. (1976). Some evidence for heightened sexual attraction under conditions of high anxiety. *Journal of Personality and Social Psychology, 30*, 510–517. doi:10.1037/h0037031.

Dykas, M.J., Woodhouse, S.S., Cassidy, J., & Waters, H.S. (2006). Narrative assessment of attachment representations: Links between secure base scripts and adolescent attachment. *Attachment and Human Development, 8* (3), 221–240.

Eastwick, P.W. (2009). Beyond the Pleistocene: Using phylogeny and constraint to inform the evolutionary psychology of human mating. *Psychological Bulletin, 135*, 794–821.

Emanuele, E. (2008). Of love and death: The emerging role of romantic disruption in suicidal behaviour. *Suicide and Life-Threatening Behaviour 38*, 482. doi:10.1521/suli.2008.38.4.482.

Erikson, E.H. (1968). *Identity: Youth and Crisis.* New York: W.W. Norton.

Fagot, B.I. (1985). Changes in thinking about early sex role development. *Developmental Review, 5*, 83–98.

Feeney, J.A. (2016). Adult Romantic Attachment: Developments in the study of couple relationships. In Cassidy, J., & Shaver, P.R. *Handbook of Attachment: Theory, research, and clinical applications. Third edition* (pp.435–463). New York: The Guilford Press.

Feeney, J.A., & Noller, P. (1990). Attachment style as a predictor of adult romantic relationships. *Journal of Personality and Social Psychology, 58*, 281–291.

Feeney, J.A., & Noller, P. (1992). Attachment style and romantic love: Relationships dissolution. *Australian Journal of Psychology, 44*, 69–74.

Feeney, J.A., & Noller, P. (1996). *Adult Attachment.* Thousand Oaks, CA: Sage.

Feingold, A. (1988). Matching for attractiveness in romantic partners and same-sex friends: A meta-analysis and theoretical critique. *Psychological Bulletin, 104*, 226–235.

Feingold, A. (1994). Gender differences in personality: A meta-analysis. *Psychological Bulletin, 116*, 429–456. doi:10.1080/00224499.2011.565429.

Fergusson, D.M., Horwood, L. J., & Beautrais, A.L. (1999). Is sexual orientation related to mental health problems and suicidality in young people? *Archives of General Psychiatry, 56* (10), 876–880. doi:10.1001/archpsyc.56.10.876.

Festinger, L. (1957). *A Theory of Cognitive Dissonance.* Stanford: Stanford University Press.

Festinger, L., Schacter, S., & Back, K. (1950). The spatial ecology of group formation. In L. Festinger, S. Schacter, & K. Back (Eds.), *Social Pressure in Informal Groups* (pp. 141–161). Palo Alto, CA: Stanford University Press.

Fischer, J., & Gochros, H.L. (1977). *Handbook of Behaviour Therapy with Sexual Problems: Approaches to specific problems (Vol 2).* New York: Pergamon Press.

Fisher, W.A. (1986). A psychological approach to human sexuality: The sexual behaviour sequence. In D. Byrne & K.Kelly (Eds.), *Alternative Approaches to the Study of Sexual Behaviour* (pp. 131–171). Hillsdale: Lawrence Erlbaum.

Fontenot, E. (2013) Unlikely congregation: Gay and lesbian persons of faith in contemporary U.S. culture. In K.I. Pargament, J.J. Exline, & J.W. Jones (Eds.), *APA Handbook of Psychology, Religion, and Spirituality: Vol. 1 Context, theory, and research* (pp. 627–633). Washington, DC: American Psychological Association.

Forbes, C.E., & Grafman, J. (2010). The role of the human prefrontal cortex in social cognition and moral judgement. *Annual Review of Neuroscience, 33*, 299–324. doi:10.1146/annurev-neuro-060909-153230.

Foster, C.A., Witcher, B.S., Campbell, W.K., & Green, J.D. (1998). Arousal and Attraction: Evidence for automatic and controlled processes. *Journal of Personality and Social Psychology, 74*, 86–101. doi:10.1037/0022-3514.74.1.86.

Freud, S. (2006). *The Psychology of Love.* London: Penguin Books.

Friedman, R. (1988). *Male Homosexuality: A Contemporary Psychoanalytical Perspective.* New Haven: Yale University Press.

Fromm, E. (1962). *The Art of Loving.* London: Unwin Books.

Furman, W. (2001). Working models of friendships. *Journal of Social and Personal Relationships, 18* (5), 583–602.

Gagnon, J.H. (1990). The explicit and implicit use of the scripting perspective in sex research. *Annual Review of Sex Research 1*, 1–43.

Gailliot, M.T., & Baumeister, R.F. (2007). Self-regulation and sexual restraint: Dispositionally and temporarily poor self-regulatory abilities contribute to failures at restraining sexual behaviour. *Personality and Social Psychology Bulletin, 33*, 173–186. doi:10.1177/1046167206293472.

Gangestad, S.W, Thornhill, R., & Garver-Apgar, C.E. (2005). Adaptations to ovulation: implications for sexual selection and social behaviour. *Current Directions in Psychological Science, 14*, 312–316. doi:10.1111/j.0963-214.2005.00388.x.

Garcia J.R., Mackillop, J., Aller, E.L., Merriwheather, A.M., Wilson, D.S., & Lum, J.K. (2010). Associations between dopamine D4 receptor gene variation with both infidelity and sexual promiscuity. *PloS ONE, 5* (11): e14162. doi:10.1371/journal.pone.0014162.

Garcia, J., Reiber, C., Massey, S.G., & Merriwether, A.M. (2016). Sexual hookup culture: A review. *Review of General Psychology, 16* (2): 161–176.

Gardner, T.A. (2002) *Sacred Sex: A spiritual celebration of oneness in marriage.* Colorado Springs, CO: Waterbrook Press.

Garnets, L., & Kimmel, D. (1991). Lesbian and gay male dimensions in the psychological study of human diversity. In Goodchilds, J.D. (Ed.), *Psychological Perspectives on Human Diversity in America*. Washington DC: American Psychological Association.

Geen, R.G. (1997). Psychophysiological approaches to personality. In J. Hogan, J. Johnson, & S. Briggs (Eds.), *Handbook of Personality Psychology* (pp. 387–416) San Diego, C.A.: Academic Press.

Gelstein, S., Yeshurun, Y., Rozenkrantz, L., Shushan, L., Frumin, I., Roth, Y., & Sobel, N. (2011). Human tears contain a chemosignal. *Science, 331* (6014), 226–230. doi:10.1126/science.1198331.

Gemmel, N. (2015). Rekindling the flame. *The Weekend Australian Magazine*, Feb 14–15:8.

Gentzler, A.L., & Kerns, K.A. (2004). Associations between insecure attachment and sexual experiences. *Personal Relationships, 11*, 249–265.

George, W.H., Norris, J., Nguyen, H.V., Masters, N. T., & Davis, K.C. (2014). Sexuality and Health. In D.L. Tolman & L.M. Diamond (Eds.), *APA Handbook of Sexuality and Psychology, Vol 1.* (pp. 655–696). Washington: American Psychological Association.

Gillath, O., Mikulincer, M., Birnbaum, G.E., & Shaver, P.R. (2008). When sex primes love: Subliminal sexual priming motivates relational goal pursuit. *Personality and Social Psychology Bulletin, 34*, 1057–1069.

Giles, J. (2008). Sex hormones and sexual desire. *Journal for the Theory of Social Behaviour, 38* (1), 45–66.

Gimpl, G., & Fahrenholz, F. (2001). The oxytocin receptor system: Structure, function, and regulation. *Physiological Reviews, 81*, 629–683.

Gladue, B.A. (1988). Hormones in relationship to homosexual/bisexual/heterosexual gender orientation. In J.M.A. Sitsen, J.M.A. (Ed.), *Handbook of Sexology: The Pharmacology and Endocrinology of Sexual Function (Vol 6)* Amsterdam: Elsevier.

Gladue, B.A. (1994). The biopsychology of sexual orientation. *Current Directions in Psychological Science, 3*, 150–154.

Goldman, J. (1990). The importance of an adequate sexual vocabulary for children. *Australian Journal of Marriage and the Family, 11*, 136–148.

Goleman, D. (1995). *Emotional Intelligence: Why it can matter more than IQ*. New York: Bantam Books.

Green, R. (1987). *The "Sissy Boy" Syndrome and the Development of Homosexuality*. New Haven: Yale University Press.

Greene, K., & Faulkner, S.L. (2005). Gender, belief in the sexual double standard, and sexual talk in heterosexual dating relationships. *Sex Roles, 53* (3), 239–251. doi:10.1007/s11199-005-5682-6.

Gray, J. (1993). *Men are from Mars; Women are from Venus: A practical guide for improving communications and getting what you want in your relationships.* London: Thorsons.

Gray, P.B., Chapman, J.F., Burnham, T.C., McIntyre, M.H., Lipson, S.F., & Ellison, P.T. (2004a). Human male pair bonding and testosterone. *Human Nature, 15* (2), 119–131. doi:10.1007/s12110-004-1016-6.

Gray, P.B., Campbell, B.C., Marlowe, F.W., Lipson, S.F., & Ellison, P.T. (2004b). Social variables predict between-subject but not day-to-day variation in the testosterone of US men. *Psychoneuroendocrinology, 29* (9), 1153–1162. doi:10.1016/j.psyneuen.2004.01.008.PMID 15219639.

Graziano, W.G., Jensen-Campbell, L., Shebilske, L., & Lundgren, S. (1993). Social influence, sex differences, and judgements of beauty: putting the 'interpersonal' back in interpersonal attraction. *Journal of Personality & Social Psychology, 65,* 522–531. doi:10.1037/0022-3514.65.3.522.

Greene, K., & Faulkner, S.L. (2005). Gender, belief in the sexual double standard, and sexual talk in heterosexual dating relationships. *Sex Roles, 53* (3), 239–251. doi:10.1007/s11199-005-5682-6.

Griffitt, W. (1974). Attitude similarity and attraction. In T.L. Huston (Ed.), *Foundations of Interpersonal Attraction.* New York: Academic Press.

Guisinger, S., & Blatt, S.J. (1949). Individuality and relatedness: Evolution of a fundamental dialectic. *American Psychologist, 49,* 104–111.

Guyton, A.C. (1981). *Textbook of Medical Physiology* (6th ed.). Philadelphia: W.B. Saunders Company.

Gullette, D.L., & Lyons, M.A. (2005). Sexual sensation seeking, compulsivity, and HIV risk behaviours in college students. *Journal of Community Health Nursing, 22,* 47–60. doi:10.1207/ s15327655jchn2201_5.

Guo, G., Tong, Y., Xie, C.W., & Lange, L.A. (2007). Dopamine transporter, gender, and number of sexual partners among young adults. *European Journal of Human Genetics, 15,* 279–287. doi: 10:1038/sj.ejhg. 5201763.

Haggstrom-Nordin, E., Hanson, U., & Tyden, T. (2005). Associations between pornography consumption and sexual practices among adolescents in Sweden. *International Journal of STD and AIDS, 16,* 102–107.

Hall, J.H., & Fincham, F.D. (2006). Relationship dissolution following infidelity. In M.A. Fine & J.H. Harvey (Eds.), *Handbook of Divorce and Relationship Dissolution* (pp. 153–168). Malwah, NJ: Erlbaum.

Hall, J.A., & Matsumoto, D. (2004). Gender differences in judgements of multiple emotions from facial expressions. *Emotions, 4*, 201–206. doi:10.1037/1528-3542.4.2.201.

Halpern, C.T. (2006). Integrating hormones and other biological factors into a developmental systems model of adolescent female sexuality. *New Directions for Child and Adolescent Development, 112*, 9–22. doi:10.1002/cd.159.

Halpern, C.T., & Kaestle, C.E. (2014). Sexuality in emerging adulthood. In D.L. Tolman & L.M. Diamond (Eds.), *APA Handbook of Sexuality and Psychology, Vol 1.* (pp. 487–522). Washington: American Psychological Association.

Halpern, C.T., Udry, J.R., & Uchindran, C. (1998). Monthly measures of salivary testosterone predict sexual activity in adolescent males. *Archives of Sexual Behaviour, 27*, 445–465. doi:101023/A:1018700529128.

Hartmann, U. (2007) Depression and sexual dysfunction. *Journal of Men's Health and Gender, 4*, 18–25. doi:10.1016/j.jmhg.2006.12.003.

Hatfield, E. (1988) Passionate and companionate love. In R.J. Sternberg & M.L. Barnes (Eds.), *The Psychology of Love.* New Haven: Yale University Press.

Hazan, C., & Shaver, P. (1987). Romantic love conceptualized as an attachment process. *Journal of Personality and Social Psychology, 52*, 511–524.

Hazan, C., & Shaver, P. (1990) Love and work: An attachment theoretical perspective. *Journal of Personality and Social Psychology, 59*, 270–280.

Hazan, C., & Shaver, P.R. (1994) Attachment as an organizational framework for research on close relationships. *Psychological Inquiry, 5*, 1–22.

Hazan, C., & Zeifman, D. (1994) Sex and the psychological tether. In K. Bartholomew & D. Perlman (Eds.), *Advances in Personal Relationships (Vol. 5): Attachment processes in adulthood* (pp. 151–178). London: Jessica Kingsley.

Hellhammer, D.H., Hubert, W., & Schürmeyer, T. (1985) Changes in saliva testosterone after psychological stimulation in men. *Psychoneuroendocrinology 10* (1), 77–81. doi:10.1016/0306-4530(85)90041-1.PMID4001279.

Herdt, G., & McClintock, M. (2000) The magical age of 10. *Archives of Sexual Behaviour, 29*, 587–606. doi:10.1023/A:1002006521067.

Hernadez, K.M., Mahoney, A., & Pargament, K.I. (2014) Sexuality and religion. In D.L. Tolman & L.M. Diamond (Eds.), *APA Handbook of Sexuality and Psychology, Vol 2.* (pp. 425–47). Washington: American Psychological Association.

Hess, N.H., & Hagan, E.H. (2006) Sex differences in indirect aggression: Psychological evidence from young adults. *Evolution and Human Behaviour, 27*, 231–245. doi:10.1016/j.evolhumbehav.2005.11.001.

Higgins, J.A., Trussell, J., Moore, N.B., & Davidson, J.K. (2010) Virginity lost, satisfaction gained? Physiological and psychological sexual satisfaction at heterosexual debut. *Journal of Sex Research, 47*, 384–394. doi:10.1080/00224491003774792.

Hilgard, E.R., & Bower, H.B. (1966) *Theories of Learning*, 3rd edition, New York: Appleton-Century-Crofts.

Hill, C.A., & Preston, L.K. (1996) Individual differences in the experience of sexual motivation: Theory and measurement of dispositional sexual motives. *Journal of Sex Research, 33*, 27–45.

Hill, C., Rubin, Z., & Peplau, L.A. (1976) Breakups before marriage: The end of 103 affairs. *Journal of Social Issues, 31*, 147–168.

Hiller, J. (2005) Gender differences in sexual motivation. *The Journal of Men's Health & Gender, 2* (3), 339–345.

Hirschenhauser, K., Frigerio, D., Grammer, K., & Magnusson, M.S. (2002) Monthly patterns of testosterone and behavior in prospective fathers. *Hormones and Behaviour 42* (2), 172–181. doi:10.1006/hbeh.2002.1815. PMID 12367570.

Hofer, J., Busch, H., Bond, M.H., Campos, D., Li, M., & Law, R. (2010). The implicit power motive and sociosexuality in men and women: Pancultural effects of responsibility. *Journal of Personality and Social Psychology, 99* (2), 380–394. doi:10.1037/a0020053.

Hull, C.L. (1943). *Principles of Behaviour*. New York: Appleton-Century-Crofts.

Hume, D. (1978) *A Treatise of Human Nature*, 2nd ed., L.A. Selby-Bigge and P.H. Nidditch Oxford: Clarendon

Huston, T.L., & Levinger, G. (1978). Interpersonal Attraction. *Annual Review of Psychology, 29*: 118–157.

Impett, E.A., Gordon, A., & Strachman, A. (2008). Attachment and daily sexual goals: A study of dating couples. *Personal Relationships,15*, 375–390. doi:10.1111/j.1475-6811.2008.00204.x.

Impett, E.A., Muise, A. & Peragine, D. (2014). Sexuality in the context of relationships. In D.L. Tolman & L.M. Diamond (Eds.), *APA Handbook of Sexuality and Psychology, Vol 1*. (pp. 269–316). Washington: American Psychological Association.

Isay, R.A. (2009). *Being Homosexual: Gay men and their development*. New York: Vintage Books.

Izard, C.E. (1991). *The Psychology of Emotions*. New York: Plenum.

Janssen, E., & Bancroft, J. (2007). The dual control model: The role of sexual inhibition and excitation in sexual arousal and behaviour. In E. Janssen (Ed.), *The Psychophysiology of Sex* (pp. 197–222). Bloomington: Indiana University Press.

James, P.J., Nyby, J.G., & Saviolakis, G.A. (2006). Sexually stimulated testosterone release in male mice (Mus musculus): Roles of genotype and sexual arousal. *Hormones and Behaviour 50* (3), 424–431. doi:10.1016/j.yhbeh.2006.05.004. PMID 16828762.

Jessor, R. (1992). Risk behaviour in adolescence. *Developmental Review, 12*, 374–390.

Jones, A., Hwang, D.J., Duke, C.B.3rd, He, Y., Siddam, A., Miller, D.D., & Dalton, J.T. (2010). Nonsteroidal selective androgen receptor modulators enhance female sexual motivation. *The Journal of Pharmacology and Experimental Therapeutics, 334* (2), 439–448.

Jose, A., O'Leary, K.K., & Moyer, A. (2010). Does premarital cohabitation predict subsequent marital stability and marital quality? A meta-analysis. *Journal of Marriage and Family, 72*, 105–116. doi:10.1111/ j.1741-3737.2009.00686.x.

Kashdan, T.B., Adams, L., Savostyanova, A., Ferssizidis, P., McKnight, P.E., & Nezlek, J.B. (2011). Effects of social anxiety and depressive symptoms on the frequency and quality of sexual activity: A daily process approach. *Behaviour Research and Therapy, 49*, 352-360. doi:10.1016/j.brat.2011.03.004.

Katz-Wise, S.L. & Hyde, J.S. (2014) Sexuality and gender: the interplay. In D.L. Tolman & L.M. Diamond (Eds.), *APA Handbook of Sexuality and Psychology, Vol 1.* (pp. 29–62). Washington: American Psychological Association.

Kelly, D. (2011). *Yuck!: The Nature and Moral Significance of Disgust.* Cambridge: The MIT Press.

Kenrick, D.T., Groth, G.E., Trost, M.R., & Sadalla, E.K. (1993). Integrating evolutionary and social exchange perspectives on relationship: Effects of gender, self-appraisal, and involvement level on mate selection criteria. *Journal of Personality and Social Psychology, 64*, 951–969.

Kenrick, D.T., Montello, D.R., Gutierres, S.E., & Trost M.R. (1993). Effects of physical attractiveness on affect and perceptual judgements: When social comparison overrides social reinforcement. *Personality and Social Psychology Bulletin, 19*, 195–199. doi:10.1177/0146167293192008.

Kerr, D.L., Santurri, L., & Peters, P. (2003). A comparison of lesbian, bisexual and heterosexual undergraduate women on selected mental health issues. *Journal of American College Health, 61* (4), 185–194. doi:10.1080/07448481.2013.787619.

Kiecolt-Glaser, J.K., & Newton, T.L. (2001). Marriage and health: His and hers. *Psychological Bulletin, 127*, 472–503. doi:10.1037/0033-2909.127.4.472.

King, C.D. (1945). The meaning of normal. *Yale Journal of Biological Medicine,18*, 493–501.

Kleinplatz, P.J. & Diamond, L.M. (2014). Sexual diversity. In D.L. Tolman & L.M. Diamond (Eds.), *APA Handbook of Sexuality and Psychology, Vol 1.* (pp. 245–268). Washington: American Psychological Association.

Kobal, H.I., Moiduddin, E., Henderson, J., Goesling, B., & Besculides, M. (2010). What do we know about the link between marriage and health? *Journal of Family Issues, 31*, 1019–1040.

Komarovsky, M. (1976). *Dilemmas of Masculinity.* New York: W.W. Norton.

Kraemer, H.C., Becker, H.B., Brodie, H.K., Doering, C.H., Moos, R.H., & Hamburg, D.A. (1976). Orgasmic frequency and plasma testosterone levels in normal human males. *Archives of Sexual Behaviors 5* (2), 125–132. doi:10.1007/BF01541869.PMID 1275688.

Kraus, S. W., & Russell, B. (2008). Early sexual experiences: The role of internet access and sexually explicit material. *CyberPsychology and Behavior, 11* (2), 162–168.

Kringelbach, M.L. (2005). The human orbitofrontal cortex: Linking reward to hedonic experience. *Nature Reviews Neuroscience, 6*, 691–702. doi:10.1038/nrn1747.

Kuehne, D.S. (2009). *Sex and the iworld: Rethinking relationship beyond an age of individualism.* Grand Rapids, Michigan: Baker Academic.

Laan, E., & Both, S. (2008). What makes women experience desire? *Feminism & Psychology, 18*, 505–541. doi:10.1177/0959353508095533.

Lamb, S., & Plocha, A. (2014). Sexuality in childhood. In D.L. Tolman & L.M. Diamond (Eds.), *APA Handbook of Sexuality and Psychology, Vol 1.* (pp. 415–432). Washington: American Psychological Association.

Laner, M.R., & Ventrone, N.A. (1998). Egalitarian daters/traditionalist dates. *Journal of Family Issues, 19*, 468–477.

Lanning, K.V. (2010). *Child Molesters: A behavioural analysis for professionals investigating the sexual exploration of children* 5th Edition. Retrieved from https://www.ncjrs.gov/pdffiles1/Digitization/14925NCJRS.pdf

Laumann, E.O., Gagnon, J., Michael, R., & Michaels, S. (1994). *The Social Organization of Sexuality: Sexual practices in the United States*, Chicago: University of Chicago press.

Laurent, S.M., & Simons, A.D. (2009). Sexual dysfunction in depression and anxiety: Conceptualizing sexual dysfunction as part of an internalizing dimension. *Clinical Psychology Review, 29*, 573–585. doi:10.1016/j.cpr.2009.06.007.

Lawrence, K., & Byers, E.S. (1995). Sexual satisfaction in long-term heterosexual relationship: The interpersonal exchange model of sexual satisfaction. *Personal Relationships, 2*, 267–285. doi:10.1111/j.1475-6811.1995.tb00092.x.

Lehmiller, J.J. (2014). *The Psychology of Human Sexuality*. Chichester: Wiley Blackwell.

Lehmiller, J.J., & Agnew, C.R. (2006). Marginalised relationships: The impact of social disapproval on romantic relationship commitment. *Personality and Social Psychology Bulletin, 32*, 40–51. doi:10.1177/0146167205278710.

Lehmiller, J.J., & Agnew, C.R. (2007). Perceived marginalization and the prediction of romantic relationship stability. *Journal of Marriage and Family, 69*, 1036–1049. doi:10.1111/j.1741-3737.2007.00429.x.

Lepore, S.J. (1992). Social-conflict, social support, and psychological distress: Evidence of cross-domain buffering effects. *Journal of Personality and Social Psychology, 63*, 857–867.

Lerner, H. (1989). *The Dance of Intimacy*. New York: Harper.

LeVay, S. (1991). A difference in hypothalamic structure between heterosexual and homosexual men. *Science, 253*, 1034–1037.

Levy, M.B., & Davis, K.E. (1988). Lovestyles and attachment styles compared: Their relations to each other and to various relationship characteristics. *Journal of Social and Personal Relationships, 5*, 439–471.

Li, N.P., Bailey, J.M., Kenrick, D.T., & Linsenmeier, J.A.W. (2002). The necessities and luxuries of mate preferences: Testing the tradeoffs. *Journal of Personality and Social Psychology, 82*, 947–955.

Li, S.-C. (2003). Biocultural orchestration of developmental plasticity across levels: The interplay of biology and culture in shaping the mind and behaviour across the life span. *Psychological Bulletin, 129*, 171–194. doi:10.1037/0033-2909.129.2.171.

Lishner, D.A., Nguyen, S., Stocks, E.L., & Zillmer, E.J. (2008). Are sexual and emotional infidelity equally upsetting to men and women? Making sense of forced-choice responses. *Evolutionary Psychology, 6*, 667–675.

Little, A.C., Jones, B.C., & Burriss, R.P. (2007). Preferences for masculinity in male bodies change across the menstrual cycle. *Hormones and Behaviour, 51*, 633–639. doi:10.1016/j.yhbeh.2007.03.006.

Lou, H.C., Gross, J., Biermann-Ruben, K., Kjaer, T.W., & Schnitzler, A. (2010). Coherence in consciousness: Paralimbic gamma synchrony of self-reference links conscious experiences. *Human Brain Mapping, 31*, 185–192.

Mackay, H. (2013). *What Makes Us Tick?* Sydney: Hachette Australia.

MacNeil, S., & Byers, E.S. (2005). Dyadic assessment of sexual self-disclosure and sexual satisfaction in heterosexual dating couples. *Journal of Social and Personal relationships, 22*, 169–181. doi:10.1177/0265407505050942.

MacNeil, S., & Byers, E.S. (2009). Role of sexual self-disclosure in the sexual satisfaction of long-term heterosexual couples. *Journal of Sex Research, 46,* 3–14. doi:10.1080/00224490802398399.

Madigan, S., Vaillancourt, K., McKibbon, A., & Benoit, D. (2012). The reporting of maltreatment experiences during the Adult Attachment Interview in a sample of pregnant adolescents. *Attachment and Human Development, 14* (2), 119–143.

Mahoney, E.R. (1983). *Human Sexuality.* New York: McGraw-Hill.

Manne, A. (2015). *The Life of I: The new culture of narcissism* Melbourne: Melbourne University Publishing.

Mangalwadi, V. (2011). *The Book That Made Your World: How the Bible created the soul of Western civilization.* Nashville, Tennessee: Thomas Nelson.

Mansfield, H.C. (2006). *Manliness.* New Haven: Yale University Press.

Marazziti, D., & Canale, D. (2004). Hormonal changes when falling in love. *Psychoneuroendocrinology 29* (7), 931–936. doi:10.1016/j.psyneuen2003.08.006.PMID 15177709.

Markey, P.M., & Markey, C.N. (2007). The interpersonal meaning of sexual promiscuity. *Journal of Research in Personality, 41,* 1199–1212. doi:10.1016/j.jrp.2007.02.004.

Marquis, J.N. (1978). Orgasmic reconditioning: changing sexual object choice through controlling masturbation fantasies. In Fischer, J. and Gochros, H.L. *Handbook of Behaviour Therapy with Sexual Problems* New York: Pergamon.

Marshall, A.G. (2007). *'I love you but I'm not in love with you': Seven steps to saving your relationship.* London: Bloomsbury.

Marshall, T.C. (2010). Gender, peer relations, and intimate romantic relationships. In J.C. Chrisler & D.R. McCreary (Eds.), *Handbook of Gender Research in Psychology: Vol. 2,* New York: Springer-Verlag.

Maslow, A.H. (1968). *Toward a Psychology of Being (2nd ed.).* Princeton N.J.: Van Nostrand.

Mathy, R.M. (2003). Transgender identity and suicidality in a non-clinical sample – Sexual orientation, psychiatric history, and compulsive behaviours. *Journal of Psychology and Human Sexuality, 14,* 47–65. doi:10.1300/J056v14n04_03.

Mazur, A., & Booth, A. (1998). Testosterone and dominance in men. *Behavioural and Brain Sciences, 21,* 353–397.

McLean, S. (2014). *Sexts, Texts & Selfies: How to keep your children safe in the digital space.* Melbourne: Viking.

Meade, C.S., Fitzmaurice, G.M., Sanchez, A.K., Griffin, M.L., McDonald, L.J., & Weiss, R.D. (2011). The relationship of manic episodes and drug abuse to sexual risk behaviour in patients with co-occurring bipolar and substance use disorders: A 15-month prospective analysis. *AIDS and Behaviour, 15,* 1829–1833. doi:10.1007/BF01550953.

Mehta P.H., Jones A.C., & Josephs, R.A. (2008). The social endocrinology of dominance: basal testosterone predicts cortisol changes and behavior following victory and defeat. *Journal of Personality and Social Psychology 94* (6), 1078–1093. doi:10.1037/0022-3514.94.6.1078. PMID 18505319.

Mehta, P.H., & Josephs, R.A. (2006). Testosterone change after losing predicts the decision to compete again. *Hormones and Behaviour 50* (5), 684–692. doi:10.1016/j.yhbeh.2006.07.001. PMID 16928375.

Meston, C.M., & Buss, D.M. (2007). Why humans have sex. *Archives of Sexual Behaviour, 36,* (4), 477–507. doi:10.1007/s10508-007-9175-2.

Meyer, J.P., & Pepper, S. (1977). Need compatibility and marital adjustment in young married couples. *Journal of Personality and Social Psychology, 35,* 331–342.

Meyer-Bahlburg, H.F.L. (1980) Sex hormone changes during puberty and sexual behaviour. In J. Samson (Ed.), *Childhood and Sexuality* (pp. 113–122). Montreal, Quebec, Canada: Editions Etudes Vivantes

Meyer-Bahlberg, H.F.L., Ehrhardt, A.A., Rosen, L.R., Gruen, R.S., Veridiano, N.P., Vann, F.H., & Neuwalder, H.F. (1995). Prenatal estrogens and the development of homosexual orientation. *Developmental Psychology, 31,* 12–21.

Michael, A., & O'Keane, V. (2000). Sexual dysfunction in depression. *Human Psychopharmacology: Clinical and Experimental, 15,* 337–345. doi:10.1002/1099-1077 (200007)15:5<337::AID-HUP207>3.0.CO;2-H.

Mikulincer, M., & Goodman, G.S. (2006). *Dynamics of Romantic Love: Attachment, caregiving, and sex.* New York: The Guilford Press.

Mikulincer, M., & Shaver, P.R. (2007). A behavioural systems perspective on the psychodynamics of attachment and sexuality. In D. Diamond, S.J. Blatt, & J.D. Lichtenberg (Eds.), *Attachment and Sexuality* (pp. 51–78). New York: Analytic Press.

Mikulincer, M., & Shaver, P.R. (2015). *Attachment in Adulthood: Structure, dynamics, and change (2nd ed.).* New York: Guilford Press.

Miller, J.D., Lynam, D., Zimmerman, R.S., Logan, T.K., Leukefeld, C., & Clayton, R. (2004). The utility of the Five Factor Model in understanding risky sexual behaviour. *Personality and Individual Differences, 36,* 1611–1626. doi:10.1016/j.paid.2003.06.009.

Miller, N.E. (1959). Liberalization of basic S-R concepts: Extensions to conflict behaviour, motivation, and social learning. In S. Koch (Ed.) *Psychology: A study of science (Vol. 2).* (pp. 196–292). New York: McGraw-Hill.

Mitchell, A., Patrick, K., Haywood, W., Blackman, P., & Pitts, M. (2014). *National survey of Australian secondary students and sexual health 2013,* (ARCSHS Monograph Series No 97). Melbourne: Australian Research Centre in Sex, Health and Society, Latrobe University.

Mitterauer, M., & Sieder, R. (1982). *The European Family: Patriarchy to partnership from the Middle Ages to the present.* Oxford: Basil Blackwell.

Montoya, R., Horton, R.S., & Kirchner, J. (2008). Is actual similarity necessary for attraction? A meta-analysis of actual and perceived similarity. *Journal of Social and Personal Relationships, 25,* 889–922. doi:10.1177/0265407508096700.

Mullen, P.E., Martin, J.L., Anderson, J.C., Romans, S.E., & Herbison, G.P. (1993). Childhood sexual abuse and mental health in adult life. *The British Journal of Psychiatry, 163* (6), 721–732. doi:10.1192/bjp.163.6.721.

Murray, H.A. (1937). *Explorations in Personality.* New York: Oxford University Press.

Murstein, I. (1972). Physical attractiveness and marital choice. *Journal of Personality and Social Psychology, 22,* 8–12.

Musick, K., & Bumpass, L. (2012). Re-examining the case for marriage: Union formation and changes in well-being. *Journal of Marriage and Family, 74* (1), 1–18. doi:10.1111/j.1741-3737.20111.00873.x.

Neave, N., & Wolfson, S. (2003). Testosterone, territoriality and the 'home advantage'. *Physiology and Behavior, 78,* 269–275.

Newcomb, T.M. (1961). *The Acquaintance Process.* New York: Holt, Rinehart and Winston, Inc.

Newman, B.S., & Muzzonigro, P.G. (1993). The effect of the coming out process of gay male adolescents. *Adolescence, 28,* 213–226.

Nobre, P.J., & Pinto-Gouveia, J. (2006). Emotions during sexual activity: differences between sexually functional and dysfunctional men and women. *Archives of Sexual Behaviour, 35,* 491–499. doi:10.1007/s10508-006-9047-1.

Nobre, P.J., & Pinto-Gouveia, J. (2008). Cognitive and emotional predictors of female sexual dysfunctions: Preliminary findings. *Journal of Sex and Marital Therapy, 34,* 325–342. doi:10.1080/00926230802096358.

Noller, P., Feeney, J.A., & Peterson, C. (2001). *Personal Relationships Across the Lifespan.* Philadelphia, PA: Taylor & Francis.

Norton, G.R., & Jehu, D. (1984). The role of anxiety in sexual dysfunctions: a review. *Archives of Sexual Behaviour, 13,* 165–183. doi:10.1007/BF01542150.

Oliver, M.B., & Hyde, J.S. (2001). Gender differences in sexuality: A meta-analysis. In Baumeister, R.F. (Ed.), *Social Psychology and Human Sexuality: Key readings in Social Psychology* (pp. 29–43). Philadelphia, PA: Psychology Press.

Ostrow, R. (2017). Might it be infidelity? Experts wrestle with ethical dilemmas as sexbots get more sophisticated. *The Weekend Australian, Inquirer, July 15–16,* 17.

O'Sullivan, L.F., & Thompson, A.E. (2014). Sexuality in adolescence. In D.L. Tolman & L.M. Diamond (Eds.), *APA Handbook of Sexuality and Psychology, Vol 1.* (pp. 433–486). Washington: American Psychological Association.

Oswalt, S.B., & Wyatt, T.J. (2011). Sexual orientation and differences in mental health, stress, and academic performance in a national sample of U.S. college students. *Journal of Homosexuality, 58* (9), 1255–1280 doi:10.1080/00918369.2011.605738.

Ott, M.Q., Corliss, H.L., Wypij, D., Rosario, M., & Austin, S.B. (2011). Stability and change in self-reported sexual orientation identity in young people: Application of mobility metrics. *Archives of Sexual Behaviour, 40* (3), 519–532.

Paolucci, E.O., Mark L., & Violato, C. (2001). A meta-analysis of the published research on the effects of child sexual abuse. *The Journal of Psychology, 135* (1), 17–36.

Patrick, M.E., & Lee, C.M. (2010). Sexual motivations and engagement in sexual behaviour during the transition to college. *Archives of Sexual Behaviour, 39* (3), 674–681. doi:10.1007/s10508-008-9435-9.

Paul, E.L., McManus, B., & Hays, A. (2000) "Hook-ups": Characteristics and correlates of college students' spontaneous and anonymous sexual experiences. *Journal of Sex Research, 37,* 76–88.

Paulk, A., & Zayac, R. (2013). Attachment style as a predictor of risky sexual behaviour in adolescents. *Journal of Social Sciences, 9,* 42–47.

Peck, S. (1978). *The Road Less Travelled.* London: Hutchinson & Co.

Perel, E. (2006). *Mating in Captivity: Reconciling the Erotic and the Domestic.* New York, NY: HarperCollins.

Perelman, M.A. (2006). A new combination treatment for premature ejaculation: A sex therapist's perspective. *Journal of Sexual Medicine, 3,* 1004–1012. doi:10.1111/J.1743-6109.2006.00238.x.

Perilloux, C., & Buss, D.M. (2008). Breaking up romantic relationships: Costs experienced and coping strategies deployed. *Evolutionary Psychology, 6,* 164–181.

Peter, J., & Valkenburg, P.M. (2007). Adolescents' exposure to a sexualized media environment and their notions of women as sex objects. *Sex Roles, 56,* 381–395. doi:10.107/s11199-006-9176-y.

Peter, J., & Valkenburg, P.M. (2008). Adolescents' exposure to sexually explicit Internet material and sexual preoccupancy: A three-wave panel study. *Media Psychology, 11,* 207–234. doi:10.1080/15213260801994238.

Peter, J., & Valkenburg, P.M. (2009a). Adolescents' exposure to sexually explicit internet material and notions of women as sex objects: Assessing causality and underlying processes. *Journal of Communication, 59*, 407–433. doi:10.1111/j.1460-2466.2009.01422.x.

Peter, J., & Valkenburg, P.M. (2009b). Adolescents' exposure to sexually explicit Internet material and sexual satisfaction: A longitudinal study. *Human Communication Research,35*, 171–194. doi:10.1111/j.1468-2958.2009.01343.x.

Peter, J., & Valkenburg, P.M. (2011). The use of sexually explicit Internet material and its antecedents: A longitudinal comparison of adolescents and adults. *Archives of Sexual Behaviour, 40*, 1015–1025. doi:10.1007/s10508-010-9644-x.

Peterson, C. (2004). *Looking Forward through the Lifespan.* Frenchs Forest: Pearson Education Australia.

Peterson, J.B. (2018) *12 Rules for Life: An antidote to chaos.* Vancouver: Penguin Random House.

Pettit, M., & Hegarty, P. (2014). Psychology and sexuality in historical time. In D.L. Tolman & L.M. Diamond (Eds.), *APA Handbook of Sexuality and Psychology, Vol 1.* (pp. 63–78). Washington: American Psychological Association.

Pfaus, J.G. (1999). Revisiting the concept of sexual motivation. *Annual Review of Sex Research, 10*, 120–156.

Pfaus, J.G. (2009). Pathways of sexual desire. *Journal of Sexual Medicine, 6*, 1506–1533. doi:10.1111/j.1743-6109.2009.01309.x.

Pfaus, J.G., Kippin, T.E., Coria-Avila, G.A., Gelez, H., Alfonso, V.M., Ismail, N., & Parada, M. (2012). Who, what, where, when, (and maybe even why)? How the experiences of sexual reward influences sexual desire, preference, and performance. *Archives of Sexual Behaviour, 41*, 31–62. doi:10.1007/s10508-012-9935-5.

Pfaus, J.G., Scepkowski, L.M., Marson, L., & Georgiadis, J.R. (2014). Biology of the sexual response. In D.L. Tolman & L.M. Diamond (Eds.), *APA Handbook of Sexuality and Psychology. Vol 1.* (pp. 145–204). Washington: American Psychological Association.

Pierce, G.R., Sarason, B.R., & Srarson, I.G. (1991). General and specific support expectations and stress as predictors of perceived supportiveness: An experimental study. *Journal of Personality and Social Psychology, 63*, 297–307.

Pirke, K.M., Kockott G., & Dittmar F. (1974). Psychosexual stimulation and plasma testosterone in man. *Archives of Sexual Behavior 3* (6), 577–584. doi:10.1007/BF01541140.PMID 4429441.

Plichta, S., & Falik, M. (2001). Prevalence of violence and its implications for women's health. *Women's Health Issues, 11*, 244–258. doi:10.1016/S1049-3867(01)00056-8.

Pratt, R. (2015). The "porn genie" is out of the bottle: Understanding and responding to the impact of pornography on young people. *InPsych* (Bulletin of the Australian Psychological Society Limited), *38*:2.

Pronk, T.M., Karremans, J.C., & Wigboldus, D.H.J. (2011). How can you resist? Executive control helps romantically involved individuals stay faithful. *Journal of Personality and Social Psychology, 100*, 827–837, doi:10.1037/a0021993.

Purnine, D.M., & Carey, M.P. (1997). Interpersonal communication and sexual adjustment: The role of understanding and agreement. *Journal of Consulting and Clinical Psychology, 65*, 1017–1025. doi:10.1037/0022-006X.65.6.1017.

Putnam, F.W. (2003). Ten-year update review: Child sexual abuse. *Journal of the American Academy of Child & Adolescent Psychiatry, 42* (3), 269–278. doi:10.1097/00004583-200303000-00006.

Raffaelli, M., & Crockett, L.J. (2003). Sexual risk taking in adolescence: The role of self-regulation and attraction to risk. *Developmental Psychology, 39*, 1036-1046. doi:10.1037/0012-1649.39.6.1036.

Reeve, J. (2005). *Understanding Motivation and Emotion*. Hoboken: John Wiley and Sons.

Rimm, D.C., and Masters, J.C. (1979). *Behaviour Therapy: Techniques and empirical findings* 2nd Ed. New York: Academic Press.

Rodrìguez-Manzo, G., & Fernández-Guasti, A. (1995). Opioid antagonists and the sexual satiation phenomenon. *Psychopharmacology, 122*, 131–136. doi:10.1007/BF02246087.

Roney, J.R., Mahler, S.V., & Maestripieri, D. (2003). Behavioral and hormonal responses of men to brief interactions with women. *Evolution and Human Behavior 24* (6), 365–375. doi:10.1016/S1090-5138(03)00053-9.

Rosario, M., & Schrimshaw, E.W. (2014). Theories and etiologies of sexual orientation. In D.L. Tolman & L.M. Diamond (Eds.), *APA Handbook of Sexuality and Psychology, Vol 1.* (pp. 555–596). Washington: American Psychological Association.

Rosser, B.R.S., Bockting, W.O., Ross, M.W., Miner, M.H., & Coleman. E. (2008). The relationship between homosexuality, internalized homo-negativity, and mental health in men who have sex with men. *Journal of Homosexuality, 55* (2), 185–203. doi:10.1001/archpsyc.56.10.883.

Rubin, Z. (1973). *Liking and Loving* New York: Holt, Rinehart & Winston.

Ryan, R.M. (1991). The nature of the self in autonomy and relatedness. In J. Strauss & G.R. Goethals (Eds.), *The Self: Interdisciplinary approaches.* (pp. 208–238). New York: Springer-Verlag.

Ryan, R.M., & Lynch, J.H. (1989). Emotional autonomy versus persistence: When free-choice behaviour is not intrinsically motivated. *Motivation and Emotion, 15*, 185–205.

Ryan, R.M., Stiller, J., & Lynch, J.H. (1994). Representations of relationships to teachers, parents, and friends as predictors of academic motivation and self-esteem. *Journal of Early Adolescence, 14*, 226–249.

Ryken, L. (1986). *Worldly Saints: The Puritans as they really were.* Grand Rapids, Michigan: Zondervan Publishing House.

Sabina, C., Wolak, J., & Finkelhor, D. (2008). The nature and dynamics of internet pornography exposure for youth. *CyberPsychology and Behavior, 11*, 691–693.

Sacks, O. (2015). *On the Move: a Life* London: Picador.

Sarason, B.R., Pierce, G.R., Shearin, E.N., Sarason, I.G., Waltz, J.A., & Poppe, L. (1991). Perceived social support and working models of self and actual others. *Journal of Personality and Social Psychology, 60*, 273–287.

Savin-Williams, R.C., & Diamond, L.M. (2000). Sexual identity trajectories among sexual-minority youths: Gender comparisons. *Archives of Sexual Behaviour, 29*, 607–627. doi:10.1023/A:1002058505138.

Savin-Williams, R.C., & Ream, G.L. (2007). Prevalence and stability of sexual orientation components during adolescence and young adulthood. *Archives of Sexual Behaviour, 36* (3), 385–394.

Schaffer, H.R., & Emerson, P. (1964). The development of social attachments in infancy. *Monographs of the Society for Research in Child Development, 29*, 3, (94).

Schenk, J., & Pfrang, H. (1986). Extraversion, neuroticism, and sexual behaviour: Interrelationships in a sample of young men. *Archives of Sexual Behaviour, 15*, 449–455. doi:10.1007/BF01542309.

Schneider, T. (2013). *The Brain, the Clinician and I: Neuroscience findings and the subjective self in clinical practice.* London: Routledge.

Schachner, D.A., & Shaver, P.R. (2004). Attachment dimensions and motives for sex. *Personal Relationships, 11*, 179–195.

Schnatz, P.E., Whitehurst, S.K., & O'Sullivan, D.M. (2010). Sexual dysfunction, depression, and anxiety among patients of an inner-city menopause clinic. *Journal of Women's Health, 19*, 1843–1849. doi:10.1089/jwh.2009.1800.

Secord, P.F., & Backman, C.W. (1965). Interpersonal approach to personality. In B.H. Maher (Ed.), *Progress in Experimental Personality Research. Vol 2* (pp. 91–125). New York: Academic Press, Inc.

Seligman, M.E.P. (1994). *What you can Change and What You Can't.* Sydney: Random House Australia.

Seto, M.C. (1992). A review of anxiety and sexual arousal in human sexual dysfunction. *Annals of Sexual Research, 5*, 33–43. doi:10.1177/107906329200500102.

Shaver, P.R., & Hazan, C. (1988). A biased overview of the study of love. *Journal of Social and Personal Relationships, 5*, 473–501.

Shaver, P.R., Hazan, C., & Bradshaw, D. (1988). Love as attachment: The integration of three behavioural systems. In R.J. Sterberg & M. Barnes (Eds.), *The Psychology of Love* (pp. 68–99). New Haven, CT: Yale University Press.

Shechner T. (2010). Gender identity disorder: A literature review from a developmental perspective. *The Israel Journal of Psychiatry and Related Sciences,47*, 132–138.

Siegel, D. (2012). *The Developing Mind: How relationships and the brain interact to shape who we are.* New York: The Guilford Press.

Silverman, I. (1971). Physical attractiveness and courtship. *Archives of Sexual Behaviour, 1*, 22–5.

Simon, W., & Gagnon, J.H. (1986). Sexual scripts: Permanence and change. *Archives of Sexual Behaviour, 15*, 97–120.

Simpson, J.A., Rholes, W., Campbell, L., & Wilson, C.L. (2003). Changes in attachment orientations across the transitions to parenthood. *Journal of Experimental Social Psychology, 39*, 317–331. doi:10.1016/S00221031(03)00030-1.

Singh, D. (2012). *Follow-up Study of Boys with Gender Identity Disorder.* PhD Thesis, Department of Human Development and Applied Psychology, University of Toronto.

Slaby, R.G., & Frey, K.S. (1975). Development of gender constancy and selective attention to same-sex models. *Child Development, 46*, 849–856.

Snyder, M., & Cantor, N. (1998). Understanding personality and social behaviour: A functionalist strategy. In D.T. Gilbert, S.T. Fiske, & G Lindzey (Eds.), *The Handbook of Social Psychology, Vol 1, 4th Ed,* (pp.635–679). Boston: McGraw-Hill.

Smith, D. (2015). Pornography: Pleasure or pain? *InPsych (Bulletin of the Australian Psychological Society Limited), 38*: 2.

Spielmann, S.S, Joel, S., MacDonald, G., & Kogan, A. (2013). Ex appeal current relationship quality and emotional attachment to ex-partners. *Social Psychological and Personality Science, 4*, 175–180.

Stefanou, C., & McCabe, M.P. (2012). Adult attachment and sexual functioning: A review of past research. *Journal of Sexual Medicine, 9*, 2499-2507. doi:10.1111/j.1743-6109.2012.02843.x.

Steinberg, L. (1988). Reciprocal relation between parent-child distance and pubertal maturation. *Developmental Psychology, 24*, 122–128.

Stephenson, K., Ahrold, T., & Meston, C. (2011). The association between sexual motives and sexual satisfaction: Gender differences and categorical comparisons. *Archives of Sexual Behaviour, 40* (3), 607–618. doi:10.1007/s10508-010-9674-4.

Stevenson, R.J., Case, T.L., & Oaten, M.J. (2011). Effect of self-reported sexual arousal on responses to sex-related and non-sex-related disgust cues. *Archives of Sexual Behaviour, 40* (1), 79–85. doi:10.1007/s10508-009-9529.

Sternberg, R.J., & Weis, K. (Eds.) (2006). *The New Psychology of Love*. New Haven, C.T.: Yale University Press.

Stoller, R.J. (1979). *Sexual Excitement: Dynamics of erotic life*. New York: Simon & Schuster.

Storms, M.D. (1983). *Development of sexual orientation. Module of the Committee on Gay Concerns of the American Psychological Association* (Available from the Office of Social and Ethical Responsibility, American Psychological Association, DC).

Symons, D. (1979). *The Evolution of Human Sexuality*. New York: Oxford.

Szymanski, D.M., & Stewart-Richardson, D.N. (2014). Psychological, relational, and sexual correlates of pornography use on young adult heterosexual men in romantic relationships. *Journal of Men's Studies, 22*, 64–82.

Szielasko, A.L., Symons, D.K., & Price, E.L. (2013). Development of an attachment-informed measure of sexual behaviour in late adolescence. *Journal of Adolescence, 36*, 361–370.

Temple, J., Weston, R., Roderiquez, B., & Marshall, L. (2007). Differing effects of partner and non-partner sexual assault on women's mental health. *Violence Against Women, 13*, 285–297. doi:10.1177/1077801206297437.

Tennov, D. (1999). *Love and Limerence: The experience of being in love*. Lanham: Scarborough House.

Thibaut, J.W., & Kelley, H.H. (1959). *The Social Psychology of Groups* New York: Wiley.

Tiefer, L. (2001). A new view of women's sexual problems: Why new? Why now? *Journal of Sex Research, 38*, 89–96. doi:10.1080/00224490109552075.

Tiefer, L. (2004). *Sex is Not a Natural Act, and Other Essays*. New York, NY: Westview Press.

Toates, F. (2014). *How Sexual Desire Works: The enigmatic Urge*. Cambridge: Cambridge University Press.

Tolman, D.L., & Diamond, L.M. (Eds.) (2014). *APA Handbook of Sexuality and Psychology Vol 1 & 2*. Washington: American Psychological Association.

Tolman, D.L., & Diamond, L.M. (2014). Sexuality Theory: A review, a revision, and a recommendation. In D.L. Tolman & L.M. Diamond (Eds.), *APA Handbook of Sexuality and Psychology, Vol 1.* (pp. 3–28). Washington: American Psychological Association.

Tolman, D.L., Bowman, C.P., & Fahs, B. (2014). Sexuality and embodiment. In D.L. Tolman & L.M. Diamond (Eds.), *APA Handbook of Sexuality and Psychology, Vol 1.* (pp. 759–804). Washington: American Psychological Association.

Tomkins, S.S. (1962). *Affect, Imagery, and Consciousness: The positive effects (Vol 1).* New York: Springer.

Tomkins, S.S. (1963). *Affect, Imagery, and Consciousness: The negative effects (Vol 2).* New York: Springer.

Tomkins, S.S. (1984). Affect Theory. In K.R. Scherer & P. Ekman (Eds.), *Approaches to Emotion* (pp. 163–196). Hillsdale, NJ: Lawrence Erlbaum.

Tracy, J.L., Shaver, P.R., Albino, A.W., & Cooper, M.L. (2003). Attachment styles and adolescent sexuality. In P. Florsheim (Ed.) *Adolescent Romance and Sexual Behaviour: Theory, research, and practical implications* (pp. 137–159). Mahwah, N.J.: Erlbaum.

Træen, B., & Martinussen, M. (2008). Extradyadic activity in a random sample of Norwegian couples. *Journal of Sex Research, 45*, 319–328. doi:10.1080/00224490802398324.

Treas, J., & Giesen, D. (2000). Sexual infidelity among married and cohabiting Americans. *Journal of Marriage and the Family, 62*, 48–60. doi:10:1111/j.1741-3737.2000.00048.x.

Traupmann, J., & Hatfield, E. (1981). Love and its effects on mental and physical health. In J.G. March (Ed.), *Aging: Stability and change in the family* New York: Academic Press.

Tripp, C.A. (1975). *The Homosexual Matrix.* New York: McGraw-Hill.

Turchik J.A., Garske, J.P., Probst, D.R., & Irvin, C.R. (2010). Personality, sexuality, and substance use as predictors of sexual risk taking in college students. *Journal of Sex Research, 47*, 411–419. doi:10.1080/00224490903161621.

Uchino, B.N., Cacioppo, J.T.,& Kiecolt-Glaser, J.K. (1996). The relationship between social support and physiological processes: A review with emphasis on underlying mechanisms and implications for health. *Psychological Bulletin, 119*, 488–531. doi:10.1037/0033-2909.119.3.488.

Udry, J.R., Talbert, L.M., & Morris, N.M. (1986). Biosocial foundations for adolescent female sexuality. *Demography, 23*, 217–230. doi:10.2307/2061617.

Urada, L.A., Goldenberg, S.A., Shannon, K., & Strathdee, S.A. (2014). Sexuality and sex work. In D.L. Tolman & L.M. Diamond (Eds.), *APA Handbook of Sexuality and Psychology, Vol 2.* (pp. 37–76). Washington: American Psychological Association.

van Anders, S.M., Goldey, K.L., & Kuo, P.X. (2011). The steroid/peptide theory of social bonds: Integrating testosterone and peptide responses for classifying social behavioural contexts. *Psychoneuroendocrinology, 36*, 1265–1275. doi:10.1016/j.psyneuen.2011.06.001.

van Anders, S.M., Hamilton, L.D., & Watson, N.V. (2007). Multiple partners are associated with higher testosterone in North American men and women. *Hormones and Behavior, 51*, 454–459.

van Anders S.M. & Watson N.V. (2006). Relationship status and testosterone in North American heterosexual and non-heterosexual men and women: Cross-sectional and longitudinal data. *Psychoneuroendocrinology, 31* (6), 715–723.

von Drehle, D. (2013). How gay marriage won *TIME*, April 8, 16–24.

Vohs, K.D., & Baumeister, R.F. (2004). Sexual passion, intimacy, and gender. In D.J. Mashek & A. Aron (Eds.), *Handbook of Closeness and Intimacy* (pp.189–199). Mahwah, New Jersey: Lawrence Erlbaum Associates.

Wallen, K. (2001). Sex and context: Hormones and primate sexual motivation. *Hormones and Behavior, 40* (2), 339–357.

Wallmyr, G., & Welin, C. (2006). Young people, pornography, and sexuality: Sources and attitudes. *Journal of School Nursing, 22*, 290–295. doi: 10.1177/10598405060220050801.

Walster, E., & Walster, G.W. (1978). *A New Look at Love.* Reading, MA: Addison-Wesley.

Walter, M. (1971). *Introduction to Personality.* New York: Holt, Rinehart and Winston.

Walum, H., Westberg, L., Henningsson, S., Neiderhiser, J.M., Reiss, D, Igl, W., Ganiban, J.M., Spotts, E.L., Pedersen, N.L., Eriksson, E., & Lichtenstein, P. (2008). Genetic variation in the vasopressin receptor 1a gene (AVPR1A) associates with pair-bonding behaviour in humans. *Proceedings of the National Academy of Sciences of the United States of America 105* (37), 14153–14156. doi:10.1073/pnas.0803081105.

Wegner, D.M. (1986). Transactive memory: A contemporary analysis of the group mind. In B. Mullen & G.R. Goethals (Eds.), *Theory of Group Behaviour*, (pp. 185–208). New York: Springer-Verlag.

Wegner, D.M., Erber, R., & Raymond, P. (1991). Transactive memory in close relationships. *Journal of Personality and Social Psychology, 61*, 923–929.

Weinberg, M.S., Lottes, I.L., & Shaver, F.M. (1995). Swedish or American heterosexual college youth: Who is more permissive? *Archives of Sexual Behavior, 24,* 409–437.

Weiten, W. (2001). *Psychology: Themes and Variations: Briefer Version* (Fifth Edition). Stamford: Wadsworth/ Thompson Learning.

Whisman, M., Gordon, K., & Chatav, Y. (2007). Predicting sexual infidelity in a population-based sample of married individuals. *Journal of Family Psychology, 21,* 320–324. doi:10.1037/0893-3200.21.2.320.

Whisman, M., & Snider, D. (2007). Sexual infidelity in a national survey of American Women: Differences in prevelance and correlates as a function of method of assessment. *Journal of Family Psychology, 21,* 147–154. doi:10.1037/0893-3200.21.2.147.

White, G.L., & Knight, T.D. (1984). Misattribution of arousal and attraction: Effects of salience of explanations for arousal. *Journal of Experimental Social Psychology, 20,* 55–64. doi:10.1016/0022-1031(84)90012-X.

Williams, J.G., & Solano, C.H. (1983). The social reality of feeling lonely: Friendship and reciprocation. *Personality and Social Psychology Bulletin, 9,* 237–242.

Wilson, G., & Rahman, Q. (2005). *Born Gay: The Psychobiology of Sex Orientation.* London: Peter Owen Publishers.

Wilson, P. (1981). *The Man they called a Monster: Sexual Experiences between Men and Boys.* North Ryde: Cassel Australia Ltd.

Windle, M. (1992). Temperament and social support in adolescence: Intercorrelations with depression and delinquent behaviour. *Journal of Youth and Adolescence, 21,* 1–21.

Wingfield, J.C., Hegner, R.E., Dufty, A.M. & Ball, G.F. (1990). The "challenge hypothesis": Theoretical implications for patterns of testosterone secretion, mating systems, and breeding strategies. *The American Naturalist, 136,* 829–846.

Winter, D.G. (1988). The power motive in women – and men. *Journal of Personality and Social psychology, 54,* 510–519. doi:10.1037/0022-3514.54.3.510.

Young, J.E., Klosko, J.S., & Weishaar, M. (2003). *Schema Therapy: A Practitioner's Guide.* New York: Guilford Publications.

Zajonc, R.B. (1968). Attitudinal effects of mere exposure. *Journal of Personality and Social Psychology, 9* (2, Pt. 2), 1–27. doi:10.1037/h0025848.

Ziefman, D.M., & Hazan, C. (2016). Pair bonds as attachments: Mounting evidence in support of Bowlby's hypothesis. In: Cassidy, J., & Shaver, P.R. (2016) *Handbook of Attachment: Theory, research, and clinical applications. Third edition.* (pp. 416–434). New York: The Guilford Press.

Ziegler, T. E. (2007). Female sexual motivation during non-fertile periods: a primate phenomenon. *Hormones and Behavior, 51* (1), 1–2.

Zilmann, D. (1984). *Connections between Sex and Aggression*. Hillsdale: Lawrence Erlbaum.

www.ingramcontent.com/pod-product-compliance
Lightning Source LLC
Chambersburg PA
CBHW070352270326
41926CB00014B/2511